THE ORIGIN OF BRANDS

THE ORIGIN OF
BRANDS

DISCOVER THE NATURAL LAWS
OF PRODUCT INNOVATION AND
BUSINESS SURVIVAL

AL RIES and LAURA RIES

HarperBusiness
An Imprint of HarperCollins*Publishers*

HarperCollins books may be purchased for educational, business, or sales promotional use. For information please write: Special Markets Department, HarperCollins Publishers Inc., 10 East 53rd Street, New York, NY 10022.

FIRST EDITION

Designed by Richard Oriolo

Library of Congress Cataloging-in-Publication Data

Ries, Al.
    The origin of brands : discover the natural laws of product innovation and business survival / Al Ries and Laura Ries.—1st ed.
        p. cm.
Includes bibliographical references and index.
ISBN 0-06-057014-8
    1. Brand name products. 2. Brand name products—Marketing.
3. Brand name products—Management. 4. New products—Management. I. Ries, Laura. II. Title.

HD69.B7R538 2004
658.8'27—dc22

                                                                2004042466

04 05 06 07 08 RRD 10 9 8 7 6 5 4 3 2 1

DEDICATED TO
"DIVERGENCE,"
THE LEAST UNDERSTOOD,
MOST POWERFUL FORCE
IN THE UNIVERSE.

CONTENTS

ON

THE ORIGIN OF SPECIES

BY MEANS OF NATURAL SELECTION,

OR THE

PRESERVATION OF FAVOURED RACES IN THE STRUGGLE FOR LIFE.

By CHARLES DARWIN, M.A.,

FELLOW OF THE ROYAL, GEOLOGICAL, LINNÆAN, ETC., SOCIETIES;
AUTHOR OF 'JOURNAL OF RESEARCHES DURING H. M. S. BEAGLE'S VOYAGE
ROUND THE WORLD.'

LONDON:
JOHN MURRAY, ALBEMARLE STREET.
1859.

The right of Translation is reserved.

THE FIRST EDITION OF *THE ORIGIN OF SPECIES* BY CHARLES DARWIN
WAS PUBLISHED ON NOVEMBER 24, 1859. IT SOLD OUT THAT DAY.

INTRODUCTION

IT HAS BEEN TWENTY-THREE YEARS since the publication of Al's first book, *Positioning: The Battle for Your Mind*.

Coincidentally, twenty-three years elapsed between the day Charles Darwin completed his journey on the HMS *Beagle* and the day his magnum opus was published.

Time distills ideas and concepts so they become refined and purified. In spite of the hundreds of thousands of words we have already written on branding, we believe the essence of the subject has still eluded us. We believe there's an important principle at work that has never been isolated, defined, or explained.

We believe this principle is so fundamental that the only analogy that would do it justice is contained in Darwin's definitive book on biology, *The Origin of Species*.

That principle is *divergence*, the least understood, most powerful force in the world.

What has happened in nature is also happening in the world of products and services. Eventually every category will diverge and become two or more categories, creating endless opportunities to build brands.

The interplay of evolution and divergence provides a model for understanding both the Universe and the universe of brands.

Evolution has received all the publicity, but evolution alone cannot account for the millions of diverse and unusual species that populate the Earth. If it weren't for divergence, evolution by itself would have created a world populated by millions of single-cell prokaryotes the size of dinosaurs.

So, too, it is in the world of brands. Brands evolve to become stronger and more dominant. But it's divergence that generates the conditions that allow the introduction of new categories and new brands.

Comparing branding with biology might seem far-fetched, but we could think of no other analogy that so clearly and simply explains the branding process.

As Thomas Huxley said upon reading *The Origin of Species*, "How extremely stupid not to have thought of that."

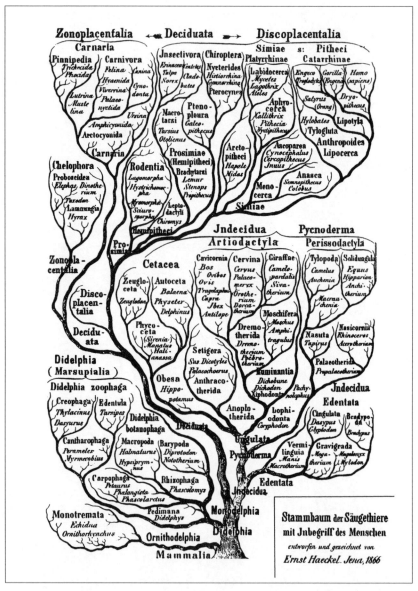

ONE OF GERMAN BIOLOGIST ERNST HAECKEL'S 19TH CENTURY
EVOLUTIONARY TREES OFTEN REPRODUCED IN MODERN TEXTBOOKS.

Chapter 1

The Great Tree
of Life

THE "GREAT TREE OF LIFE" is how Charles Darwin described his metaphor for the origin of species.

"The affinities of all the beings of the same class have sometimes been represented by a great tree. . . . The green and budding twigs may represent existing species; and those produced during each former year may represent the long succession of extinct species. At each period of growth all the growing twigs have tried to branch out on all sides, and to overtop and kill the surrounding twigs and branches, in the same manner as species and groups of species have tried to overmaster other species in the great battle for life."

How do new branches arise? By divergence of existing branches. How do new species arise? By divergence of existing species.

When he was just twenty-eight years old, Charles Darwin jotted down his view of nature in his notebook: "If we choose to let conjecture run wild, then animals, our fellow brethren in pain, disease, suffering and famine—our slaves in the most laborious works, our companions in our amusements—they may partake of our origin in one common ancestor—we may be all melted together."

Melted together, looking backward but spread apart and diverging, looking forward.

The Great Tree of Products and Services

In the "great tree of products and services," how do new categories arise? By divergence of existing categories.

- First there was a branch called computer. Today that computer branch has diverged and now we have mainframe computers, midrange computers, network computers, personal computers, laptop computers, and handheld computers. The computer didn't converge with another technology. It diverged.

- First there was a branch called television. Today that television branch has diverged and now we have analog and digital television. Regular and high-definition television. Standard (4/3) and wide-screen (16/9) formats. Television didn't converge with another medium. It diverged.

- First there was a branch called radio. Today that radio branch has diverged and now we have portable radios, car radios, wearable radios, and clock radios. Radio didn't converge with another medium. It diverged.

- First there was a branch called telephone. Today that telephone branch has diverged and now we have regular telephones, cordless telephones, headset phones, cellphones, and satellite phones. The telephone didn't converge with another technology. It diverged.

Did you ever see a tree in which two branches converged to form a single branch? Perhaps, but this is highly unlikely in nature. It's also highly unlikely in products and services.

Some Categories Live. Some Categories Die.

Darwin explains: "Of the many twigs which flourished when the tree was a mere bush, only two or three, now grown into great branches, yet survive and bear all the other branches; so with the species which lived during long-past geological periods, very few now have living and modified descendants. From the first growth of the tree, many a limb and branch has decayed and dropped off; and these lost branches of various sizes may represent those whole orders, families, and genera which have now no living representatives, and which are known to us only from having been found in a fossil state."

A branch called typewriter, for example, diverged and formed multiple branches called manual typewriter, portable typewriter, and electric typewriter. Today the typewriter branch has decayed and is about to drop off, overshadowed by a nearby branch called personal computer.

The typewriter is a dinosaur. Today you find most typewriters, slide rules, and adding machines only in a fossil state. That is, in somebody's basement or attic and possibly listed on eBay. (Ebay recently had 1,314 typewriters for sale.)

The sailing ship, the steam engine, and the horse and buggy have all followed similar paths.

The Great Tree of Brands

If you want to build a successful brand, you have to understand divergence. You have to look for opportunities to create new categories by divergence of existing categories. And then you have to become the first brand in this emerging new category.

In the "great tree of brands," a successful brand is one that dominates an emerging branch and then becomes increasingly successful as the branch itself expands to block the sunlight from nearby branches.

Traditional marketing is not focused on creating new categories. Traditional marketing is focused on creating new customers. Traditional marketing involves finding out what consumers want and then giving them what they want, better and cheaper than the competition.

The high priest of a traditional-marketing company is the director of marketing research. To find out what consumers want, companies spend lavishly on research. In a recent year, American companies spent $6.2 billion on marketing research.

(If you've read some of our previous books, you know that we are big believers in public relations, yet PR is only a $4.2-billion business, a third less than marketing research.)

Are We Opposed to Marketing Research?

Yes and no. We're opposed to market research when it attempts to predict the future. This happens when you ask consumers what they *will* do rather than what they *have* done.

We're not opposed to market research that explores the past. Why consumers chose the brands they did, for example.

Consumers don't know what they will do until they are actually given the opportunity to make a decision. Another way of looking at the situation is that categories don't diverge until there is an available brand for consumers to purchase.

Today, four out of the five best-selling beer brands are light beers. Before the 1975 national launch of Lite beer, what good would it have done Miller Brewing to ask consumers if they would buy a watered-down beer? As a matter of fact, the 1967 launch of Gablinger's should have answered that question with a resounding no.

Named after the Swiss chemist who developed the beer (Hersch Gablinger), the new light-beer product was launched with a massive advertising program. It was all for naught. Gablinger's died a quick death.

The Role of the Name

Why was Lite successful and Gablinger's not? One reason is the name. "Give me a Gablinger's"? Sounds like you're asking for a Polish sausage. If you are going to invent a new type of beer, make sure you have a nice German name like Adolph Coors or August Busch.

Names don't matter, many managers believe; it's the product that matters. With the right product at the right price, goes the thinking, we can win the battle of the marketplace.

Names do matter. Depending on the category, the name alone can represent the primary reason for the brand's success.

A company might spend hundreds of millions of dollars to develop a new product and then give that new product a brand name that almost guarantees failure. Innovation alone is never enough.

Along with innovation, a company needs marketing to assure the brand's eventual success and survival. The heart of a good marketing program is a great name.

If marketing research is a useless tool for predicting consumer behavior, how can a company figure out what might happen to a new brand in the marketplace?

The Role of Test Marketing

What about another component of traditional marketing, test marketing? Should a new product be tested in a regional or local market before a national introduction?

Test marketing has some benefits, but we believe the negatives far outweigh the benefits. Some of the negatives include:

WASTED TIME. You can't afford to waste the time that test marketing takes, especially since the essence of branding is getting into the mind first.

TIPPING OFF THE COMPETITION. Test marketing will alert competitors and perhaps stimulate one or more of them to introduce similar products.

UNPROJECTABLE RESULTS. Test marketing for Enamelon toothpaste projected $50 million in annual sales nationally. Actual sales: $10 million.

One of the problems with test marketing is overstimulation of demand. To get enough tangible results to measure, you usually have to run a local marketing program that you can't afford to run nationwide.

Most test marketing is not done to make a go/no-go decision. Most test marketing is done to measure the effectiveness of the brand's advertising. And since you shouldn't do much, if any, advertising in launching a brand, the value of test marketing is greatly reduced. (See chapter 16, "Launching the Brand.")

Launching a new product the traditional way includes market research, test marketing, and a big advertising budget. We are opposed to all three of these activities.

If you want to improve your odds, you need to forget all you have learned about traditional marketing. You need a new theory of how to build a brand.

You need to learn the Darwinian principle of divergence.

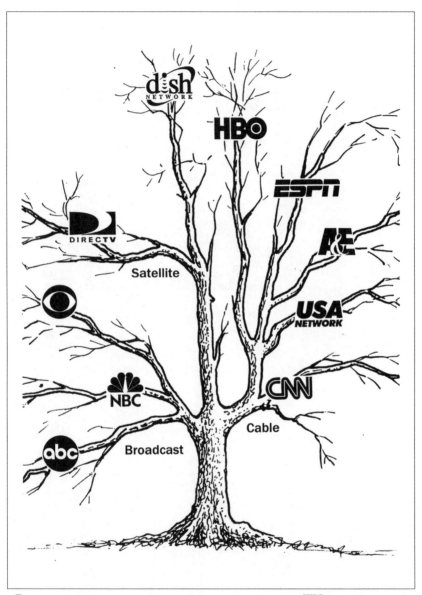

BROADCAST TELEVISION BRANCHED OUT INTO CABLE TV AND SATELLITE
TV, CREATING MANY NEW BRANDING OPPORTUNITIES.

Chapter 2

Predicting the Future

CHARLES DARWIN WAS A VISIONARY. He could see effects that took place over millions of years even though these effects couldn't be directly observed in the real world.

In *The Origin of Species*, Darwin describes how natural selection gradually increases the number of species that populate the earth:

"This gradual increase in number of the species of a group is strictly conformable with the theory, for the species of the same genus, and the genera of the same family, can increase only slowly and progressively; the process of modification and the production of a number of allied forms necessarily being a slow and gradual process,— one species first giving rise to two or three varieties, these being slowly converted into species, which in their turn produce by equally slow steps other varieties and species, and so on, like the branching of a great tree from a single stem, till the group becomes large."

It's easier for us. We can see the evolution of brands because the process is taking place right in front of our face. Everywhere you look, you see the same thing: categories are evolving and diverging.

In nature, changes in the environment create the conditions that cause species to diverge. In business, changes in technology and in the cultural environment create the conditions that cause categories to diverge.

The Television Tree

First there was broadcast television, which allowed the creation of three network TV brands: CBS, NBC, and ABC. Then cable television emerged and a proliferation of cable TV brands followed: HBO, ESPN, CNN, and many others. Then satellite television arrived on the scene, creating opportunities for DirecTV and the Dish Network.

Put yourself in the shoes of an executive of a company wanting to get into television just as cable TV was emerging. On the one hand, broadcast television, with three networks, was generating hundreds of millions of dollars in revenues. On the other hand, cable television had near-zero revenues and an uncertain future.

Where Does Opportunity Lie?

Are you better off trying to take a piece of an established market like network TV or are you better off trying to establish a new brand in an uncertain new category like cable TV?

Hindsight is twenty-twenty. Today the answer to the question is cable TV, but that wasn't so obvious back in 1968 when the FCC first authorized pay-cable transmission.

- It wasn't ABC, CBS, or NBC that started CNN, the first cable-television news network. It was billboard tycoon Ted Turner, who also put the first local TV station on a satellite creating "superstation" WTBS.

- It wasn't ABC, CBS, or NBC that started ESPN, the first cable-television sports network. It was Scott Rasmussen and his father, Bill Rasmussen, who launched ESPN with a $9,000 cash advance on a credit card.
- It wasn't ABC, CBS, or NBC that started HBO, the first premium cable television network. It was Charles Dolan, the man running Sterling Manhattan, a cable system controlled by Time Inc. (Dolan moved on to found Cablevision Systems, now the nation's fifth-largest cable operator.)

   Now part of Time Warner, HBO has become a massive moneymaker. In a recent year, for example, HBO was reported to have made more money than ABC, CBS, NBC, and Fox put together.

And so it goes. Big companies tend to see things the way they are. Entrepreneurs tend to see things the way they could be.

Improving Your Foresight

Forget hindsight. This book was written to improve your foresight. To show you that you don't need to be a visionary to predict the future.

All categories will diverge. They always have and they always will. It's this divergence that creates opportunities for new brands. What direction this divergence will take is another matter. The only thing you can count on is that divergence will happen, in one direction or another.

Of course, there are brands and there are brands. Most brands are worthless, some brands have value, and a few brands are among the most valuable assets a company can own. Our objective is to help you build one of those valuable brands. A brand like Starbucks or Red Bull or Lexus.

A brand is valuable for one reason and for one reason only. It dominates a category. Coca-Cola, the world's most valuable brand, is valuable because it dominates the cola category worldwide.

Microsoft, the world's second-most-valuable brand, is valuable because it dominates the personal-computer-software category worldwide.

It's hard to find a brand more dominant in its category than Microsoft. Someday soon, we predict, Microsoft will be the world's most valuable brand.

Most New Brands Don't Stand a Chance

Each year consumer-product makers in the United States introduce more than thirty thousand new products and services. That's thirty thousand opportunities to introduce another Southwest Airlines, another Swiffer, another Google, another Gatorade.

That's just the consumer side of the street. On the industrial side, U.S. companies introduce at least that many new products and services with corresponding opportunities to introduce another Adobe, another FedEx, another Gulfstream, another Oracle.

The vast majority of these new products and services (and the brands that are hung on them) don't stand a chance to become big brands because they were introduced to serve a market rather than to create a market.

How do you increase your chance of success in the new-product game? It's simple. You just predict the future.

That's what launching a new brand is all about. You make a bet on your ability to predict what is likely to happen to your new product or service in the future.

Something Is Wrong with Our Predictions

A recent Nielsen BASES and Ernst & Young study put the failure rate of new U.S. consumer products at 95 percent and new European consumer products at 90 percent.

Nor are our successes much to brag about either. An analysis done a few years ago found that fewer than two hundred of the hundreds of thousands of new products introduced in a ten-year period had sales of more than $15 million a year, and only a handful produced sales of more than $100 million.

We need to do better than that. We need to have a better way to predict the future.

Sadly, there is no way to predict the future. The only chance you have of increasing your odds is by studying the past. And what do you find when you compare the brands of yesterday with the brands of today?

An Explosion of Choice

Fifty years ago, a grocery store might have stocked some four thousand items. Today, the average supermarket stocks more than forty thousand items. What's happened in grocery stores has also happened in drugstores, clothing stores, appliance stores, hardware stores, liquor stores, department stores. More items, more categories, more brands, more choice.

Consumers might complain about confusion, but fundamentally they like choice. Try opening a supermarket with some twenty thousand items across the street from a supermarket with forty thousand items and you'll see what we mean. In rivers, the big fish eat the small fish. In retailing, the big stores eat the small stores.

Wherever you look, you see the same phenomenon at work. A category might start with a single product, often a single brand. And over time, it explodes into many different categories and many different brands.

Take television, for example. Not only has the sending side of television exploded into different categories, the receiving side has, too. In television sets, you now have a choice of CRT (cathode-ray tube), LCD (liquid crystal display), rear-projection LCD, rear-projection LCOS (liquid crystal on silicon), DLP (digital light processing) and plasma TV. And in the near future you're likely to see OLED (organic light-emitting diode.)

With more to come.

A New Category Needs a New Name

Each new category creates an opportunity for a new brand. Sadly, most companies "stretch" an existing brand to cover the new category.

This represents the biggest mistake in marketing.

Consider computers. Initially all computers were mainframe computers, a category dominated first by Remington Rand and then by IBM. Then the category diverged and we had minicomputers (Digital Equipment), home personal computers (Apple), workstations (Sun Microsystems), 3-D workstations (Silicon Graphics), laptops (Toshiba), business personal computers (Compaq), and personal computers sold direct (Dell).

What happened in mainframe computers is happening today in many other categories. Big companies jump in with their brands to try to take market share from the leader while entrepreneurs pioneer new categories and become multimillionaires.

In mainframe computers, General Electric, RCA, Motorola, and Xerox, big companies all, tried to muscle in on IBM's territory. All failed.

Meanwhile entrepreneurs Kenneth Olsen and Harlan Anderson started a minicomputer company named Digital Equipment and made a fortune. Ditto entrepreneurs Steve Jobs and Steve Wozniak with Apple Computer. And entrepreneurs Andreas Bechtolsheim, Scott McNealy, Vinod Khosla, and William Joy with Sun Microsystems. And entrepreneur James Clark with Silicon Graphics. And entrepreneurs Rod Canion, James Harris, and William Murto with Compaq Computer. And entrepreneur Michael Dell with Dell Computer.

In computers, the only exception to the general rule that entrepreneurs who launch new brands beat big companies that line-extend is the laptop category currently dominated by Toshiba.

Interestingly enough, Compaq Computer started as a portable-computer company (hence the name Compaq) before branching out into the desktop category, thereby losing both its focus and its opportunity to dominate an emerging category.

What if Compaq had stayed a portable (or laptop) computer company? Would Compaq today be a bigger and more successful company than Dell?

We think so. Last year, for example, laptop computers outsold desktop computers.

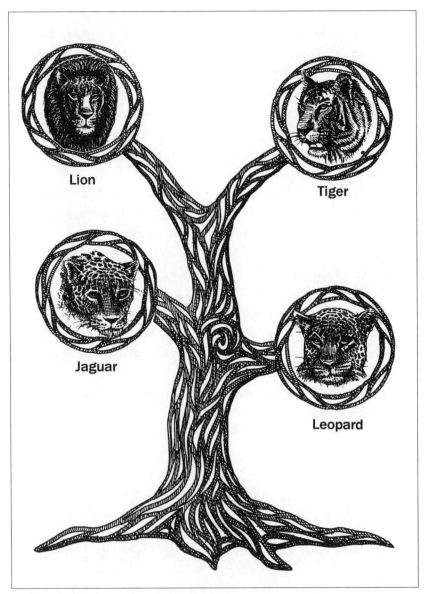

THE PANTHERA, AN ANCIENT ANIMAL, DIVERGED OVER TIME TO CREATE
THE LEOPARD, THE JAGUAR, THE TIGER, AND THE LION.

Chapter 3

Divide and Conquer

WHAT'S THE SIZE OF THE MARKET?

That's the first question normally asked before starting a branding program. It's also the wrong question to ask.

Branding opportunities do not lie in the pursuit of existing markets. Branding opportunities lie in the creation of new markets.

A new brand is like a new species. A new species does not evolve from an existing species. If the "lion" is a brand, you can't create a new brand by improving the lion. No matter how much you improve the breed, a lion is still a lion.

New species are created by divergence of an existing species. Somewhere in the distant past, the ancestor of the lion (panthera) diverged and a new species was created called a leopard. In the same way, the panthera diverged a number of times creating the jaguar, the tiger, and the lion. That's the way nature works.

That's Also the Way Branding Works

If you want to create a powerful new brand, you should look for ways that your product or service can diverge from an existing category. In other words, the best way to build a brand is not by going after an existing category, but by creating a new category you can be first in.

Divide and conquer is the way you build a powerful new brand.

What's the size of the market? The best answer to this question, from a branding point of view, is zero.

To build a new brand, you must overcome the logical notion of *serving* a market. Instead you must focus on *creating* a market.

Consider the world's ten most valuable brands and their estimated values, as determined by Interbrand, the leading brand-valuation company.

No. 1: Coca-Cola ($70 billion)

This is an astounding number because it is almost three times the physical assets of the Coca-Cola Company, which are on the books at $24.5 billion.

How did the Coca-Cola brand achieve such a lofty value? It wasn't because the brand was launched to serve an existing market. The soft-drink market in those days consisted of root beer, sarsaparilla, ginger ale, orange drink, lemonade, and other concoctions. Coca-Cola became a big brand because it created a new market called cola.

Coca-Cola created a tiger in a market populated by lions, leopards, and jaguars. Powerful new brands are always created this way . . . by divergence of an existing category. Never by improving an existing category or combining two or more categories.

No. 2: Microsoft ($65 billion)

How did mighty Microsoft achieve branding preeminence in such a relatively short time? (The company is just 29 years old compared with 118 for Coca-Cola.)

Microsoft didn't get mighty by building a better personal-computer operating system. Most experts give the nod to Macintosh for its superior look and feel. Microsoft won the operating system war by being first. As sixteen-bit personal-computer operating systems diverged from eight-bit systems like the Apple OS and Digital Research's CP/M, Microsoft was the first to establish itself as the leading sixteen-bit brand, thanks to IBM.

In August 1981, IBM introduced the PC along with its Microsoft operating system. Apple's Macintosh brand (and operating system) was not introduced until January 1984.

You can't give a powerful competitor like IBM a two-and-a-half-year head start and expect to win the race. By the time the Mac appeared, the IBM PC (and its clones) were well on its way to becoming the industry standard.

No. 3: IBM ($52 billion)

What built the IBM brand? In a word, the *mainframe* computer. IBM wasn't the first company to introduce a commercial computer. (Remington Rand was first with its Univac brand, which was introduced in 1951.)

But Remington Rand was a conglomerate and IBM concentrated all of its efforts on information machines for business.

Even so, Remington Rand might have prevailed with its Univac brand except for the rapid evolution of the mainframe product. The first IBM computer, the 701, was introduced in 1953. Less than a year later, IBM introduced the 702, which processed information twice as fast as a Univac machine.

It's interesting to note that what worked for IBM in mainframes didn't work for them in personal computers. IBM was the first company to introduce a sixteen-bit, serious personal computer (the IBM PC), but still lost the personal computer war to copycats like Compaq, Hewlett-Packard, and Dell.

Why? The IBM name on the brand was wrong. IBM meant *mainframe* computer, not *personal* computer. We discuss this paradox in chapter 16, "Launching the Brand."

No. 4: General Electric ($42 billion)

GE can trace its history back to Thomas Edison, who invented the electric lightbulb in 1879. His company (Edison Light Company) eventually became the General Electric Company.

As revolutionary in its time as the Internet is today, the electric lightbulb fundamentally altered society, turning twelve-hour days into twenty-four-hour days.

No. 5: Intel ($31 billion)

Like all of the world's most valuable brands, it was a single inspired development that built the Intel brand. In a word, the *microchip*. Intel was the first company to introduce a microprocessor, the Intel 4004.

Furthermore, Intel wisely shut down its computer-memory chip business to focus on its new line of microprocessors. An example of the power of pruning. (See chapter 13.)

No. 6: Nokia ($29 billion)

What built the Nokia brand? In a word, the *cellphone*.

Quite honestly, the world's sixth most valuable brand should have been Motorola, the first company to introduce a cellphone. Yet Motorola lost out to Nokia for the same reason that IBM lost out to

Compaq, Hewlett-Packard, and Dell in personal computers. Nokia meant "cellphone" and Motorola meant a wide range of products from communications equipment to global satellite systems.

Nokia did the opposite. The company dropped everything (paper, rubber products including tires and boots, electronics, machinery, and computers) to focus on cellphones. Once again, the power of pruning.

No. 7: Disney ($28 billion)

What built the Disney brand? In a word, *Mickey Mouse*.

Disney was the first brand identified with motion-picture animation, or fantasy. Snow White and the Seven Dwarfs, Donald Duck, Pluto, and other animated characters helped to create the Disney brand.

No. 8: McDonald's ($25 billion)

What built the Big Mac brand? Billions and billions of hamburgers.

The first McDonald's restaurant had exactly eleven items on the menu, even if you count all sizes and flavors as different items. If you weren't going to order a hamburger (or its upscale cousin, a cheeseburger), there was no reason to go to a McDonald's. Everything else on the menu complemented the burgers.

Today, of course, a typical McDonald's restaurant has some fifty items on the menu (more than 100 if you count all sizes and flavors) and the brand is in trouble. Pruning, anyone?

No. 9: Marlboro ($22 billion)

We're not happy celebrating the glories of cigarette marketing, but there's no question that Marlboro has become one of the world's most powerful brands. How did Marlboro do it? It was a long way from being the first cigarette brand.

Conventional wisdom suggests that advertising was the dominant element in Marlboro's success. But advertising is only a tool.

You can build a house with a hammer, but you need an architect to build a home you can be proud of.

Marlboro represents pure Darwinism at work. Until Marlboro, all cigarettes were unisex brands in the sense that they appealed to women as well as men. Marlboro diverged from the cigarette mainstream by using cowboy imagery to create a masculine brand.

Forget that almost as many women smoke Marlboros as men. Marketing is not about markets; marketing is about minds. And in the mind, Marlboro is a masculine cigarette, which is exactly why women smoke the brand, to express their masculine side.

No. 10: Mercedes-Benz ($21 billion)

Karl Benz invented the automobile in 1885 (a three-wheeler), followed by Gottlieb Daimler, who introduced a four-wheeler in 1886. Later the companies started by the two automotive pioneers merged to form Daimler-Benz AG.

Mercedes-Benz was the brand created by the Daimler-Benz company. Today, Mercedes is one of the most prestigious automobile brands in the world, although the company is doing its best to destroy that prestige. First by merging with a down-market company, Chrysler, and then by introducing a series of down-market Mercedes models.

The Irrelevance of Market Size

What was the size of the cola market the day Coca-Cola was launched?

What was the size of the sixteen-bit personal-computer operating-system market the day Microsoft MS/DOS was launched?

What was the size of the electric-lightbulb market the day Thomas Edison introduced his history-making invention?

What was the size of the microprocessor market the day the Intel 4004 was launched?

What was the size of the motion-picture animation market the day Walt Disney's Mickey Mouse appeared for the first time?

What was the size of the fast-food hamburger market the day the McDonald brothers opened their first unit?

What was the size of the masculine-cigarette market the day Marlboro was repositioned as a male-oriented brand?

What was the size of the automobile market the day Karl Benz introduced his first vehicle?

In all of these eight cases, the size of the market, for all practical purposes, was zero. Eight of the world's ten most valuable brands were created by divergence from an existing category.

The Power of a Narrow Focus

The two remaining cases (IBM and Nokia) are the exceptions to the general rule that brands are built by divergence. But these two cases do demonstrate another branding principle. You can win by doing the right thing or you can win when your competitor does the wrong thing.

In the case of IBM and Nokia, their competitors did the wrong things.

Take Remington Rand, for example. The company made a wide variety of products including electric shavers, industrial television systems, punch-card machines, and computers. It couldn't keep up with the intense product development taking place in the computer field.

Four years after the first Univac was introduced, IBM seized the mainframe computer leadership, which the company has never lost.

Take Motorola, for example. The company made the classic line-extension mistake. Putting the Motorola name on an emerging new category called the cellphone.

But didn't IBM do the same thing as Motorola? Put the IBM name on mainframe computers even though the company made other products, most notably punch-card machines? True, but IBM's intense focus on computers turned the IBM brand into a "mainframe computer" brand.

That never happened at Motorola. The Motorola brand never stood alone as a cellphone brand. It was, and still is, a conglomerate brand that stands for semiconductors, global communications equipment, cable modems, television set-top boxes, home theater equipment, emergency radios, and military and space electronic equipment in addition to cellphones.

Motorola even made ill-fated forays into personal computers and mainframe computers. With the Motorola name, of course.

The Market versus the Mind

Critical to making correct branding decisions is the ability to differentiate between the market and the mind.

The primary objective of a branding program is never the market for the product or service. The primary objective of a branding program is always the mind of the prospect. The mind comes first; the market follows where the mind leads.

Many managers try to short-circuit this process. They think in terms of markets and ignore the need to first influence minds. This thinking can be the source of much confusion about market definitions and positions.

Take Marlboro cigarettes, for example. One could argue that the target market for the Marlboro brand was the entire cigarette category. And that the cowboy was only a clever way to appeal to this market.

This is the approach that drives the advertising industry. Marlboro got lucky with cowboys, so the search went on for other clever visuals that could sell cigarette brands. Animals (Camel), swimming pools (Parliament), race car drivers (Winston), and so forth.

The mind doesn't think markets. The mind thinks categories.

In this respect, the visual is only a means to an end. In Marlboro's case the end is a category the mind identifies as "masculine" cigarette.

Sure, ultimately you would like your brand to dominate the entire market, as the Marlboro brand eventually did. But the way to do this is to start small, not big.

The first question to ask is, does a category exist in the mind called "masculine" cigarette? The second question to ask is, can you create a brand that could start a divergence from the mainstream cigarette market? A divergence that would eventually create a "masculine" cigarette category?

The Process Does Not Depend on the Market

Dozens of masculine cigarette brands may have been on the market the day that Marlboro was relaunched as a masculine brand. What matters is not what's on the market. What matters is what's in the mind. Is there an open hole or position for a new category?

Dozens of expensive watch brands were on the market on July 2, 1908, the day Hans Wilsdorf registered the trademark Rolex. (The Swiss watch industry started in Geneva in the middle of the sixteenth century.) But there was no category in the average mind called "expensive watch," and certainly no brands were in that category even if the average watch buyer was dimly aware that you could buy a $5,000 watch.

Like the launch of Marlboro, the launch of Rolex created the perception of a new category (expensive watch), identified the category with a new brand (Rolex), and eventually drove the market in that direction. Before Rolex the market for expensive watches was insignificant. Today, expensive watches represent a substantial share of the watch market.

What's the size of the market?

Zero. That's great! That's the market we want to target.

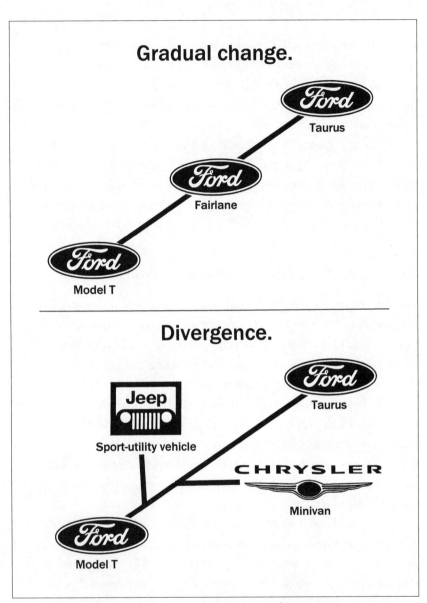

FORD SEDANS HAVE GRADUALLY CHANGED. ABRUPT CHANGE, OR DIVERGENCE, OCCURS WHEN NEW TYPES OF VEHICLES ARE INTRODUCED.

Chapter 4

Gradual Change vs. Divergence

DARWIN RECOGNIZED THAT EVOLUTION had two aspects. One is a gradual change from an ancestral to a current condition (called anagenesis). The other is divergence, or a spitting of the ancestral tree to create new branches (called cladogenesis).

In biology, anagenesis (gradual change) and cladogenesis (divergence) are largely independent processes. Anagenesis produces strawberries the size of plums. It just won't produce a plum. It takes divergence to do that.

In business, the two processes are largely independent, too. What can cause problems is confusing the two. You need to recognize what is normal, natural change and what conditions can lead to divergence, which is abrupt change.

A 2004 Ford Taurus doesn't look like a 1955 Ford Fairlane, but they are still both sedans.

There have been a lot of changes in Ford sedans over the years, but they didn't evolve into minivans or sport-utility vehicles.

If you see divergence as natural change, you will miss the opportunity to create a profitable new brand. If you see natural change as divergence, you might launch a new brand that turns out to be a disaster.

Principle No. 1: Gradual Change

The first fundamental principle of evolution is survival of the fittest. The competition between individuals improves the species over an extended period. Darwin believed that all living things are engaged in a fierce struggle for existence and that this tended to kill off those plants and animals that inherit unfavorable traits.

Over time, a species evolves and because of competition becomes stronger and more resistant to the unfavorable conditions of life.

One hundred years ago, the average American infant could expect to live to the age of forty-seven. Today his or her life expectancy is seventy-seven years.

Two hundred years ago, the average American adult male was five feet seven inches tall. Today the average American adult male is five feet nine inches tall. Two inches over two centuries doesn't seem like much change until you multiply it by the thousands of centuries of human existence.

In addition to *Homo sapiens*, birds, bees, plants, and animals improve as nature discriminates against the weak.

In the Olympic Games of 1896, Thomas Burke of the United States won the hundred-meter run in 12.0 seconds. In the Olympic Games of 2000, Maurice Green of the United States won the event in 9.87 seconds. Individuals don't improve much over time, but the species does. All the competitors in the 1896 event (in their prime) would not have qualified for a spot in the 2000 games.

Principle No. 2: Divergence

The second fundamental principle of evolution is derived directly from the first. It's the principle of divergence. The competition between species drives them further and further apart.

Darwin describes the process as follows: "Therefore, during the modification of the descendants of any one species, and during the incessant struggle of all species to increase in numbers, the more diversified the descendants become, the better will be their chance of success in the battle for life. . . . Natural selection, as has just been remarked, leads to divergence of character and to much extinction of the less improved and intermediate forms of life."

A famous experiment in biology demonstrates the principle. Place two different species of paramecia in a test tube and come back in a few days. One species will have occupied the top of the test tube and the other species will have occupied the bottom. The border between the two is a desert.

Likewise with barnacles. One species takes the high-tide line and another species takes the low-tide line. (In marketing, a brand that tries to occupy two different positions is often referred to as being stuck in the "mushy middle.")

Two Kinds of Competition

These two principles of nature have great relevance in the unnatural field of marketing. Competition between individuals (brands) improves the species. Competition between species (categories) drives the categories further and further apart.

Take brands in the category called personal computers. A manufacturer of personal computers that didn't continually improve and upgrade its products would soon find itself out of business. The same fate holds true for most products and services. You can't sell yesterday's products to today's consumers.

Darwin's second principle is equally valid in marketing. Competition between species (categories) drives the categories further and further apart. Compaq introduced the first portable computer, which weighed eighteen pounds. It was essentially a slimmed-down desktop with a handle. Instead of calling the product a "portable" computer, users called it a "luggable" computer.

Compare today's desktop computer with today's portable computer (now called a laptop). On Laura's desk is a Dell Dimension XPS T550 computer (29 pounds,) a nineteen-inch Sony LCD monitor (17 pounds), and a Microsoft ergonomic keyboard and mouse (3.5 pounds). Total weight: 49.5 pounds.

On the road, however, Laura carries a Toshiba Protégé, which weighs in at just 4.5 pounds. No longer can you put a handle on a desktop computer and call it a "portable." The portable or laptop computer has diverged from the desktop computer.

Visually it would be difficult to see the common ancestry of the laptop and the desktop computer. But intellectually we see the connection because they use common software and both are called personal computers.

The process never stops. Today the laptop category is dividing into full-featured machines that weigh six to eight pounds and ultralight machines that weigh three to four pounds.

This is an important concept because your instincts might lead you in the opposite direction. If you think of "the" customer as a single identity (and many companies do), your instincts are to satisfy "the" customer's every wish. As a result, a laptop computer needs to be full-featured, yet ultralight. In other words, you put yourself right in the mushy middle where there is no market.

The "sweet spot" of a market is an illusion that will soon give way to multiple sweet spots. So which spot do you want your brand to occupy? The top of the test tube or the bottom of the test tube? Trying to occupy both spots leads directly to the mushy-middle.

The automobile industry has often fallen into the trap of satisfying the consumer's every wish. So every year, cars become a little longer, a little wider, a little more loaded with chrome, and a little more expensive. Sooner or later, automobile brands are pushed out of their natural niches.

The Pressure to Diverge

Darwin writes about a human example of the pressure that nature exerts on species to diverge. "As with mariners shipwrecked near a coast, it would have been better for the good swimmers if they had been able to swim still further, whereas it would have been better for the bad swimmers if they had not been able to swim at all and had stuck to the wreck."

If sailors were a species, given enough time and enough shipwrecks, there would eventually be two species of sailors: swimmers and nonswimmers. Again, the mushy middle is the place to avoid.

If there were only two sports in the world, basketball and horse racing, you'd eventually wind up with only two types of athletes. The big and the small. Centers and jockeys. Giraffes and gazelles.

In marketing, it's easy to see how a brand "evolves" over time. The 1908 Model T Ford has become the 2004 Ford Taurus. What isn't as obvious is how the brand has also "diverged" over the same period.

In 1908, Ford had one model, one color, one price. Today, Ford has ten different models you can buy:

- Ford Crown Victoria (luxury car)
- Ford Econoline (van)
- Ford Excursion (large sport-utility vehicle)

- Ford Explorer (sport-utility vehicle)
- Ford Focus (compact car)
- Ford F-series (pickup truck)
- Ford Mustang (sports car)
- Ford Ranger (compact pickup truck)
- Ford Taurus (standard car)
- Ford Windstar (minivan)

The models in today's Ford lineup look different and perform different functions, but they obviously had a common ancestor, the Model T Ford.

Gradual change has improved the breed at Ford, while divergence has created nine additional categories where once there was only one.

Notice that each category pretty much stands on it own. The pickup truck is not a modified compact car. The sport-utility vehicle is not a modified sports car. Although they obviously have some elements in common.

Man, according to Charles Darwin, is not descended from monkeys, although they may have had a common ancestor. Somewhere in the distant past, *Homo sapiens* diverged or branched off from the limb of the same tree that also produced apes, gorillas, chimpanzees, orangutans, gibbons, and monkeys.

Keeping Up with Competition

Any brand that wants to keep up with competition has to "evolve." You couldn't sell a 1908 Model T Ford in competition with a 2004 Chevrolet Malibu. The Ford brand is the same (even the logotype remains relatively unchanged), but the product has drastically changed to take advantage of technological developments in the automobile industry.

To a greater or lesser extent, this is true of all brands. Change is the price you pay to stay in the evolutionary ball game.

Most leading brands have nothing to fear from the passage of time. As long as they do a reasonably good job of "keeping up with competition," they should manage to keep their positions in the marketplace. Even if Chevrolet introduces a better car, Ford is unlikely to lose its automotive leadership.

Why is this so? Because it takes time for a better product to change the minds of automobile buyers. And time is on the side of the leader. Monitoring competition and then matching (or outdoing) their developments is the name of the brand-maintenance game today.

It's Darwin's second principle that creates opportunities (and causes problems) for marketers. Divergence is the evolutionary principle responsible for the creation of new species. And a new species can easily wipe out an existing species (or product category). Witness what the personal computer has done to the typewriter. And what the Internet is doing to facsimile.

The Word "Evolution" Is Misleading

The word *evolution* implies a gradual transformation from one species to another. This is not what happens in nature.

Charles Darwin did not use the word *evolution* in the original edition of *The Origin of Species*. As a matter of fact, he only used it reluctantly in later editions when it became obvious that the word *evolution* would forever be connected to his work.

To Darwin, the divergence principle was equally as important as the principle of gradual change. If nature took an "evolutionary" path only, it would mean that many species would be so closely related that it would be hard to tell one from another. Is that animal a cat or a dog? Well, it's hard to tell. Could be one or another.

Darwin's genius was in recognizing that species like cats and dogs might have a common ancestor, but that they had "branched off" or diverged in response to environmental changes. Over time, the differences between species become exaggerated. In Darwin's terms, "nature favors the extremes."

(In branding, too, nature favors the extremes. Look at the success of Rolex, Starbucks, and Ritz-Carlton at the high end. And Swatch, Wal-Mart, and Costco at the low end.)

If "evolution" were the only thing that ever happened in the history of Earth, the world would be populated by the biggest, strongest, toughest single-cell individuals you can possibly imagine.

Too bad. Evolution of brands is widely accepted as a marketing concept. What's not widely accepted is the divergence of brands. Yet over the long haul, it's divergence, not evolution, that creates the most opportunities to build a brand.

Take the Ford Motor Company. Along the way, Ford missed many "divergence" opportunities to launch new brands. The sports car branch, for example, which is currently dominated by Porsche, or the luxury car branch, which is currently dominated by Mercedes-Benz. Ford also missed the sport-utility vehicle branch (Jeep), and even the minivan branch (Chrysler.)

"Evolution" or gradual change is an obvious strategy: "Every year we need to make our products better, cheaper, and more reliable than ever." But divergence is not. In fact, your instincts might lead you in exactly the wrong direction.

Kmart, Wal-Mart, and Target

Take Kmart versus Wal-Mart. Kmart was obviously losing the battle of mass merchandisers to their archrival from Bentonville, Arkansas. So what did Kmart do?

They hired new management, who cut back on the weekly

circulars that promoted an endless array of specials and instead instituted an "everyday low pricing" policy similar to Wal-Mart's.

Do customers like what the industry calls ELP, or everyday low pricing? Of course, that's why they shop at Wal-Mart, the chain that promotes (and delivers) on its promise of "always low prices."

Target, on the other hand, went out of its way to "branch off" from the Wal-Mart pattern. Wide aisles, neat displays, and designer merchandise help to differentiate the Target brand from the Wal-Mart brand. "Cheap chic" is the theme. (Oprah Winfrey calls the store "Tar-ZHEY.")

Target is branching off from the mass merchandiser category to become an "upscale" mass merchandiser.

If you put the Target, Wal-Mart, and Kmart brands in a test tube marketed "mass merchandisers" and mixed them up, you would find Target at the top, Wal-Mart at the bottom, and Kmart, the company that went bankrupt, in the mushy middle.

If you study the history of Sam Walton and his Wal-Mart chain, you'll find that the brand went through periods of both divergence and gradual change.

Initially, the Wal-Mart brand was a classic divergence story. Kmart was the leading discount chain with stores in most of the big cities. Instead of competing head-to-head with Kmart, Wal-Mart opened stores only in smaller communities.

With little or no competition, Wal-Mart became stronger every year through gradual change. Once the company had strengthened its warehouses and distribution systems, Wal-Mart was strong enough to move into Kmart's territory. "Survival of the fittest" determined the outcome in this classic battle.

Two Brands Cannot Occupy the Same Position

In the struggle for life, no two species (or two brands) can occupy the same position. If they try to do so, one species (or one brand) will drive the other to extinction.

What's true in the long run is often hard to see in the short run. A clever promotion, a string of good luck, or some other marketing miracle might boost the fortunes of a brand . . . in the short term. But unless the brand finds an effective strategy, it is usually doomed to die in the long run.

Take Miller Lite. After years of declining market share, the brand recently registered a slight uptick due to its "low-carb" campaign. (Everybody is talking about low-carb diets these days.)

But is low-carb a viable long-term strategy for a mass market Joe Six-pack brand? Miller Lite needs a mainstream idea if it is going to stay in the same league as Bud Light and Coors Light. "Healthy beer" is not going to do it.

Especially since Michelob Ultra was launched first, focused exclusively on low-carbs and has fewer carbs than Lite. Ultra is the low-carb beer of choice. Miller might pick up some sales in the short term, but in the long term they will be right back where they started.

Saving an existing brand is only half the story. The other half of the story is the creation of new brands. Far too much time and effort is devoted to saving brands when the same resources invested in new brands might produce a lot more bang for the buck.

Darwin believed that all living organisms (plants as well as animals) must be related through their common descent from some simple original stock. If so, the amount of divergence is awesome. Today about 1.7 million species are known to exist, with about fifty thousand described in detail. That's a small fraction of the 10 to 100 million species estimated to populate the earth.

Nor does this number take into consideration the millions of species that have become extinct over the years. The dinosaurs, the mammoths, and many others. Probably more species have become extinct than are currently alive. (The same is true of brands.)

"Endless Forms Most Beautiful and Wonderful"

This multiplication of life-forms created by divergence can be seen as a positive force. Darwin sums up his view of life in the last two sentences of *The Origin of Species.* "Thus, from the war of nature, from famine and death, the most exalted object which we are capable of conceiving, namely, the production of the higher animals, directly follows. There is grandeur in this view of life, with its several powers, having been originally breathed into a few forms or into one; and that, whilst this planet has gone cycling on according to the fixed law of gravity, from so simple a beginning endless forms most beautiful and most wonderful have been, and are being evolved."

Look at the endless forms of products that did not exist fifty or a hundred years ago. Computers, cellphones, digital cameras. Light beer, diet cola, energy drinks. English muffins, freeze-dried coffee, yogurt. Microwave ovens, cable television, videocassette recorders, DVDs.

Will a cornucopia of new products continue to spew out of research-and-development laboratories in the future? Sure.

In truth, the vast majority of the most beautiful and the most wonderful new products are still to come. And each one of them creates an opportunity for the introduction of a new brand.

A new brand that can make you wealthy beyond your wildest dreams. But first you have to resist the lures of the convergence crowd.

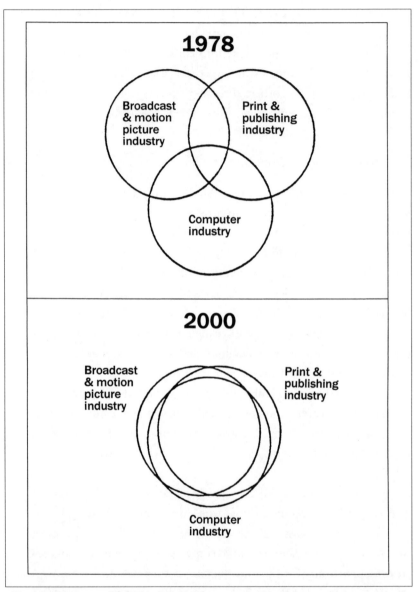

1978

Broadcast
& motion
picture
industry

Print &
publishing
industry

Computer
industry

2000

Broadcast
& motion
picture
industry

Print &
publishing
industry

Computer
industry

THE FOUNDER OF M.I.T.'s MEDIA LAB USED A CHART LIKE THIS IN 1978
TO SHOW THE FUTURE CONVERGENCE OF THREE MAJOR INDUSTRIES.

Chapter 5

The Curse of the Clock Radio

THE CLOCK RADIO HAS DONE MORE DAMAGE than all the government agencies and Wall Street investment bankers combined.

The success of the ubiquitous clock radio has convinced thousands of otherwise rational business leaders that the future belongs to a concept called convergence.

If the clock can combine with the radio to produce an interesting and useful device, then what might happen if entire industries were to converge?

What Sculley Hath Wrought

Some people give the credit (or blame) to the recent surge of interest in convergence to a *New York Times* interview that appeared on September 15, 1992: "John Sculley, chairman of Apple, has been preaching about a post-industrial promised land where four giant industries (computers, consumer electronics, communications and information) will converge.

"Mr. Sculley describes an emerging industry that he says will be a $3.5-trillion business within a decade.

"It will, he says, be more than half as large as the combined economies of the United States, Canada, and Mexico are today."

The following year the *Wall Street Journal* jumped on the convergence bandwagon: "Shock is a common feeling these days among leaders of five of the world's biggest industries: computing, communications, consumer electronics, entertainment and publishing. Under a common technological lash—the increasing ability to cheaply convey huge chunks of video, sound, graphics and text in digital form—they are transforming and converging."

That same year, *Fortune* magazine, commenting on the proposed acquisition of Tele-Communications Inc. by Bell Atlantic, fanned the convergence fire this way: "*Convergence* will be the buzzword for the rest of the decade. This isn't just about cable and telephone hopping into bed together. It's about the cultures and corporations of major industries—telecommunications (including the long-distance companies), cable, computer, entertainment, consumer electronics, publishing, and even retailing—combining into one mega-industry that will provide information, entertainment, goods, and services to your home and office."

Also that same year, the *New York Times* was just as enthusiastic about convergence: "Digital convergence is not a futuristic prospect or a choice to be made among other choices; it is an onrushing train. The digitalization of all forms of information (including the transmission of sensations) has proven itself to be accurate, economical, ecologically wise, universally applicable, easy to use, and fast as light."

Headline of a recent article in the *New York Times:* "As 2 Powerful Industries Converge, Change Will Abound." The paper went on to report, "The convergence of media and technology, long predicted but not yet fulfilled, is at last showing signs of happening—with high-speed Internet access making much of it possible."

Putting Their Money Where Their Mouths Are

Furthermore, many major publications are putting their money where their mouths are. The *Wall Street Journal* publishes a European magazine insert called *Convergence*. *Business Week* runs an annual conference entitled "The Global Convergence Summit."

Dow Jones conducts an annual conference in London entitled *"The Wall Street Journal Europe*'s Annual CEO Summit on Converging Technologies." Speakers at the seventh annual summit included Michael Dell, CEO of Dell, and Michael Capellas, the former CEO of Compaq and now CEO of WorldCom.

In 1999, *Forbes ASAP* magazine published a special issue entitled "The Great Convergence." The editorial writer for the issue got carried away: "Great ideas have changed us many times before. We divide much of human history by the dates they emerged: fire, the domestication of animals, farming and trade, democracy, empire, the divine right of kings, perspective, Newtonian mechanics, liberty, mass production, the nation-state, evolution and relativity, fission, abstraction, digitization, equality. The emerging idea of our time is convergence. It is the governing metaphor of the turn of the millennium."

Democracy, liberty, equality, convergence? Which one of these four "great ideas" seems out of place to you?

Convergence versus Divergence

This is the most important issue in marketing today. The path you choose has enormous implications for the success of your brand.

Creating a new category and then making sure that your brand name stands for that new category in the mind is not easy. Especially today when the emphasis in product design and development is not on creating new categories, but on combining existing categories.

If categories are converging, then existing brand names (and the companies that own these brand names) are going to become more powerful. If the handheld computer (or PDA) converges with the cellphone (as many pundits have predicted), then the resulting PDA/cellphone market would likely be dominated either by Palm, the dominant PDA brand, or by Nokia, the dominant cellphone brand.

If categories are diverging, then the opportunity arises for new brands.

You know where our beliefs lie. In spite of the overwhelming media hype to the contrary, we strongly believe that convergence will never happen. Technologies don't converge. They diverge. And thankfully they do, otherwise it would be almost impossible to create new brands.

In the best of circumstances, branding is not an easy task. Especially today when the convergence philosophy has made such enormous inroads in the corporate psyche.

The Hype Marches On

George Orwell once said that some ideas are so foolish you had to belong to the intelligentsia to believe them. (Think communism.)

Convergence is another one of those ideas. And interactive television is one of the convergenists' favorite subjects.

According to futurist Faith Popcorn, "Someday in the near future I'll be watching Ally McBeal. I like the outfit she's wearing. So I put my hand on the TV screen and she'll interrupt the program and say, 'Faith, do you like what I'm wearing?' 'Yeah,' I say, 'I like your suit.' And she'll say, 'Here are the colors it comes in.' I tell Ally that I'll take just navy or black, maybe both. And she'll say, 'No, you won't, Faith. You've already got too many navy and black outfits in your closet right now. I think you should try red this time.' And I say okay, and the next day the red suit is delivered in my size to my home."

When asked how soon this would happen, Ms. Popcorn replied, "Within the next five years." (Ally McBeal is gone, so Faith Popcorn will never get a chance to try Ally's personal shopping service.)

Virtually all the intelligentsia are solidly lined up in support of the convergence concept. Here is a sampling:

- Alvin Toffler, author of *Future Shock:* "Today we are once again racing toward a metaconvergence—this time at superaccelerated speeds."
- John Naisbitt, author of *Megatrends:* "Everything is finally coming together. That is what will create the telecommunications revolution we have heard about for so long. Here is a list of the ideas and media that are in the process of coming together: fiber optics, interactive, digital, wireless,

computer, entertainment, television, computer software, telephone, multimedia, cellular, global, pagers, virtual reality, networks."

- Denis Waitley, author of *Seeds of Greatness:* "We have recently entered one of the great historic pivotal points that will forever change the way all society will work. A brave new world is here."
- John Malone, cable pioneer: "Media, computers, and telecommunications are converging into a gazillion-dollar worldwide information industry."
- Mitch Kapor, founder of Lotus Development Corporation: "The idea that there are separate telephone and cable industries—that idea is dead."
- Bill Gates, Microsoft chairman: "The convergence of the PC and consumer electronics markets is a tremendous opportunity. More of the consumer devices are becoming as powerful, connected, and programmable as the PC, so it's more important than ever to create software that makes these devices work well together."
- Bob Palmer, former CEO of Digital Equipment Corporation: "Computing, telecommunications, publishing, education, entertainment, and consumer electronics are converging. The distinctions between their products and services is fading rapidly."
- Nicholas Negroponte, founding director of MIT's Media Laboratory: "Don't worry about the difference between the TV set and the PC; in the future there will be no distinction between the two."
- Barry Diller, CEO of InterActive Corp.: "Everyone knows that television, the computer, and the communications network are racing to become one seamless entity."

And, would you believe, the city of Denver is promoting itself as Convergence Corridor. According to an advertisement in *Forbes* magazine: "It's here. It's now. It's Denver, Colorado, where companies are redefining the way the world communicates by bringing voice, data and video together (convergence) for faster, more reliable global interaction. It's all happening in a city that has reinvented itself as the 21st century's Convergence Corridor."

Not to be outdone is the state of Illinois, which is calling itself the Convergence Economy. Here is how the state describes itself: "An economy where different technological platforms are coming together, driving the success of business and creating new opportunities for the future. To thrive in this challenging business dynamic, companies are seeking a state that provides them with a solid foundation that supports industries that make convergence possible. Illinois is where it all comes together."

The Case for Convergence

Steve Case, former CEO of America Online, was one of the earliest and most fervent believers in convergence. According to the *New York Times*, "So he called Mr. Levin (CEO of Time Warner) to describe a future in which the media and Internet seem increasingly likely to converge—as the personal computer, the television and the telephone become parallel digital pathways to new types of information and entertainment services.

"My motivation is to position this company to capitalize on the era of convergence," Mr. Case explained.

USA Today ballyhooed the benefits of the merger this way: "The marriage of America Online and Time Warner is a giant step toward the kind of future once previewed in science fiction. . . ."

Fortune commented on the Case case as follows: "He paints a picture of a customer-focused behemoth—if that's not a contradiction in terms—that will be a force in media, communications, retailing, financial services, health care, education, and travel, competing with everything from newspapers, TV, and radio stations to phone companies, banks, brokerage firms, auto dealerships, travel agencies, the local photo shop, and the corner bar. 'Interactivity will become more and more a part of everyday life for more and more people,' Case says. 'This company is perfectly positioned at the epicenter of change.'"

Perfectly positioned? Steve Case is gone. Jerry Levin is gone. But convergence is still here.

On February 7, 2000, American Online and Time Warner together were worth $240 billion on the stock market. Currently the company (now called simply Time Warner) is worth $76 billion, a drop of 68 percent.

Corporations for Convergence

Convergence has the solid backing of the electronics industry. Electronics, of course, is more than just an industry. It's the leading edge of a country's economy. As electronics goes, so goes the nation.

- **Sony.** According to *Advertising Age*, the company has just completed a sweeping reorganization "to capitalize on the convergence of consumer electronics, information technology, communications and entertainment."

  At Sony's annual "Dream World" convention, held in Paris this year, Sir Howard Stringer, chairman of Sony Corporation of America, said, "In Europe, we're a hardware brand, not a convergence brand. We're trying to exhibit our digital convergence leadership, which is still a battle we have to fight over and over."

  When asked about the collapse of Vivendi Universal,

France's version of a convergence company, Sir Howard replied, "Vivendi is getting out of this business, but no one is asking us to get out of the business."

According to a story in the *New York Times*, "At Sony, he insists, the idea of convergence is now so deeply ingrained that it manifests itself in myriad collaborations among its film and record executives, video game designers and engineers."

Dream on, Sir Howard.

- **Samsung.** "Making Digital Convergence Come Alive" is the headline of a recent Samsung advertisement.

  The copy goes on to say: "Samsung DigitAll is all about making the promise of digital convergence come alive no matter where you are, who you are, or what you do. It's TVs made for websurfing (as well as watching hot episodes of your favorite TV shows). Refrigerators that keep your food cold (and let you watch a spicy cooking DVD wirelessly from your DVD player while standing at the stove). Phones that let you see as well as talk and listen."

  According to Samsung Electronics vice chairman Jong Yong Yun, the convergence of technologies is destined to completely change our society. "Evolution will eventually lead to the ubiquitous network," Yun noted. He believes that this future society will be free of the distinction between, and the individual limitations of, networks, devices, and time.

  Take a trip on HMS *Beagle*, Mr. Yun. Evolution moves in the opposite direction. Towards divergence, not convergence.

- **Philips.** Europe's largest electronics company is pursuing a similar strategy, which it calls the Connected Home. Its strategy is to "position the company as a leader as we move from stand-alone boxes to smart networks whose 'intelligent' components are integrated into furniture, clothing, windows, and walls."

The Connected Home, according to Philips, is "a place where devices are linked through wireless and Internet technologies, where they speak to each other and exchange data." For example, says a Philips brochure, "If someone is watching a film in the living room and wants to move to the kitchen to make some popcorn, the film will follow them without interruption."

- **Microsoft.** The world's largest software company is currently mounting a massive effort to build software that will link everything together. "Bill Gates who is now ensconced as chairman and chief software architect," according to *Fortune* magazine, "is determined to make Microsoft code even more ubiquitous, linking all kinds of computing and communications and consumer electronics devices in a mesh of software that will make the entire Internet and everything on it a single, programmable entity. . . . It also means finding ways to implant Microsoft code in cellphones, game machines, and other consumer devices—pretty much anything with an electrical current—so they will play together with a minimum of human tinkering."

- **Intel.** The world's largest microchip company recently announced a new silicon chip that can "blur the line between computing and communications."

   "It is yet another step in the path to convergence we have been discussing for the past few years," said Paul Otellini, Intel's president.

"Before there were two worlds, computing and communications," said Alan Huang, a former Bell Labs physicist. "Now they will be the same, and we will have powerful computers everywhere."

- **Legend.** China's largest personal-computer maker has just introduced the Supremia2, a product that bridges the gap between computers, stereos, and television sets. With a Supremia2, a Chinese family can view TV programs and photographs as well as do their household accounts.

  Legend believes that convergence plays to its strengths, given that the company's product range already spans digital cameras, laptops, and pocket PCs.

  It's interesting that companies that make a wide range of products (Sony, Samsung, Philips and Legend) are strong believers in convergence.

  Management looks at its product line and thinks, how can we put all these things together?

- **NEC Corporation.** Ever since 1977, Japan's NEC Corporation has been dedicated to a convergence concept it calls C&C, for "computers and communications." A pet project of former CEO Koji Kobayashi, C&C has become wellnigh a religion inside NEC.

  A few years ago, Hisashi Kaneko, another former CEO, predicted, "There will be convergence between the PC and other electronic products. In about ten years, all these technologies will come together."

- **Hitachi.** "Where will the convergence of computing, communications and content lead?" is the headline of a Hitachi advertisement in the *Wall Street Journal* several years ago. (Nowhere, we say.)

- **Siemens.** The company's Web site says it all: www. siemens.convergenceadvantage.com.

- **Canon.** Why did the company introduce a line of personal computers to complement its copier and camera products? According to a company vice president, "Canon needs to have a presence in PCs to take advantage of the merging technologies of computing, print, copying, and faxing."

Everything came to a head at a 2004 Las Vegas convention that attracted more than 110,000 attendees and 2,500 exhibitors. According to *Newsweek*, "Last week's Consumer Electronics Show in Las Vegas was all about crowing that the long-promised 'digital convergence' was finally underway."

At the Las Vegas show, the Japanese electronic giants rallied around a convergence theme called ubiquity. According to the *Wall Street Journal*, "In its narrowest sense, 'ubiquitous' refers to a network of gadgets—the kind Japanese companies are famous for—that pass information around. . . . But for those in the know, 'ubiquitous' describes a grandiose vision where everything—from potatoes to people to the garbage—is linked up to a big network that's accessible any place, any time."

What the Clock Radio Hath Wrought

Is it possible these crazy convergence concepts got their start from the ubiquitous clock radio? If so, it might be worthwhile to take another look at this seminal convergence product. Is the clock radio really the revolutionary development it seems to be?

How many clocks in the world receive radio signals? Very few.
How many radios in the world have clocks? Very few.

Nor is the clock radio universally loved, especially the ones found in hotel rooms, which no one in America seems to know how to work. "I have an MS in industrial engineering and an MBA," said one user. "The first thing I do when I get to a room is to unplug the radio to make sure it does not awake me in the middle of the night with the traffic report because a prior guest set the alarm for four A.M."

Another user tried asking the hotel. "I went to the desk during the evening to ask them how to set the alarm. Both people at the front desk said many people asked that question, but the staff had no idea how to set the clock."

It's not just the clock radio that gets the convergenists excited. Another device has had an even greater effect.

NEVER ONE TO MISS A TREND, ABSOLUT VODKA JUMPED ON THE
CONVERGENCE CONCEPT WITH THIS ADVERTISEMENT.

Chapter 6

Swiss Army Knife Thinking

EVERY MACHO MALE HAS ONE, but when was the last time you saw someone actually use the scissors on a Swiss Army knife to cut something? Or the screwdriver to screw something? Or the tweezers to tweeze something?

Many "Swiss Army knife" products are on the market. They get a lot of publicity, they capture the public's imagination, they get bought by the millions, and then they wind up in dresser drawers where they sit idle for decades.

Swiss Army knife thinking is rampant up and down the corridors of corporate America. (Even Absolut vodka celebrated the convergence concept in one of its famous "bottle" advertisements.)

What are the three biggest, most exciting, most dynamic industries in America? Most people would probably say television, computers, and the Internet. Great, why not combine the Internet with your television set as well as your computer? And so the cry goes up, interactive TV, the wave of the future.

Some wave.

Interactive TV, Microsoft Version

In 1997, Microsoft bought WebTV Networks for $425 million and has since poured more than half a billion dollars into the venture. Results have been dismal. Today, WebTV (whose name has been changed to MSN TV) has about 1 million subscribers, a trivial number compared to the more than 100 million TV sets in use.

Convergence has clearly become an obsession with Microsoft. "Has William H. Gates become the Captain Ahab of the information age?" asked the *New York Times*. "Mr. Gates's white whale remains an elusive digital set-top cable box that his company, the Microsoft Corporation, is hoping will re-create the personal computer industry by blending the PC, the Internet and the television set into a leviathan living-room entertainment and information machine."

Also in 1997, Microsoft invested $1 billion for 11.5 percent of Comcast Corporation, at the time the nation's fourth-largest cable operator. According to the *New York Times*, "Comcast will become a seedbed for Mr. Gates to test his vision of a converging world."

But that was just a start. In 1999, Microsoft pumped $5 billion into AT&T and secured a contract to install Microsoft TV software in as many as 10 million AT&T set-top boxes. Not a single box made it to the top of a television set serviced by an AT&T cable system, and since AT&T is now out of the cable business, the contract is just another convergence dead end.

Microsoft keeps trying. After the lukewarm reception of WebTV, Microsoft moved on to UltimateTV. Putting a clock together with a radio is nothing compared to what Microsoft has in mind for today's couch potato.

UltimateTV consists of a DirecTV satellite subscription ($22 to $83 a month), a special rooftop dish capable of pulling in two channels at once ($50 plus $200 installation), a thirty-five-hour satellite receiver and digital video recorder ($399), and a subscription to UltimateTV ($9.95 a month). You save money, of course, by using your own television set.

What can you do with UltimateTV? Everything, it's the ultimate in television. You can record and store up to thirty-five hours of programming. You can pause and instant-replay live TV. You can watch and record two shows at once. You can send email and chat online while watching TV.

Fred Allen once said that television is 85 percent confusion and 15 percent commission. UltimateTV may turn out to be 100 percent confusion. "If programming the clock on the VCR gives you a migraine," reported *Fortune* magazine, "UltimateTV will trigger a full nervous breakdown."

Interactive TV, AOL Version

Even before the Time Warner merger, America Online was a strong supporter of convergence. In 1999, the company invested $1.5 billion in Hughes Electronics and got a deal to launch AOLTV on its DirecTV satellite service.

In July 2000, AOL rolled out its AOLTV service, a $249 set-top box that allows users to send instant messages, read email, chat online, and surf the Web while watching a TV show. AOL subscribers, who now pay $21.95 a month, would fork over an additional $14.95 for AOLTV. For nonmembers, the monthly cost would be $24.95 plus the cost of the box.

For all that money what could you actually do with AOLTV? *USA Today* imagined it this way: "Imagine lying on a sofa, watching a program produced by *Cooking Light* magazine on your wall-size plasma television. AOL Time Warner serves up a digital version of the recipe. You send the recipe to your refrigerator; it knows you need milk, which it orders online."

USA Today calls interactive television "the holy grail for AOL Time Warner. It will eventually enable TV viewers to communicate, shop, play games, call up information and order news and entertainment on demand from the TV screen." (It might be churlish of us to point out that in two thousand years no one has ever found the Holy Grail.)

As you might have expected, AOLTV is now on hiatus and is no longer accepting new subscribers.

Interactive TV, NASCAR Version

If you are a subscriber to NASCAR in Car service, currently offered by Time Warner, Cox, and Comcast, you can watch the races from the cockpits of seven different drivers. Push the button on a special remote-control unit to switch from one driver's perspective to the next, or instead simply watch the standard broadcast version of the program.

For something like $20 a month, you can put yourself in the driver's seat and even hear his conversations with the pits. But when the novelty wears off, when you miss a big crash because you were watching the action from the wrong car, when you'd rather be eating popcorn and drinking a beer than pushing buttons, you might have second thoughts about the value of interactive TV.

Times have changed, reasons the convergence crowd. Young people in particular want to interact with an entertainment medium like television. As proof, industry pundits cite the success of video games like NASCAR Thunder. (More money is spent on the interactive medium of video games than is spent on the passive medium of motion pictures.)

True, but when you play NASCAR Thunder, you are the driver and you control the car. When you watch NASCAR in Car racing, you control nothing. You're just a backseat driver.

"People do not want to be passive when they watch TV," says Nicholas DeMartino, the director of new media ventures for the American Film Institute. "Old people want to be passive. Young people do many things at once, from looking at the Internet to talking on the phone, while they watch television."

The old people we know often read a magazine while they watch TV. But they don't necessarily want the magazine on half the screen and the TV program on the other half.

Nor do young people necessarily want to combine television with the telephone and the Internet just because they might be using several devices at once. You pay a price when you try to put things together. And the price is usually the sacrifice of simplicity, flexibility, and ease of use.

Interactive TV, ABC Version

"We believe in interactive television," says Rich Mandler, general manager of ABC's Enhanced TV group, "because it encourages live TV and live commercial viewing." Give consumers something active to do during a scheduled show, the reasoning goes, and they will watch it, commercials and all.

The first test of that reasoning was *Celebrity Mole II*, starting in January 2004. ABC also offers simple interactive versions of some shows, but most use a two-screen approach. The viewer watches the regular show on a TV set while using a personal computer to get additional material via ABC's Web site.

Celebrity Mole II is different, but you need a personal computer running Windows XP Media Center to get the full picture. A TV card within the PC captures the standard broadcast image, and the network's Web site supplies the additional graphics.

Sounds complicated and it is. Furthermore, how many viewers are going to bother booting up their PCs to watch one show when it's a lot easier to push the power button on the TV remote?

Interactive TV, Newsweek *version*

Here is how *Newsweek* magazine describes television of the future. "You come home from work and grab the remote. As you putter around, removing tie or pantyhose, and occasionally checking the picture, your personal video navigator brings you up to date. You find out what TV shows the kids watched after school and hear a reminder from the florist: it's time to send Aunt Agnes's birthday bouquet; how about this arrangement? You look at a copy of Tommy's report card, issued that day, and a list of movies you could watch that night, based on how much you loved *The Age of Innocence*. You click on the beef bourguignon how-to that you selected this morning; you've got all the ingredients because the program automatically faxed a list to Safeway, which delivered."

That's the hype, but the reality is different. The Internet is an active medium. Nothing happens until the user clicks away at a computer keyboard. Interactivity is an essential element of the Internet experience. Television, on the other hand, is a passive medium.

Convergence is fundamentally a flawed concept, but it's even worse when you try to put an active medium (the Internet) together with a passive medium (television).

Will the average couch potato want to put down his Bud Light long enough to change the camera angle or surf the Net? We don't think so. TV directors get paid for doing that. Why would the average viewer want to do it for nothing?

What's astounding about interactive television is how long this concept has been around and how little progress has been made. Warner Amex Cable introduced QUBE, the first interactive TV system, in Columbus, Ohio, in 1977. That's twenty-seven years ago.

The first airplane flight was made by Wilbur and Orville Wright in 1903. Twenty-four years later Charles Lindbergh flew the Atlantic Ocean solo and the airplane was firmly established as a viable transportation device. Twenty-seven years after the Wright brothers first flew, American, Eastern, and TWA were flying passengers.

Where is interactive television twenty-seven years after its founding? Not ready for its first transatlantic flight, that's for sure.

Semi-interactive Television

Even semi-interactive television hasn't done well at the box office. TiVo and ReplayTV were introduced in 1999 with a blaze of publicity. Called the "personal video recorder," these cool electronic gadgets allow users to zap through commercials and record shows at the touch of a button.

Michael Lewis writing in a cover story in the August 13, 2000, issue of the *New York Times Magazine* equated the founding of TiVo with the end of the mass market. "August 4, 1999, was the beginning of the end of another socialistic force in American life: the mass market." By the end of 2002, the author predicted there would be 5 to 7 million of these personal video recorder boxes in use. Within a decade, 90 million.

Mike Wallace devoted a chunk of *60 Minutes* to singing the praises of TiVo. (The following Monday, TiVo stock rose 27 percent.)

Five years after its unveiling, TiVo has fewer than a million subscribers and the entire personal video recorder industry as a whole has about 2 million subscribers.

Will TiVo and its clones survive? Undoubtedly. For a certain percentage of viewers, a personal video recorder is one of those "I can't live without it" services. Will TiVo's arrival mean the end of the mass market? Unlikely.

Too many business executives see each technological development as "all or nothing at all." Either TiVo is a failure or it's the end of the mass market.

Reality is usually somewhere in between. There's a market for convergence concepts even though they may be out of the mainstream and not represent a trend, which is almost always in the direction of divergence. We predict that the personal video recorder market share will ultimately wind up to be about 10 to 15 percent of the television market, about the same market share enjoyed by supermarket private label brands.

What makes convergence seem successful is the concept's ability to generate massive amounts of publicity. No convergence product, no matter how trivial, is announced without a blaze of favorable PR.

Interactive Telephones

"Everyone seems to agree," reported *The Economist* four years ago, "that the mobile phone will quickly overtake the personal computer as the means by which most people gain access to online services." By 2005, according to Forrester Research, 97 percent of the 177 million cellphones in operation that year will have wireless Web access.

Nobody asked us, but we believe that this is also highly unlikely. Cellphone/Internet devices are complicated and hard to use.

Their tiny screens are suitable only for short messages and simple visuals.

The European telecommunications industry has bought into the interactive telephone fantasy in a big way. In developing their systems for the next generation of interactive phones (the so-called 3G phones), the industry has gone heavily into debt. According to the *New York Times*, "The early mad dash to buy licenses and build networks has left telephone operators saddled with some $330 billion of debt." (It's doubtful that operators will ever get their money back.)

In justifying this kind of investment, telephone operators are quick to quote the success of iMode service introduced by NTT Do-CoMo in Japan. It's the fastest-growing telephone service in the world with around 40 million subscribers.

With iMode service, you can swap notes, buy tickets, and download tunes to play on your phone. In principle you can use an iMode phone to look at Internet sites, but you will likely see only a small portion of the page and what you see may not be meaningful.

Most users spend most of their iMode time on the three thousand or so iMode partner sites operated by some two thousand content providers. What seems to be happening is a classic branching process where iMode sites are diverging from traditional Internet sites.

Instead of one Internet, there will be two: traditional Internet sites and truncated "iMode-type" sites that can be accessed by phone.

Smart Phones

The latest example of Swiss Army knife thinking is called the smart phone. It combines a PDA, or handheld computer, with a cellphone with Internet access. Many smart phones also have a digital camera thrown in. All the major cellphone manufacturers are marketing the devices, including Nokia, Motorola, Samsung, Siemens, and Hitachi. In addition, PDA makers like Handspring (now part of palmOne) have introduced smart phones.

And how smart is it to combine a cellphone with a video-game machine and an MP3 player, as Nokia's new N-Gage does? How many teenage gamers can pay $300 for the phone plus $25 a month for a voice plan, $10 a month to play online games, $30 to $50 for each new game, and $50 for a multimedia card so they can listen to MP3 tunes? Meanwhile, the gold standard of handheld games, the $100 Nintendo Game Boy Advance SP, sells like hotcakes.

Some manufacturers have been adding a keyboard and calling their products communicators rather than smart phones or cell-phones. Take the Nokia 9210 Communicator. It's a cellphone, PDA, wireless email, and Internet device with connections for a digital camera. The software includes a word processor, spreadsheet, pre-sentation viewer, and file manager. What more could you want?

How about simplicity, reliability, convenience, low cost, ease of use, small size, light weight, and protection against obsolescence?

And how smart is it to pay $10 a month to get television on a cellphone. That's what Sprint is charging for a new service called MobiTV, billed as "live television, anywhere, anytime." Or as one re-viewer noted, "live slide show, some places, sometimes."

The Migration Problem

If a convergence technology is going to take hold, it must attract users from the pool of available prospects.

Who would most likely buy a combination cellphone/PDA? Broadly speaking there are two groups of prospects. The first group consists of the "early adopters," who are, generally speaking, the primary targets of any new technology. Can anyone imagine an early adopter who doesn't already have either a cellphone or a PDA? We can't.

Furthermore, these early adopters are more than likely to have the latest, most up-to-date cellphone or PDA. That means that an early adopter would have to throw away a perfectly good cellphone and a perfectly good PDA if he or she bought a combination product. How many people are likely to do that?

The second group consists of prospects who don't own either a cellphone or a PDA. For the most part these are lower-income, unsophisticated people. Most of us walk before we run. Does anyone really expect the non-cellphone, non-PDA user to rush out and buy a $500 or $600 combination device?

One category the transition problem *doesn't* affect are the columnists who write the glowing reviews about all these convergence products. They already get all the free stuff they could possibly use. It's no problem for a columnist to dump a free cellphone and a free PDA into a desk drawer and move on to a free combination unit.

The migration problem mitigates against even some practical convergence products. A DVD player is useless without a television set or monitor. You might expect that most people would buy a combination TV/DVD player rather than individual units, but they don't.

Walk into any Best Buy or Circuit City store and observe the action. Most people come in to buy either a replacement TV set or a replacement DVD player. Few customers want to buy both products at the same time. If the manufacturers of these devices could figure out a way to have your TV and your DVD player break down at exactly the same time, convergence products might find a much larger market. (*The One-Horse Shay*, a poem by Oliver Wendell Holmes, finds the humor in the rarity of such events.)

Camera Phones

Camera phones are doing relatively better than smart phones in the marketplace and there's a reason. It's the convenience factor. A camera phone allows you to take a picture and then send it via email almost immediately. You can accomplish the same thing with a separate digital camera and laptop or desktop computer, but it's not nearly as convenient. You have to wire the two units together and then juggle the software.

Convenience is a powerful motivating factor which can assure the success of some convergence products. Does a camera phone take as good a picture as a separate digital camera? No, but it doesn't matter because the camera phone is more convenient.

On the other hand, some major employers are banning camera phones on the job amid fears the gadgets pose threats to workers' privacy and company secrets. Now what? Do employees of these companies need to buy an on-the-job phone and an off-the-job phone?

In one sense, however, the camera phone is not a true convergence product because it doesn't replace the digital camera. Anyone interested in photography would probably have a digital camera in addition to a camera phone. (The clock radio didn't replace the clock either.)

Interactive Everything

In spite of the relative lack of success of most convergence products, companies have been in a mad rush to build interactivity into their products.

- **Interactive automobiles.** Fidelity Investments has teamed up with General Motors to let you check your portfolio and even trade stocks while you're behind the wheel. The service is offered through GM's OnStar system.

- **Interactive gas pumps.** BP (formerly British Petroleum) is spending $200 million to install Web-linked gasoline pumps at twenty-eight thousand stations so that drivers can fill their minds with news headlines and traffic reports while they're filling their tanks with gas.
- **Interactive homes.** Gannett, the parent company of *USA Today*, made a $270-million investment in ZapMedia.com, a company developing an appliance that blends Internet access with a hard drive, DVD/CD player, and MP3 player. Armed with a remote control and wireless keyboard, TV viewers would be able to access and store videos, music, email, and other Web content, which could then be directed to TVs, radios, personal computers, and other devices.
- **Interactive pianos.** You can download instrumental song files on Yamaha and Casio interactive pianos as lights shine on the keys in time with the notes, to show would-be pianists how to play the tune.
- **Interactive watches.** For ten bucks a month you not only get the correct time but also sports, news, weather, stock quotes, and personal messages and appointments. Made by Fossil, Citizen, and Suunto, the watches use Microsoft's smart personal objects technology, SPOT for short. Microsoft hopes to place SPOT on alarm clocks, refrigerator magnets, and key chains.
- **Interactive toys.** British start-up Intrasonics has invented a technology that would allow toys to respond to sound from a television, radio, CD, digital videodisc, or personal computer. A toy dog, for example, could wag its tail and bark when another dog appears on the television screen. (No big deal, our real dog already does that.)

- **Interactive recliners.** La-Z-Boy introduced the world's first "e-cliner," a product that comes with a foldout wireless keyboard that, with the right hardware, lets you access the Internet via your TV set.

- **Interactive clothing.** Reimar, a Finnish company, introduced the Smart Shout jacket, which lets wearers communicate on the run. The coat's detachable body belt has a built-in microprocessor, speaker, microphone, and phone adapter. The processor stores the numbers of everyone in a group. Pull a tag, speak into a mike by your shoulder, and your voice will be heard by other group members. Can Web access be next?

- **Interactive print advertising.** The Digital Convergence Corporation (prophetic name) introduced the CueC.A.T., which allows users to scan special bar codes in printed advertisements. You then plug the CueC.A.T. scanner into your computer, which directs you to the Web site of the advertiser.

  James Berrien, president of *Forbes* magazine, got so excited about the technology he sent CueC.A.T.s to his 850,000 subscribers: "We are proud to debut: CueC.A.T. technology from DigitalConvergence.Com, a *Forbes* 'first' that ushers in a new era in communication—the convergence of magazine publishing and the digital age."

- **Interactive pens.** Cross Pen introduced its new Convergence Pen, which features a built-in scanner enabling users to connect to Web sites.

- **Interactive paper.** Both E Ink and Gyricon Media (spun off from the Xerox Palo Alto Research Center) are working on e-paper, a paperlike sheet made up of thousands of microcapsules that are electrically charged to display white or black ink or any other pair of colors. E Ink's general manager says that e-paper is something of a cross between broadcast and print. (That's a bad sign.)

- **Interactive refrigerators.** Samsung has introduced an $8,000 side-by-side refrigerator/freezer with doors that double as a docking station for a nine-by-eleven-inch Web tablet, which is wired and ready for connection to a high-speed Internet service as well as satellite and cable services. You can also hook up the unit to DVD players and VCRs, which means that you can read and send email, surf the Web, watch TV or movies on a ten-inch screen, and leave text or video messages for family and friends. (We use magnets for that chore.)

- **Interactive washing machines.** Speech experts in Germany have created the ultimate washing machine. Called Hermine, the interactive clothes washer understands such spoken-word commands as "Prewash, then hot wash at ninety-five degrees, then spin at fourteen hundred revolutions, and start in half an hour."

- **Interactive soda fountains.** In May of 2001, Coca-Cola introduced a flashy soda-fountain dispenser that promised to combine the company's powerful brands with the Internet's marketing and technological potential. Know as the iFountain, the dispensers were beset with technical flaws. "Ultimately, Coke's iFountain experiment," commented *USA Today*, "might be the company's biggest marketing bust since the introduction and withdrawal of New Coke a generation ago."

- **Interactive toilets.** This development combines traditional plumbing with the electronics needed to analyze its contents and monitor the user's temperature and blood pressure. (Convergence hits a new low.)

- **Interactive home appliances.** LG Electronics has introduced HomNet, a network that allows LG appliances to talk to one another. The heart of the system is an $8,000 Internet refrigerator, the "server" for the other units, which include a washing machine, microwave oven, air conditioner, and digital projection TV.

  What can you do with a $30,000 HomNet system? In one scenario laid out in LG's literature, a woman forgot to push the start button on her HomNet washing machine when she left home, so she logged on to www.dreamlg.com at the office and started it up.

Save money. For only $1,800 you could have bought a Salton iCEBOX unit (terrible name) that was a combination television, DVD/audio CD player, Internet access device, FM radio, and home monitoring unit.

Most of these interactive ideas are foolish, some have an ounce of merit, and some might even make if they provide a convenience angle.

The Role of Convenience

Take the aptly named "convenience store," usually connected to a gasoline station. Do convenience stores have lower prices? No. Better brands? No. Greater selections? No. Their single reason for existence is convenience. You can buy a number of grocery and toiletry items while you are stopping for gasoline.

Note, too, that the convenience segment is normally only a small slice of any category. Classic convenience stores, for example, account for only a small percentage of beer, soft drink, food, and toiletry sales. Similarly, we expect that camera phones, TV/DVD/VCR combinations, and other convergence products that have a convenience benefit will ultimately represent only a small slice of their respective markets.

If your company is a major player in your category, why bother with niche convergence products? Let the companies that supply Brookstone, Hammacher Schlemmer, Herrington, and The Sharper Image hustle these hybrids.

From Palm to Handspring and Back Again

Donna Dubinsky and Jeffrey Hawkins, the duo who invented the PalmPilot, started a company called Handspring, which introduced a Palm look-alike called the Visor. Key point of differentiation was an expansion slot that could carry a wide range of modules, everything from cameras to a Global Positioning System to voice recorders. More than two thousand developers signed up to create Visor modules.

The module market was more or less a disaster, so Handspring moved on to the Treo, a communications device that combines a cellphone with a PDA, wireless email, SMS messaging, and Web browsing. The Treo received a raft of favorable publicity.

- "This communicator is a breakthrough in handheld devices . . . the best personal digital assistant I have ever used and the most capable cellphone." Walter S. Mossberg, *Wall Street Journal*.
- "Handspring's clever Treo pocket communicator is just my type: voice, email, browsing, and more." Peter Lewis, *Fortune*.
- "Finally, a hybrid that really works." Stephen H. Wildstrom, *Business Week*.

Treo sales never matched the hype, and Handspring, which was once worth billions on the stock market, was acquired by Palm, in a $190-million deal. (Jeff Hawkins alone had Handspring stock that was once worth $3.9 billion.)

These products pale in comparison to the effort being put into the infrastructure necessary to handle media convergence. One example: In 1999, networking-industry veteran Mory Ejabat raised a record $500 million in private funding for a start-up called Zhone Technologies. His objective was to create a single piece of equipment capable of handling telephone, Internet, cable television, broadcast television, and wireless services. *Business Week* predictably called his concept "the Holy Grail of digital convergence."

Sales of the Zhone box so far are close to zhero.

What is discouraging about these and other stories is not the failures themselves. In a free enterprise system, failures are to be expected. What is discouraging is that managers are learning the wrong lessons.

It's never the concept. It's always the execution. "We have learned the hard way," said Donna Dubinsky, "that these are difficult products to make and that the network operators are difficult relationships to manage."

Not a word about leading Handspring down the wrong path. Not a word about convergence or even questioning the convergence concept.

Nothing clouds objective thinking like media hype. Handspring was on the right track because the *Wall Street Journal*, *Fortune*, and *Business Week* said it was. Any failure to live up to the media's expectations must be due to execution problems.

Over time, hype builds up behind a dam called "belief" until the dam can't hold it anymore and then belief bursts. The results aren't pretty. It happened with Internet start-ups and it will happen with convergence.

The longer the hype goes on, the more painful the ending. The Internet dam burst after only three or four years of buildup. The hype has been piling up against the convergence dam for more than ten years now.

Media Hub, Media Player, Media Center

Buttressing the convergence dam is a flurry of new "media" products with names like media hub, media player, and media center. "Convergence, the long-promised Holy Grail of consumer electronics, has arrived," reported *Fast Company* magazine. "This time, the enabling device du jour is the network media hub—a set-top box that allows you to share files between PCs and home theater systems."

Hewlett-Packard, GoVideo, and Gateway were first out of the box with media hubs. For less than $300, you can buy a box that will bring all of your PC-based entertainment into your living room. It stacks on top of your existing home theater devices and connects to a TV and stereo receiver by standard video- and audio-output cables.

Meanwhile over at Microsoft, the push is on the media player, a piece of software that resides on the user's computer or other device and opens a portal to what the industry calls rich media— movies, music, video—delivered over the Internet, just as the browser is a portal for viewing Web pages. Microsoft and RealNetwork's RealOne player currently share the media player market.

Microsoft has also developed a "media center" edition of its Windows XP software. It has a special interface that allows you to control a computer with a built-in TV tuner. Now you can watch television or view photos, videos, and DVDs on your computer from across a room using a remote control.

Sony, Hewlett-Packard, Gateway, and Dell have introduced media center computers. But will these combination products find a market? Sure, they might find a place in college dorm rooms or tiny apartments, but the vast majority of people are much more likely to watch television on a television set and do their computing on a computer.

A Step in the Wrong Direction

The all-purpose box is a step in the wrong direction. The trend in television is towards large, flat screens. The trend in computers is toward small laptops. A media-center box is going to be a mediocre viewing device and a mediocre computing device.

When evaluating the prospects of a new technology, it's always a red flag when the name of a product uses an all-encompassing term like *media*.

"What are you going to do tonight?"

"I'm going to go home and watch media."

People don't talk like that and they don't usually buy products with names like that.

Steve Jobs had the right take on the media center. When asked if Apple Computer would introduce a product like that, he said that it would make as much sense as Apple introducing a computer also capable of making toast.

We agree. The media center is toast.

But Jobs is only one voice in the wilderness. Convergence has almost universal acceptance. In an article about the consumer electronics industry, Mike Langberg, of the influential *San Jose Mercury News*, said, "Pay attention when all the buzzwords point in the same direction."

The hype is building down at the convergence dam.

The Pen Computer

Let's take a closer look at how convergenists think. Before the invention of the personal computer, there were two major forms of written communications. You could use a pen or pencil to put words on paper. Or you could use a typewriter to do the same thing.

We still put a lot of words on paper with pens and pencils, but the typewriter has been pretty much replaced by the personal computer.

Power corrupts and computing power is no different. The geniuses in the high-tech industry saw a way to use the PC's computing power to combine the pen and paper form of communications with the typewriter.

So the pen computer was born and the hype soon followed.

"The computer is entering its third incarnation," boasted *The Economist* magazine in April 1992. "The first number-crunchers were behemoths locked in air-conditioned rooms. In the 1980s they shrunk and crept onto the desktop, as personal computers."

The third incarnation? The pen computer? *The Economist* predicted, "Computers that take commands from pen-sized stylus instead of a desktop mouse or keyboard, and a variety of other new creations will transform the market as dramatically—and potentially as profitably—as the emergence of PCs did just over a decade ago."

"Competition to dominate this new market has begun in earnest," reported *The Economist*. "Microsoft began deliveries of software for pens at the start of April. Go, a young Silicon Valley company, soon followed. IBM has just started delivering—to big customers, by special order a pen-based computer called the ThinkPad. Probably around a dozen companies will by the end of the year join IBM, NCR, NEC, Grid and Momenta in the market for pen computers."

It was over as soon as it started. By the fall of 1992, John Sculley, Apple Computer's chairman at the time, said, "A year ago we were all talking about pen computers. Who would have thought that the industry would come and go in a year?"

First the Pen. Now the Tablet

You have to give the convergenists credit. They never give up. Even though the pen computer was a failure, went the convergenists' thinking, maybe we could combine the pen computer with a keyboard computer?

Sure enough, the latest in a long line of combination computer products hit the market in 2001. It's called the tablet computer, and it has both a screen to write on and a keyboard to type on.

Microsoft was the major backer. In 2002 alone, eight manufacturers introduced versions of the Microsoft-designed tablet PC. And Bill Gates confidently predicted that tablet PCs would overtake laptops in five years.

Not a chance. By the end of 2003 only half a million tablet PCs were sold compared with 36 million laptops that year.

Be prepared for the next round of hype when someone realizes that there's a third way that humans communicate. By pen, by keyboard, and by mouth.

Will the voice computer be next?

THE 1945 HALL FLYING CAR AND THE 1961 AMPHICAR ARE TWO OF THE
MANY CONVERGENCE FAILURES IN TRANSPORTATION.

Chapter 7

Bad Ideas Never Die

WITH THE PRESS, THE PUNDITS, and virtually the entire high-tech community firmly behind the convergence concept, who could possibly doubt that one day it will all happen?

Any student of history, that's who. "Those who cannot remember the past," wrote George Santayana, "are condemned to repeat it."

To help jog your memory, here is an outline of the long, sad history of convergence.

* Remember the aerocar? When general aviation started to take off after World War II, the convergenists looked for ways to combine the airplane with the automobile.

    In 1945, Ted Hall introduced the flying car. Roads would become obsolete, traffic jams a thing of the past. You could go anywhere, anytime, with complete freedom of movement.

    Every major aircraft manufacturer in America hoped

to cash in on Hall's invention. The lucky buyer was Convair. In July of 1946, Convair introduced Hall's flight of fancy as the Convair Model 118 ConvAirCar. Company management confidently predicted minimum sales of 160,000 units a year. The price was $1,500 plus an extra charge for the wings, which would also be available for rental at any airport.

In spite of the hype, only two ConvAirCars were ever built. Both are now said to rest in a warehouse in El Cajon, California.

Three years later, Moulton Taylor introduced the Aerocar, a sporty runabout with detachable wings and tail. The Aerocar received enormous publicity at the time. The Ford Motor Company considered mass-producing it. But the Aerocar met with the same predictable fate as Hall's flying car.

Bad ideas never die. As recently as August 2, 2002, the *New York Times* carried a major story (nearly a full page) on the Taylor Aerocar. "A car with wings," said the *Times*, "is many a flyboy's dream machine."

Then there's Paul Moller, who has spent four decades developing the M400 Skycar, a personal flying machine that's as easy to use as a car. Today, $50 million, forty-three patents, and three wives later, his dream has still not taken off.

Millions of dollars were spent trying to get the combination airplane/automobile off the ground. Like many such projects, the flying car tries to solve an unsolvable problem. An automobile has to be heavy enough to stay on the road and an airplane has to be light enough to get off the runway.

Nor were these post–World War II efforts the first attempts to put an automobile into space. The Wrights first flew in December 1903. *Popular Mechanics* featured its first flying-car story in its April 1906 issue.

It's divergence that triumphs, not convergence. Instead of a flying car, today we have many types of airplanes (jet planes, prop planes, helicopters) and many types of automobiles (sedans, convertibles, station wagons, minivans, sport-utility vehicles).

• Remember the autoboat? Would-be convergenists should study the combination automobile/boat introduced with great fanfare in 1961 by Amphicar, a German company. Like all convergence products, the Amphicar performed neither function well. Drives like a boat, floats like a car, was the buyers' verdict.

Bad ideas never die. Many millions of dollars have been spent trying to successfully launch an autoboat. In 1983, the Amphi-Ranger. In 1992, the Hobbycar. In 1994, the Aquastrada Delta. In 1996, the Dutton Mariner. In 2003, the March WaterCar and the Gibbs Aquada.

The 2003 Gibbs announcement captures the flavor of previous autoboat introductions. "Gibbs Technologies Ltd. announced on Wednesday the achievement of one of the most exciting engineering projects in British history, the successful development of High Speed Amphibian (HSA) technology. After seven years of research and development of HSA technology, Gibbs demonstrated the vehicle that can reach 30 mph on water and speeds over 100 mph on land."

Then there's the Dobbertin HydroCar coming soon to a lake near you.

- Remember the videophone? Despite strenuous efforts by AT&T and others dating back to the 1920s, only 650,000 videophone systems are in worldwide use today, most of them in businesses. (Who wants to get dressed up to make a phone call?)

  Bad ideas never die. Recently Vialta introduced the Beamer TV, a $150 gadget that allows you to make video phone calls with a standard television set. (Figure $300 for a pair.) After eight decades of trying, does anyone believe that the videophone has a future?

- Remember 3-D movies? Every couple of decades, they make a comeback, creating a lot of excitement at the box office. Teleview introduced the first 3-D movie in 1922. In the 1930s, *Campus Sweethearts* was a big hit. In 1952, *Bwana Devil*. In 1960, *13 Ghosts*. In 1983, *Jaws 3-D*. And last year, *Spy Kids 3-D: Game Over*.

  Sharp and two U.S. companies (X3D and Stereo-Graphics) are producing 3-D monitors for trade shows, window displays, and video arcade games. But don't expect 3-D to replace 2-D. It's a novelty that's unlikely to become a mainstream product.

  (Actually we already have 3-D movies. They're called plays and they're a big hit on Broadway and other places.)

- Remember the television set that was going to print your daily newspaper for you in your living room? When TV turned on the public in the 1950s, the convergenists looked for ways to combine TV with print media. You were going to be able to get your newspapers and magazines printed right out of your TV set. Furthermore, you could print out just those sections of the paper you wanted to read.

  Don't laugh. Epson has just introduced a line of television sets that can display and print still photos. "In five years," said the director of Epson's home entertainment division, "we expect this to be a $300 million business for us."

- Remember the Bendix washer/dryer introduced with great hype in the 1940s? How come most people still have separate washers and separate dryers?

- Remember EVR, electronic video recording? CBS invested many millions of dollars in EVR, a fruitless attempt to combine electronic images with photographic ones. In the EVR system, color images were recorded on black-and-white film in the form of a coded pattern. When the film was run through a small EVR player attached to a color TV set, the coded patterns were scanned electronically and reconverted into color images on the screen.

- Remember the "office of the future," promoted by Xerox and other companies? In the office of the future, all office equipment would be linked together in one master system. It never happened. (Today, all the hype is about the "home of the future." In the current scheme every electronic gadget in the home would be linked together in one master system. Same bad idea.)

- Remember the "road of the future," promoted by General Motors at the 1964 New York World's Fair? The road of the future would be built by a road-builder, a machine that was a block long and eighty feet high. Operated by thirty men, the road-builder was capable of producing from within itself one mile of four-lane, elevated superhighway every hour, leveling everything in its path (presumably including the environmentalists and their lawyers who fight every highway construction project).

- Remember the fax/phone? When facsimile became a big deal in the 1970s, the convergenists looked for ways to combine the fax with the telephone. The fax/phone was going to be the hot product of the decade. (Do you have a fax/phone? Do you know anyone who does?)

- Remember the computer/phone, a computer with a telephone attached? Compaq, Northern Telecom, Rolm, Wang, and AT&T introduced computer/phones in the mid-1980s. The manufacturers believed that it was a natural to combine a computer with a telephone because voice and data traffic were already flowing over the same lines. Needless to say the computer/phone went nowhere.

- Remember the home entertainment center? A company called Advent invented projection television, TV sets with forty- to sixty-inch screens. But projection TV wasn't good enough for Bernie Mitchell, Advent's high-powered chief executive recruited from a successful run at Pioneer, the high-fidelity company. Let's take Advent and spread our wings into home entertainment, decided Mr. Mitchell. Of course, Advent wound up in bankruptcy court and the home entertainment center did, too, in a way.

  Interestingly enough, projection television went on to become a big success. If Advent had focused on its original product, the company might still be around today.

- Remember the combination baseball/football stadiums? Professional teams would save a fortune by playing their games in combination stadiums. One monument to this type of convergenist thinking, Three Rivers Stadium in Pittsburgh, was just blown up to be replaced by separate baseball and football facilities. More recently, Veterans Stadium in Philadelphia met the same fate.

Opened in 1982, the Hubert H. Humphrey Metrodome in Minneapolis was the last multipurpose facility built in America. Little more than two decades later, the Minnesota Twins, the Minnesota Vikings, and the University of Minnesota's football team would each like a new stadium, and we don't blame them.

- Remember the Ford Ranchero and the Chevrolet El Camino, combination car/trucks? In spite of the modest sales of these convergence vehicles, today's automakers are bringing back the concept. The Chevrolet Avalanche and SSR, the Cadillac Escalade EXT, the Subaru Baja, and the Hummer H2 SUT (for sport-utility truck) are the latest car/trucks on the market. Also the Lincoln Blackwood, which came and went so fast it will do down in automobile history as one of the shortest-lived models on record.
- Remember the Bell-Boeing V-22 Osprey, a combination helicopter/airplane? Our government has spent more than $12 billion so far on the Osprey, which has crashed three times in test flights, leading to the deaths of thirty people, twenty-six of them marines.

What might be surprising about the Osprey program is the almost overwhelming endorsement by industry experts. "Don't abandon a concept that is the most revolutionary thing that has come out of aerospace on the aeronautics side in the last probably forty to fifty years," said Dr. Daniel P. Schrage, director of the Center of Excellence in Rotorcraft Technology at the Georgia Institute of Technology.

Maybe this isn't so surprising. The aerocar and auto-boat programs also had the almost universal support of transportation experts. Perhaps it's the forest and the trees. The insider sees the trees; the outsider sees the forest.

- Remember the multipurpose fighter-bomber, the F-111. Years ago, Secretary of Defense Robert McNamara convinced everyone that it was wasteful for each military service to have separate aircraft models to perform specialized tasks. Instead, he said, we'll design and create a single aircraft that can perform all of them.

  The result was a disaster from the point of view of cost, training, and tactical applications. The F-111 is still in the Pentagon's inventory, but it is rarely used. And all the services continue to order and use a variety of aircraft, each suited to specialized tasks.

- Remember the zip-out lining that converted an overcoat into a topcoat? How come most people today have separate topcoats and overcoats? And how come my shirt didn't convergence with my pants, my socks with my shoes, my T-shirt with my shorts?

- Remember missile mail? In 1959, the postal service, in conjunction with the U.S. navy, experimented with a new form of mail delivery. Before man reaches the moon, a postal official confidently predicted, mail will be delivered within hours from New York to California, to Britain, to India, and to Australia, by guided missiles. (Duck, incoming mail!)

No Convergence in the Home

In almost every aspect of life, things don't converge. The engagement ring didn't converge with the wedding ring, the pen didn't converge with the pencil, the chair didn't converge with the sofa, the carpet didn't converge with the carpet underlay.

Sure, if you try hard enough, you can find examples of convergence. Usually, however, these are fringe products where convenience is the driving force.

After all, the eraser did combine with the pencil. Did this combination result in a better pencil? No. A better eraser? No. But the combination was *convenient*.

What seems to be the best of both worlds is usually the worst of both worlds. The convertible sofa that turns into a bed is not a better bed, nor is it a better sofa. But for some people it is convenient. (Yet most people buy separate sofas and separate beds when they have the money and the space to do so.)

The combination shampoo/conditioner is not a better shampoo or a better conditioner, but it is convenient. (Yet most people buy separate shampoos and conditioners because they think they are better.)

Most homes have bathtub/shower combinations. Yet when people can afford separate units, they usually buy separate units.

They Never Stop Trying

Years ago, a friend of ours left a cushy job at a major company to join a fast-food start-up called Celebrity House. It was a dynamite idea, he claimed, because it would combine the two retail concepts that were most attractive to the younger crowd, namely records and hamburgers. (As if Tower Records converged with Burger King.)

It was a mess. Not only did the records get greasy, the concept got clobbered as well. The partners lost their entire equity.

They never learn. In Europe, McDonald's tried to put hamburgers together with hotels. Called the Golden Arch, the new chain combined a conventional business hotel with a McDonald's restaurant. (We're sure that many company employees complained about holding a business meeting at a hamburger hotel. We're holding the meeting *where?*)

The Arch turned out to be less than golden. Three years after they opened, McDonald's sold its two Golden Arch hotels to Rezidor SAS, which promptly changed their names to Parks Inn.

Here in the United States, McDonald's is trying to put a Starbucks-type coffeehouse together with a hamburger restaurant. Called McCafe, the coffeehouse features espresso drinks, pastries, and gourmet sandwiches inside a traditional McDonald's restaurant offering a full burger-and-fries menu.

We get our hair cut and our clothes dry-cleaned at two different places, but we're quite sure that doesn't spell opportunity for some would-be entrepreneur to combine the two.

On the other hand, maybe it does. A company called Male Care is opening a chain of one-stop shops that combine a barbershop with a car wash and a dry-cleaning service. A French magazine, *Tendances Trends*, recognized Male Care as one of a hundred unique international enterprises.

Male Care is swimming against the tide. We used to get our hair cut and our nails done at one place. Now we go to two different places, a hair place and a nails place. That's divergence in action.

When video rentals became popular, virtually every drugstore, supermarket, and grocery store jumped into the business with kiosks that said, "Rent a movie tonight." You find few of these kiosks anymore because the video rental customers have gone to the specialists like Blockbuster. Combinations almost never work.

Convergence Will Never Die

Throughout history, convergence concepts have captured the imagination. The mermaid, the combination fish/woman, along with the merman, the combination fish/man, have fascinated the public for thousands of years.

Then there's the centaur from Greek mythology, a creature with the legs and body of a horse and the head, shoulders, and arms of a man.

Also from Greek mythology is Minotaur, part man, part bull. And Hydra, the multiheaded creature dispatched by Hercules. And also satyr, the god of the woods given to revelry and lechery, a humanlike creature with a horse's tail and the legs and ears of a goat.

Comic book heroes Batman and Spider-Man are also examples of the continuing popularity of convergence concepts.

When an idea is capable of capturing the imagination, the way convergence has done, that idea will live forever in the minds of a gullible public.

Some people are never convinced. As one observer reported, "Yet while convergence has diverged from the high road of early expectations, it remains the way of the future. It's only that the journey, executives in multimedia businesses say, will take longer, cost more money, and be far more complicated that first imagined."

To which we reply, borrowing a word from General McAuliffe at the Battle of the Bulge, "Nuts."

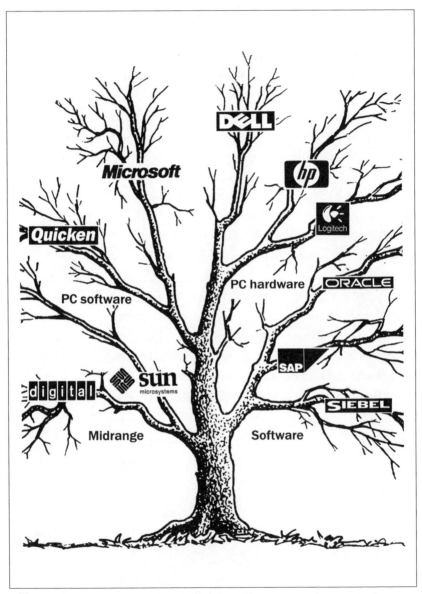

THE MAINFRAME COMPUTER BRANCHED OUT INTO SOFTWARE, MIDRANGE COMPUTERS, PC HARDWARE, AND PC SOFTWARE.

Chapter 8

The Great Tree of High-Tech Brands

IT TOOK AN ENORMOUS LEAP of the imagination for Charles Darwin to visualize his "great tree of life," a divergence process that took place over hundreds of thousands, even millions of years.

We're lucky. We can see how brands diverge over a much shorter period. Take the computer, for example. The seed was planted in 1946 by engineers at the University of Pennsylvania. Their invention, called ENIAC, was the first general-purpose, fully electronic digital computer.

Branding in the Computer Era

The introduction of Remington Rand's Univac in 1951, and the IBM's mainframe computer shortly thereafter, marked the real start of the computer era. And what an era it has been.

In a little more than fifty years, the world has witnessed an astounding array of products: minicomputers, midrange computers, personal computers, network computers, laptop computers, and handheld computers plus many thousands of software products. There are computer magazines, newsletters, Web sites and the Internet, plus an army of computer consulting firms.

The growth of the computer tree and its many branches allowed the creation of many powerful and valuable brands including IBM, Unisys, Hewlett-Packard, Sun Microsystems, Siebel, Oracle, SAP, Dell, Apple, Palm, Intel, and Microsoft.

The trunk of the computer tree (IBM) is worth $167 billion on the stock market. But the other eleven companies alone are worth $852 billion and there are thousands of other branches on the computer tree.

It's interesting to speculate what might have happened had IBM launched separate brands for each of the major computer branches. Could IBM have become the Procter & Gamble of computers with sales several times what they currently are?

What is happening in computers is also happening in every other industry. Appliances, automobiles, beverages, toiletries, food, you name it and you'll find divergence at work. Over time, categories divide and become two or more categories, creating endless opportunities to build new brands.

Time Flows in One Direction Only

Generations ago, life was simpler. Most people lived on farms and had only a few items of clothing, a few appliances, and a few bottles of stuff inside their medicine cabinets, if they had a medicine cabinet. Since then we have had generations of divergence, and life has gotten a lot more complicated.

If convergence was really a trend, it would mean that hundreds of years of divergence have suddenly come to a halt and life is going to get simpler.

Fat chance.

Life never gets simpler. It only gets more complicated. Whatever tree you are looking at, you can be sure of one thing. In the future, there will be more branches, more categories, and more brands.

Knowledge is power. Knowing that categories will eventually diverge is enormously useful to any marketer looking for an opportunity to launch a new brand.

Divergence in Personal Computers

Initially the three major brands were the Apple IIe, the Commodore Pet, and the Radio Shack TRS-80. All of the early personal computers were self-contained, in the sense that the keyboard, the central processing unit, and the monitor were integrated in one box.

Now what do you suppose might happen next in personal computer technology?

A convergenist would have looked around for useful devices to combine with the personal computer. How about a computer printer? What good is a personal computer if you can't print out your work?

Do any personal computers have integrated printers today? None that we know of. Rather the opposite trend has taken place. Instead of an integrated box, most desktop personal computers have separate keyboards and separate monitors. And, of course, separate computer printers.

Let's look at convergence from a different point of view. If you were a manufacturer and thought you saw an opportunity to integrate a printer with your line of personal computers, which type of printer would you choose?

- Laser: color or black and white?
- Ink-jet: color, black and white, or photo?
- Bubble-jet?
- Travel, desk, or heavy volume?
- Fast (expensive) or slow (inexpensive)?

Printer proliferation or (divergence) is the reason why convergence is a losing proposition. There's always a new type waiting in the wings. What printer would you combine your computer with?

Even the photo printer has branched out in a new direction. Instead of ink, the more expensive color printers use a dye sublimation technology. (Continuous tone, no dots.)

What happened to the personal computer is typical of what happens in virtually every other industry. With time, divergence creates new categories, which creates new opportunities for new brands.

Divergence in personal computers created opportunities to build a monitor brand (ViewSonic), a keyboard and mouse brand (Logitech), an operating system brand (Microsoft), a microprocessor brand (Intel), a disk-drive brand (Seagate), a modem brand (Hayes), storage brands (Zip, Migo), printer brands (Epson, Lexmark), a laser printer brand (Hewlett-Packard), a financial software brand (Quicken), a video projector brand (InFocus), a scanner brand (UMAX), a computer speaker brand (Altec Lansing), a label printer brand (Dymo), and many more to come.

What brands were created by combining the personal computer with another product? None that we know of.

Just one of these "divergent" brands (Microsoft) is worth almost twice as much on the stock market as the entire IBM company, the dominant computer brand in the early days of the industry. That's the way it goes. A segment of a category is often worth more than the entire category, at least from a branding point of view.

So where does the real opportunity lie? Putting things together or taking things apart?

Palm Computing took the "electronic organizer" function out of the personal computer to create the Palm brand, the first hand-held computer. Research-in-Motion took the email function out of the personal computer to create the BlackBerry brand, the first wireless email device.

Not every segment becomes a brand-building opportunity. In dial-up modems, for example, there's a technological barrier at 56K. It's not possible to make a faster modem that will connect to the copper wires in the telephone networks. So Hayes went from 14K to 28K to 56K, where modem evolution stopped. The modem became a commodity and Hayes Microcomputer Products Inc. went bankrupt.

In the great tree of high-tech brands, there will obviously be some dead branches (and dead brands).

Divergence Doesn't Usually Destroy

Strange as it might seem, the computer didn't put the pocket calculator out of business. Millions of calculators are sold annually. Because of evolution, however, the calculator has become smaller, lighter, and less expensive. And a new type of calculator, the scientific calculator, has also emerged.

In most cases, the new category exists side by side with the old category. The electric razor didn't put the manual razor out of business. Nor did the electric toothbrush put the manual toothbrush out of business. Life goes on. But thanks to divergence, life gets more complicated.

In personal computers, another developing category is the "smart keyboard," a cheap, simple, rugged, light, power-stingy word processor. (Everything a personal computer is not.) The leading brand is AlphaSmart, which markets a two-pound $230 device created by a pair of Apple engineers. No trackpad, no modem, no expansion slots, and only enough memory to hold about a hundred pages of typing. That's the bad news. The good news is that the AlphaSmart gets seven hundred hours of life on a set of AA batteries.

What AlphaSmart does for typing, the MailStation does for email. It only does three things, but does them extremely well: (1) compose email, (2) send email, and (3) get email. A MailStation costs less than $100 plus $10 a month for Internet service.

Warning. Stripped-down thinking isn't the same as divergence thinking. Too many companies think they can take the bells and whistles off their products to create a new category for the home market. (Automakers often take the chrome off a car to sell it as an economy model, which doesn't work well either.)

Virtually every major personal computer manufacturer has tried the stripped-down strategy with little success, starting with the IBM PCjr. Some recent examples include 3Com's Audrey, Sony's eVilla, Intel's Dot.Station, Oracle's NIC, Gateway/AOL's TouchPad, Honeywell's WebPad, Compaq's MSN Companion, and Compaq's iPaq Home Internet Appliance.

Stripping down an existing product usually means taking out value faster than taking out costs. A two-door car doesn't cost half as much to manufacture as a four-door car, which is why the auto industry sells a lot fewer coupes than they do sedans.

Palm has a winner in its Zire line of PDAs, which are simple devices excluding all the convergence extras like phone, camera, and Internet browsing. They are selling like hotcakes because Zire is what Palm is all about. A small, simple electronic organizer.

Divergence in Other Areas

Take semiconductors, for example. The vacuum tube (essentially a gigantic semiconductor) did not become smaller and smaller until it evolved into a transistor. Rather the transistor was a totally separate branch on the semiconductor limb.

None of the big vacuum-tube manufacturers (Western Electric, Sylvania, and others) made the transition to semiconductors. Instead, the big names in microprocessors are new brands like Intel and Advanced Micro Devices.

Take handheld computers. While billions of dollars are being spent trying to combine Palm-type handheld computers with cellphones and other devices, the real action has been taking place in the opposite direction. The action is with companies making specialized hardware and software tailored to specific industries.

Physicians can use software for their handhelds from companies like Epocrates and Allscripts Healthcare Solutions to check how drugs interact and figure out dosages. They can also use them to write prescriptions to send to a pharmacy. They can set prices for different services and make patients' notes.

Waiters can use handheld devices, loaded with Ameranth software, to feed orders directly into a restaurant's kitchen as well as the point-of-sales unit, leaving more time to schmooze with customers, who will presumably reward them with bigger tips.

Salespeople can use handheld devices loaded with Inventiv Pocket Advantage software to input orders and to check inventories and deliveries. It's not unusual for field staff to save as much as an hour to an hour and a half each day by eliminating much of the administrative work associated with traditional sales tools.

Will brands like Epocrates, Allscripts, Ameranth, and Inventiv become big successes? Most will probably fail, because that's the luck of the draw. But at least they have a chance to succeed because they are branching out from an existing technology. Whereas a convergence concept is almost certainly doomed to failure.

Package delivery firms have been pioneers in adapting handheld computers to the needs of a specific industry. Currently UPS, FedEx, and Airborne are outfitting their drivers with scanners and wireless handhelds that feed information into their worldwide package-tracking systems. These are not small projects either. UPS is spending $250 million on its wireless technology, and FedEx, $150 million.

The market for specialized handheld computers is likely to be four or five times as large as the market for general-purpose Palm-type devices. With a corresponding increase in brand-building opportunities.

Divergence in GPS

The microprocessor revolution has spawned a host of high-tech products (and high-tech brands).

A number of these products take advantage of the Global Positioning System. Developed for the military, GPS is the satellite-based system that allows users to pinpoint their longitude and latitude anywhere on earth within fifteen feet. GPS gadgetry has become an essential part of army life either integrated into vehicles (where it is known as the blue-force tracker) or on the ground (where it is known as the plugger).

Predictably the convergence crowd jumped on the GPS and tried to combine it with a handheld computer (GeoDiscovery Geode and Rand McNally's StreetFinder GPS) and with a personal computer (TravRoute's CoPilot). None of these brands are likely to go anywhere.

Why isn't the blue-force tracker an example of convergence at work? After all, the GPS device is integrated into a combat vehicle.

There's often a fine line between true convergence and products that are grouped together for convenience. The blue-force tracker is physically integrated with a vehicle, but functionally it remains a separate product.

It's like the radio in an automobile. You can remove the radio from an automobile and still have a functioning radio. Separating two functions in a convergence device normally produces two piles of useless parts.

A better GPS direction is the stand-alone unit. Garmin and Magellan (nice name) make units that are used by hikers, sailors, and gadget lovers. Hertz NeverLost is another GPS-based navigational system. So is General Motors' OnStar service. A GPS device can tell you where you are at any time of the day or night.

So how might a company exploit the GPS limb through branching? One way to do this is by isolating a segment of the market.

Instead of Everybody, How about Somebody?

How about a GPS device for children? Wherify Wireless (whose founder, Timothy Neher, started the company after nearly losing his brother's kids at a zoo) has a lightweight GPS device you strap on children like a watch.

Called "LoJack for kids," the Wherify watch can be programmed to notify parents when a child leaves a designated area. It also has a "panic button" that alerts parents and a 911 operator. (Applied Digital Solutions and GBSTracks make similar products.)

Then there's "LoJack for dogs." AVID Identification Systems (and Destron Fearing) make inexpensive microchips that can be inserted into an animal. Each chip has a one-of-a-kind number that allows veterinarians, shelters, animal hospitals, and others to identify the animal with a scanner. More than eighteen thousand AVID scanners are currently in use.

What AVID is doing for dogs and Wherify for kids, Road Safety International is doing for teenagers. The company makes a black box that monitors a teen's driving. Called SafeForce, the box records data like the car's speed. It will sound a warning when the driver is going too fast or turning too hard. Parents can check the box later and see for themselves just how fast their teenager was driving.

Then there's DriveCam, which some companies are installing to promote safe driving by their employees. Mounted behind the rearview mirror, the palm-sized device captures what the driver sees and hears as well as four directions of g-forces created by hard breaking, sharp acceleration, hard cornering, and collisions.

Narrowing the Market

Taking an existing technology and applying it to a narrow market segment is the surest way to build a brand. Some examples: the radar detector (Passport), the alcohol breath tester (PNI), the fish finder (Smartcast), the golf range-finder (StarCaddy), the personal mileage/speed/calorie counter (SportBrain), the weather tracker (Davis), the language translator (Phraselator), the handheld power-consumption meter (Kill A Watt), and the fake-ID detector (IDLogix.)

There's even a dog translator (Bow-Lingual) that converts canine barks into human phrases. When a dog barks into the microphone, its sound is matched against voiceprints for eighty breeds. Barks are classified into six categories: happy, sad, frustrated, angry, assertive, and needy. Bow-Lingual then randomly selects phrases to fit the category. While it's unlikely to become a big success, Bow-

Lingual illustrates the general principle that brands are built by thinking "narrow."

The New York, Boston, and other marathon races use ChampionChip transponders, which weigh about four grams and fit into a plastic container on the runner's shoelace. The transponders are capable of producing accurate, individual results for tens of thousands of runners. They track the time that runners actually spend running the course, known as chip time, as opposed to the official results, which are known as gun time. (Someday the chip time is likely to become the official time.)

The medical field has attracted a large number of entrepreneurs who have developed a range of useful new products: the diabetes tester (OneTouch), the glucose monitor (GlucoWatch), the portable defibrillator (HeartStart), the fertility monitor (PSC), the wireless heart-rate monitor (Polar), and the implantable cardioverter defibrillator (Gem III DR.)

For these and many other high-tech products, the problems are always the same: how to make the devices smaller, lighter, and less expensive in order to broaden the market. Divergence thinking helps solve these problems. Convergence thinking does the opposite.

The prototype of the GlucoWatch was about the size of a brick and much too big to carry. "We could troubleshoot and fiddle with the electronics when it was bigger," said the company's research director. "Once we got it right, the challenge was to make it small enough to market."

Divergence in Biometrics

In the aftermath of 9/11, security has become a big issue. Which is why one of the hottest areas in high-tech is biometrics, the technology that identifies people by fingerprints, eyes, and other physical characteristics.

It's interesting how "access control" devices have branched out over the years. First came the key, which is still used by more than 90 percent of the locks in the world. Then came the card, which contains a microchip that can be externally programmed. Every up-to-date hotel and motel has switched from keys to cards.

The latest is the contactless card (ProxCard), which uses radio-frequency identification technology. Just wave the card in front of the lock and it opens. (The same technology is used in tollbooths equipped with the E-ZPass system.)

Fingerprint-scanning devices (Indentix) are another branch of the access-control limb. You can easily lose a card, but it's hard to misplace a hand. Also in the race is iris-scanning (Iridian), which claims to be the most accurate biometric technology. Apparently no two irises are the same.

Eyes have an advantage over fingers. Criminals, it is claimed, can create fake fingerprints by using wax molds. (Another interesting tidbit you can learn from watching *CSI*.)

It's much harder to wax an eye.

Divergence in Component Brands

Divergence thinking should encourage innovators to ask themselves, "What component of a new product can we focus on to build a brand?" The truth is, you can make more money selling batteries (Duracell) than flashlights. Film (Kodak) than cameras. Software (Microsoft) than hardware.

The latest high-tech component that is enjoying a boom in popularity is the memory card. Last year, worldwide sales of memory cards exceeded $3 billion. CompactFlash cards, one of the leading memory-card brands, can be used in Nikon and Pentax digital cameras, Hewlett-Packard Jornada and iPaq handheld computers, and Nokia cellphones.

Someday soon radio-frequency identification (RFID) microchips used to open locks will also open up a big market in inventory control. Benetton has ordered some 15 million RFID tags (Philips) to track garments as they're made, shipped, and sold. RFID readers in some five thousand stores will collect point-of-sale data and automatically send it to Benetton.

Procter & Gamble has tested RFID chips on Pantene shampoo bottles and Bounty paper towel packages. And Gillette is testing the chips on Mach 3 razors.

But the biggest boost of RFID technology is coming from Wal-Mart. The company recently directed its top one hundred suppliers to have all their cases and pallets "chipped" by January 1, 2005. Industry experts estimated that this mandate will mean the sale of some 8 billion tags a year.

Divergence in Software

Nothing illustrates the power of divergence thinking better than computer software. Thousands of successful brands have been created by dreaming up narrow, specialized software categories.

Take Apple Computer, once the world's largest maker of personal computers, now relegated to niche status in a market dominated by Wintel machines (computers using Microsoft Windows software and Intel microprocessors).

What if? What if Apple had taken the path marked "divergence" rather than the path marked "convergence"?

In 1984, Apple introduced the Macintosh, "the first computer for the rest of us." And what was so remarkable about the Mac? It was the machine's graphical interface, which included pull-down menus and a "desktop" design. You could open multiple files on your computer screen, just like on a real desktop.

Macintosh did windows before Microsoft did Windows. Unfortunately for Apple, IBM had introduced the first sixteen-bit, serious office personal computer (the PC) in 1981, two and a half years before the Mac. (It's better to be first than it is to be better.)

By 1984, the IBM PC and its clones had already become the standard for the personal computer industry. Users were extremely reluctant to change, even to a clearly superior product. That gave Microsoft time to develop a me-too software product called Windows. (Warning to entrepreneurs: Don't knock a knockoff. Copying somebody else's idea and giving it a new twist is one of the most reliable roads to success.)

The what if? For Apple it's obvious. Instead of introducing the Macintosh, what if Apple had introduced a software-only product that just did windows? If Apple had done that, maybe they would be in the same dominant position as Microsoft. (On the stock market, Microsoft is worth thirty-six Apples.)

Convergence gets the publicity, but divergence is where the money is. If you study the history of every floundering conglomerate, you will usually find a turn in the road not taken. A turn in the road that might have taken the company to the height of success. A turn in the road marked "divergence."

Did Apple Computer ever consider this proposed strategy? Of course not. Imagine the reaction to such a proposal: "We're in the computer business. We're *not* in the computer software business."

The Computer Spreadsheet Wars

An early software superstar was VisiCalc, the first computer spreadsheet. It was so useful that business and professional people went out and bought the only machine on which it could be used, the eight-bit Apple II.

The introduction of the sixteen-bit IBM PC created an opportunity for a sixteen-bit version of VisiCalc. The first spreadsheet product to take advantage of this opportunity was Lotus 1-2-3. (Every new product, every new service, every new technological development, creates new branding opportunities that can extend in many different directions.)

Lotus 1-2-3 went on to become a tremendous success. For a number of years Lotus Development Corporation was the largest personal computer software company in the world, outselling even Microsoft.

What's perplexing about Lotus 1-2-3 and many other successful brands is the pervasiveness of convergence thinking. The reason for the unusual brand name was that the product combined "spreadsheet, information management, and graphics all in one."

The announcement advertisement for the new Lotus 1-2-3 brand contained 310 words, only one of which was the word *spreadsheet*, and it didn't appear until the eleventh sentence in the copy. A divergence success in a convergence package.

In software and other products, "bundling" can give the illusion of convergence at work. In most cases, however, bundling involves "must have" products with products that might as well be commodities. Microsoft Office, the bundle that put Lotus 1-2-3 out of business, is a good example.

Bundling is best fought in the courts, not in the marketplace.

How do you compete with a software powerhouse like Microsoft? You don't do it by emulating Microsoft, by packaging your products in a bundle, as Lotus tried to do with SmartSuite. Bundling only works for a leader with monopolistic powers. Rather you look for ways to branch off from the mainstream.

Intuit Inc. accomplished this with three brands, all of which became leaders in their fields. Quicken (personal finance), Quick-Books (small-business accounting), and TurboTax (tax preparation.)

Today Intuit does $1.4 billion in annual sales with net profit margins in excess of 10 percent. On the other hand, Microsoft Money has a minuscule market share.

Divergence in Telephones

For seventy years, the U.S. telephone business was a monopoly, tightly controlled by AT&T, a benevolent dictator. As a result the phone system was a monolithic operation with little divergence and almost no new brands.

Almost every instinct of a monopolist is against the natural laws. Keep everything under the same name and don't allow any branching-out processes to occur. (The United States Postal Service is a good example of the breed.)

Then in 1968, the Federal Communications Commission stripped AT&T of its phone equipment monopoly (the Carterfone decision) and a year later allowed rivals, led by MCI, to use its network. Finally the Justice Department prevailed in a ten-year antitrust suit, which led to AT&T's breakup in 1984.

The stage was set for decades of divergence. Cordless phones, car phones, cellphones, were just a few of the innovations.

The first cellphone, the Motorola DynaTAC 8000x, was introduced in 1983. You have probably noticed that it's de rigueur in the high-tech field to give the first of anything a long, complicated unusable name.

The first computer wasn't called a computer, it was called an "electronic numerical integrator and computer." The first personal computer was the MITS Altair 8800 microcomputer. (Hey, Motorola, what if you gave the first cellphone a simple name? Something like Nokia.)

Even though Motorola pioneered the cellphone (at one point Motorola had 45 percent of the world's market), it played a losing game. Today Nokia, a single-product company, has 35 percent of the world's market and Motorola only 15 percent.

A vigorously growing, dynamic product like the cellphone needs to break away from the confining environment of a conglomerate if it is ever going to reach its full potential. About a billion customers around the world, or one in six people, are now using cellphones.

Much the same scenario occurred in personal computers. IBM was no match for the single-product company Dell. The more dynamic the new product or service, the greater its potential, the more it needs to branch out or break away from its corporate masters. (A spin-off is one way.)

At the very least, this type of new product needs a totally new name. Yet these are exactly the new products that are least likely to be spun off or given a new identity.

When we suggested to IBM management that they use a different name for their new personal computer (the IBM PC), we were told, The product is too important to IBM's future not to use the IBM name. Regrettable result: IBM lost money on personal computers for twenty-one years in a row. Last year for the first time, IBM made a small profit on personal computers.

Divergence in Cellphones

Any vigorous category like the cellphone is bound to diverge again, and we're beginning to see some examples. There are cheaper cellphones, expensive cellphones, moderately priced cellphones.

Wristwatches went through the same process. Today we have inexpensive watches (Timex), moderately priced watches (Seiko), fashion watches (Swatch), sport watches (TAG Heuer), expensive watches (Rolex), and really expensive watches (Patek Philippe).

At the low end in cellphones is a disposable phone made by Hop-On Wireless. The size of a deck of playing cards, the phone provides sixty minutes of talk time for a flat forty dollar fee. You can buy additional time via phone cards in twelve-, sixty-, and ninety-minute increments. (If the idea of a disposable phone sounds silly, who would have predicted the enormous success of disposable cameras?)

At the high end is the Vertu, made by Nokia. Featuring a sapphire-crystal screen and ruby bearings, the Vertu is available in stainless steel, gold, and platinum finishes at prices ranging from $4,900 to $19,450. Gwyneth Paltrow owns one. So does Madonna. J.Lo is reported to own three. (Hundreds of thousands of people spend that much money on a watch to tell time. Why not spend as much money on a device to make a phone call?)

Somewhere in the middle is the fashion phone. Siemens has introduced the Xelibri, which will be available in spring and fall collections, with a choice of four models in each collection.

There are even special-purpose cellphones like the Magnavox 911, which can only be used to call a 911 operator. It's a real bargain if your only reason for owning a cellphone is for use in emergencies. There are no monthly service fees, no activation or roaming charges.

Another related telephone branch is the two-way radio, with brands like Audiovox and Cobra. And Nextel is doing a good job promoting two-way radio (or walkie-talkie) service on its wireless network.

What cellphone branches might develop in the future isn't clear since the industry is in its early stages. Yet the major manufacturers (Nokia, Motorola, and others) are a lot more focused on convergence than divergence.

They are spending their research and development dollars trying to combine the cellphone with cameras, handheld computers, and a host of other devices.

They should be looking at the cellphone tree to see what branches might be developed. Then choose the branches they want to dominate.

You can't blame companies for ignoring divergence opportunities. It's difficult to see divergence at work. Few people have ever seen a new branch grow out of a tree limb. One day you look at the tree in your backyard and think, where did all those branches come from? (We considered the possibility of using time-lapse photography to demonstrate divergence.)

Divergence in Television

Another industry that demonstrates the futility of trying to dominate every diverging branch is television. TV, of course, did not converge with another medium. It diverged. And now we have broadcast TV, cable TV, satellite TV, and pay-per-view TV. Even airport TV, elevator TV, and taxi TV, with more television branches to come.

The biggest division occurred when cable split off from broadcast. None of the big broadcast brands (ABC, CBS, NBC) became big cable brands. (Nor did any of the broadcast brands become big Internet brands either.)

Most of the successful cable brands have totally new identities. CNN, ESPN, HBO, MTV, VH1, BET, Nickelodeon, Home Shopping, QVC, Weather Channel, Discovery, E!, etc.

A majority interest in just one of these cable brands (QVC) was recently sold for $7.9 billion, valuing the entire channel at a staggering $13.6 billion.

When branching occurs, the advantage belongs to the brand that creates a separate identity. Nickelodeon, for example, is more successful than the Disney channel.

(Imagine trying to tell Michael Eisner that Disney should use a different name on its new cable channel, and you can see why most of the successful cable channels were not created by big companies with their big brands and their big egos.)

Early on, when an industry is young, management believes that the emerging branch needs the support of the core brand. And maybe it does. But when the new branch grows bigger and stronger, it separates itself from the core branch and then a line-extension name becomes a severe disadvantage.

Divergence follows a pattern. Early on, the establishment scoffs at the possibility of a competitive threat to their powerful brands. It wasn't ABC, CBS, or NBC that pioneered cable television. It was John and Margaret Walson, owners of an appliance store in Mahanoy City, Pennsylvania.

It wasn't Time Warner, Comcast, or Cablevision that pioneered satellite television. It was outsider Hughes Electronics that introduced DirecTV, the first direct-broadcast satellite television system.

Later on, when the establishment notices the outsiders' success, they launch me-too efforts using their existing names. So NBC launches a cable channel called (naturally) CNBC, which has been a moderate success at best.

Even an old communications medium like radio has shown signs of divergence recently. The two newest categories are digital radio (which will require new radio sets) and satellite digital radio (which requires both new sets and a monthly subscription fee).

Divergence in Internet Service

At first you could only tap into the Net with a dial-up modem and an Internet service provider like America Online, CompuServe, or Prodigy.

But dial-up modems are limited to speeds of 56,000 bits per second. The next category was "broadband," and you had a choice of either a digital subscriber line (DSL) or a cable modem. Both raised the speed limits to anywhere from 128,000 to 800,000 bits per second.

Today you have another choice, called fixed wireless, which uses antennas and radio signals to connect to the Net. Speeds are comparable to DSL lines, but monthly costs are less.

The dominant dial-up brand is America Online. Will AOL become the dominant broadband brand as it is trying to do?

Unlikely. As Internet service diverges, opportunities are created for new brands.

On the horizon are fiber-optic lines that can carry information one hundred times faster than today's DSL lines or cable modems. Last year, phone giants Verizon, SBC Communications, and Bell-South announced that they had agreed on standards for fiber-to-the-premises (FTTP) equipment and sent a letter to makers of telecom equipment asking for bids.

That's the way it goes. There's always room for new categories and new brands.

Nothing Stands Still for Very Long

Smart managers are quick to jump on the new technology, but not with their existing brands. A new diverging technology requires a new brand.

Another hot technology is Wi-Fi, which allows wireless Internet connections in retail stores, factories, hospitals, etc. Starbucks has teamed with T-Mobile to offer the service in some twenty-one hundred of its coffee shops. Boeing is equipping more than a hundred jets with the new Wi-Fi technology.

Will somebody build a powerful Wi-Fi brand? Sure, it's only a question of time.

Hold the phone. Airgo Networks has just introduced a new technology capable of doubling Wi-Fi's already high speed. Called MIMO, for "multiple-in, multiple-out," the technology relies on computing power to send signals from closely spaced antennas. Then there's WiMax, a new technology being promoted by Intel.

Who will win the Wi-Fi war? Maybe all systems will survive. Not every new branch kills off an existing branch. Nature often favors multiple approaches to the same problem.

Even email has diverged. Now you have regular email and "instant-messaging" email, which has become extremely popular. Some 70 million people use some sort of instant messaging service every day.

Divergence in Transportation

The Wright brothers were bicycle manufacturers, but they didn't put wings on a Schwinn bike and try to fly it on the dunes at Kitty Hawk. An airplane isn't a flying bicycle.

In a story that has been told many times, General Motors became the leading car company by segmenting the market into five different price categories: Chevrolet, Pontiac, Oldsmobile, Buick, and Cadillac. "A car for every purse and purpose" was the corporate motto.

Divergence thinking made General Motors the dominant automobile manufacturer.

But convergence thinking got General Motors into trouble. Cheap Cadillacs and expensive Chevrolets were only two of the many mistakes made by General Motors that muddied the differences between the company's five brands.

If General Motors had practiced divergence thinking, they would have increased the differences between the brands. Chevrolets would have gotten cheaper and Cadillacs would have gotten more expensive.

If GM had thought that way, today you might have been able to buy cheap Chevrolets made in China and expensive Cadillacs that have as much prestige as a Mercedes. (It's a mistake to think a domestic product can't have the prestige of an imported product. It can, but not at a cheaper price.)

Making Chevrolet cars cheaper and Cadillac cars more expensive would have left more room in the middle for Pontiac, Oldsmobile, and Buick. It would also have made Saturn (an expensive mistake) superfluous.

Nature Drives Species Apart

That's the way nature works. Over time, the competition between species drives them apart. A lion and a tiger may have had a common ancestor, but over time they have become more and more different.

Darwin puts it this way: "Natural selection, also leads to divergence of character, for the more organic beings diverge in structure, habits, and constitution, by so much the more can a large number be supported on the area. . . . Therefore, during the modification of descendants of any one species, and during the incessant struggle of all species to increase in numbers, the more diversified the descendants become, the better will be their chance of success in the battle for life."

That's not the way human nature works. Our minds look for excuses to move toward the middle. We can't stand the thought of being odd or unusual. "What's the matter with him" is an all-too-common comment when someone moves out of the mainstream.

Face it. Convergence is mainstream thinking. Divergence is not. Hence the need for a book like this. Opportunities never reside in the mainstream. They always reside on the edges where the competition is weak or nonexistent.

No innovation in automobile marketing will probably ever top Alfred Sloan's concept of the General Motors corporation. But a number of automotive innovations illustrate the power of divergence thinking:

- Volkswagen became a powerful automobile brand by being first in a new category called small cars.
- Jeep became a powerful automobile brand by being first in a new category called sport-utility vehicles.
- Hummer became a powerful automobile brand by being first in a new category called military vehicles.
- Chrysler became a powerful automobile brand by being first in a new category called minivans.
- Cadillac became a powerful automobile brand by being first in a new category called expensive American cars.
- Corvette became a powerful automobile brand by being first in a new category called American sports cars.

- Porsche became a powerful automobile brand by being first in a new category called expensive sports cars.
- BMW became a powerful automobile brand by being first in a new category called driving machines.
- Volvo became a powerful automobile brand by being first in a new category called safe cars.
- Mercedes-Benz became a powerful automobile brand by being first in a new category called expensive imported cars.
- Rolls-Royce became a powerful automobile brand by being first in a new category called ultra-expensive imported cars.

And like the personal computer, which created the opportunity for component brands like Intel and Microsoft, the automobile created the opportunity for component brands like Goodyear and DieHard. A new component brand in the making is OnStar, General Motors' security and concierge service.

Divergence in Bicycles

The bicycle traveled the same path as the automobile. Initially the big brand was Schwinn. But the category diverged and today we have road bikes (Cannondale), mountain bikes (Trek), BMX bikes (GT), and kid bikes (Huffy.) Not to mention accessory bike brands like Bell in helmets, RockShox in suspensions, and Sidi in shoes.

Schwinn developed the first spinning bicycle and launched the stationary-bike craze that swept through health clubs across the nation. Too bad they put the Schwinn name on the bike. Perhaps a new name would have saved the company from filing for bankruptcy. While spinning took off, the rest of Schwinn skidded off the road.

What should a leader like Schwinn have done to avoid being

pulled apart by a segmenting category? Conventional wisdom says move with the market. But what should you do when the market is moving in several different directions at once?

You do what General Motors did. You launch second and third brands to capture the diverging segments. You don't try to make your Schwinn name stand for everything.

Early on, the second-brand strategy can work. The upstarts are invariably small, undercapitalized companies led by entrepreneurs with vision. The category leader usually has the resources, the organization, and the facilities to mount an effective counterattack. Unfortunately the category leader usually lacks the vision to launch a second brand.

It took Delta Airlines thirty-two years to counter the threat posed by the launch of Southwest Airlines in 1971. It's too late for Song, Delta's carbon copy of a no-frills airline. The momentum is on Southwest's side. Not to mention the money and the resources.

To complicate the problem for Song (and United's Ted), the airline market is crowded with successful independent start-ups like JetBlue and AirTran.

If you are going to launch a second brand, you need to do it early, before the competition gets entrenched.

Divergence in Marketing

The hottest topic in marketing today is "integrated marketing." Some professionals are calling for advertising, PR, direct mail, sales promotion, and other functions to converge into one big entity. Already there are integrated-marketing firms offering their services to corporate America. "The wave of the future" is their rallying cry.

Will the wave include integrated operations, the close cooperation between different functions? Undoubtedly.

Will we see advertising, PR, direct-mail, and sales-promotion firms disappear into one big category called "integrated marketing" agencies? Undoubtedly not.

Divergence will continue to push the functions apart, creating more and more specialized agencies and even new categories such as Internet agencies. Advertising, for example, has seen a lot more divergence than convergence as bits and pieces of traditional ad-agency services branch off, the latest being media buying.

Look at the military and you will see what will happen in marketing.

The three classic branches for land warfare used to be infantry, artillery, and cavalry. Over time, evolution turned the cavalry branch into armor, and divergence added an air force branch.

The hottest topic in the military today is "integrated operations," the close cooperation between all branches. Today, the air force, armor, artillery, and infantry work closely together, but does that mean the Defense Department is going to merge the four branches?

Not a chance. Divergence continues to push the four branches apart, forcing the military to pour billions of dollars into communications gear to integrate their joint operations.

Marketing people should expect the same. As time goes on, new functions will develop and increase in importance until they split off from the mainstream. Both inside and outside the corporation.

Yet all the talk revolves around integration and convergence. "Although integration is often considered the Holy Grail of marketing today," reported *Advertising Age* recently, "few have uncovered its secrets." In the last ten years, according to a word count conducted by the publication, *integrated marketing* was mentioned 960 times.

It's all talk and no action. Furthermore, whenever the Holy Grail is dragged into a discussion, you can be pretty sure that whatever they're talking about is never going to happen.

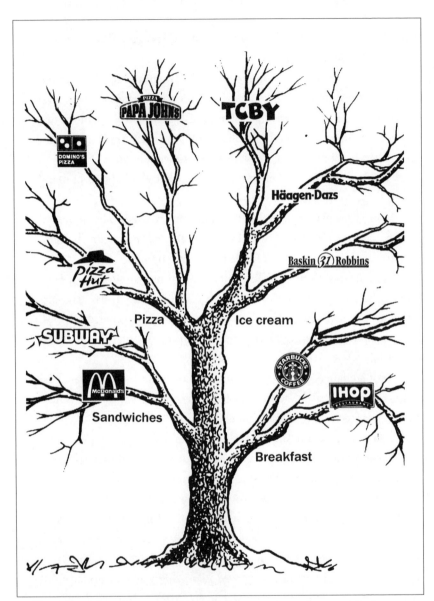

THE COFFEE SHOP OF THE FIFTIES BRANCHED OUT INTO SANDWICHES,
BREAKFAST, PIZZA, ICE CREAM, AND MANY OTHER CATEGORIES.

Chapter 9

The Great Tree of
Low-Tech Brands

CONSUMER PRODUCTS DEMONSTRATE as much divergence as high-tech products. Maybe even more.

Go back in time. Fifty years ago every town in America had a coffee shop. What did you find to eat in a coffee shop? Everything. Eggs, bacon, pancakes, hamburgers, hot dogs, chicken, soup, sandwiches, ice cream, pie, doughnuts, cake, soft drinks, and of course, coffee. Most coffee shops in the fifties and sixties were mom-and-pop operations with little or no profits except for the modest salaries taken out by the owners.

How would you improve your operations if you owned a typical coffee shop in mid-twentieth-century Middle America? Convergenists would probably focus on two issues, the menu and the location.

"As far as the menu is concerned," the convergenists would probably say, "maybe we could increase sales by adding new items. How about buying one of those new pizza machines being advertised in the trade press? Or maybe we could get one of those soft-ice-cream machines that Tom Carvel is peddling?"

Makes sense. If you want to sell more, you need more things to sell. But what makes common sense often doesn't make good marketing sense.

Today's coffee shop, the McDonald's chain, has tried adding chicken, pizza, soft ice cream, veggie burgers, and a host of other items to its menus. Yet the chain seems to get weaker, not stronger.

"As far as the location is concerned," the convergenists would probably say, "maybe we can increase sales by locating the coffee shop in a place that generates its own traffic. Shopping malls, train stations, bus stations, retail stores, hotel lobbies."

Today's coffee shops have also tried this strategy. You'll find McDonald's and Burger King restaurants in a variety of locations.

Divergence in Coffee Shops

Go back to the fifties and look at the same coffee shop from a divergenist's point of view. "What's the most popular single item in a coffee shop? Arguably it's the hamburger. Let's open a coffee shop that serves primarily hamburgers."

In 1948 in San Bernardino, California, that's exactly what Dick and Mac McDonald did. Open a "coffee shop" that served primarily hamburgers. (There were nine items on the menu: hamburgers, cheeseburgers, french fries, coffee, and five other things to drink.) If you didn't like hamburgers, you were obviously not going to eat at McDonald's.

Thirteen years later, the McDonald brothers sold out to Ray Kroc and his associates for $2.7 million. (Not a bad return for the owners of a coffee shop.) But they missed out on the big bucks. McDonald's Corporation went on to become the world's largest fast-food chain.

What do you call successful divergenists? We call them convergenists, because as soon as they become successful with a divergence strategy, they revert right back to type.

There's something about Mary and there's something about convergence. It doesn't work, but it sure sounds good in the board-room. Synergy, symbiosis, cross-selling, exploiting the equity of the brand, one plus one equals three, etc.

McDonald's has spent the last forty-three years expanding its menu. More and more, today's McDonald's looks like the coffee-house of yesterday.

Compare McDonald's with In-N-Out Burger, a California chain that has stuck to a basic burger-and-fries menu. The average McDonald's unit in the United States does $1.5 million in sales. The average In-N-Out Burger unit does $1.9 million in sales.

(The original McDonald brothers' restaurant in San Bernardino was ringing up annual sales of more than $400,000 during the 1950s, a figure that would, accounting for inflation, be $2.9 million today.)

What should McDonald's have done? Use its real estate, financial, and operating expertise to launch a second brand. Or even a third or fourth brand.

The same coffee shop that produced the hamburger as a divergence opportunity also produced a number of other brand-building opportunities.

- Chicken: Kentucky Fried Chicken
- Roast beef: Arby's
- Hot dogs: Wienerschnitzel
- Coffee: Starbucks
- Doughnuts: Dunkin' Donuts
- Cinnamon rolls: Cinnabon
- Cookies: Mrs. Fields

- Ice cream: Baskin-Robbins
- Frozen yogurt: TCBY
- Pancakes: International House of Pancakes
- Waffles: Waffle House
- Pizza: Pizza Hut
- Sandwiches: Panera
- Submarine sandwiches: Subway

Divergence in White-Tablecloth Restaurants

Fifty years ago every town in America had a white-tablecloth restaurant.

What kind of food did a white-tablecloth restaurant serve? Nobody thought to categorize the cuisine because there was no other type of high-end restaurant to differentiate from. "Fine dining" is usually what the signage on the restaurant said.

There were, of course, other types of restaurants, but these were mostly set up to serve an ethnic community. (The first pizzeria opened in New York City in 1905 to serve Italian immigrants.)

Then the fine-dining segment started to diverge. Today there are many different types of "fine-dining" establishments. In the yellow pages in Atlanta, for example, thirty-five categories of restaurants are listed:

- Barbecue
- Cajun
- Creole
- Caribbean
- Chicken
- Chinese
- Continental
- Cuban

- French
- German
- Greek
- Indian
- Irish
- Italian
- Jamaican
- Japanese
- Korean
- Kosher
- Lebanese
- Mandarin
- Mexican
- Middle Eastern
- Persian
- Peruvian
- Pizza
- Seafood
- Soul food
- Southern
- Southwestern
- Steak
- Swiss
- Thai
- Vegetarian
- Vietnamese
- And, of course, American

While they didn't call themselves "American restaurants," most dining places of the fifties served what would today be called American food. How times have changed.

In Atlanta, for example, only fifteen restaurants or 6 percent, of the 250 restaurants that pay to list themselves in the yellow pages want to be known for serving American cuisine. (The largest category? Mexican food, which accounts for thirty-five restaurants, or 14 percent of the total. Second is Chinese, and third, Japanese.)

As a category emerges, it represents an opportunity to build a brand. Some are local, some are regional, some are national, and some are global. Some of the national restaurant brands include:

- Applebee's (bar & grill)
- Arby's (roast beef)
- Benihana of Tokyo (Japanese)
- Olive Garden (Italian)
- On the Border (Mexican)
- Outback (steak)
- PF Chang's (Chinese)
- Pizza Hut (pizza)
- Ruth's Chris (steak)
- Taco Bell (Mexican)
- Tony Roma's (ribs)

Not all of these are fine-dining establishments to be sure. Branding in the food industry, as in many other industries, occurs from the bottom up. The first global restaurant brand was not a white-tablecloth operation. It was McDonald's, a brand at the bottom of the food chain.

Will high-end restaurants follow the global path taken by McDonald's, Burger King, Subway, and others at the low end? We think so, but it will take time. Brand evolution is slow.

Bice, a high-end Italian restaurant chain, is already operating twenty-eight restaurants in fourteen countries around the world. Others are certain to follow.

Divergence in Pizza

Divergence never stops. Take the pizza category. Pizza Hut was the first national pizza chain and enjoyed great success. Then Domino's Pizza branched off to focus on home delivery and became the second-largest pizza chain.

Little Caesars branched off the pizza category to focus on "take-out" and became the dominant take-out brand.

Papa John's branched off the pizza category to focus on an up-grading concept called "Better ingredients. Better pizza."

Like in nature, branching can be messy. When Domino's Pizza first got started, it sold pizza and submarine sandwiches. When Little Caesars first got started, it sold pizza, fried shrimp, fish and chips, and roasted chicken. When Papa John's first got started, it sold pizza, cheesesteak sandwiches, submarine sandwiches, fried mushrooms, fried zucchini, salads, and onion rings.

Over time, each of these three brands dropped the secondary items to focus on home delivery (Domino's), take-out (Little Caesars), and better ingredients (Papa John's), much like a growing plant will shed its secondary branches.

This is divergence in action. Over time, each successful brand becomes as different as it possibly can from the core brand and the other brands that have branched off from the same category.

A new branch on the pizza limb is Papa Murphy's Take 'N' Bake Pizza which competes with the take-out and home-delivery chains. A pizza that survives a thirty-minute trip in a heat bag is just not going to taste the same as a pizza fresh out of the oven.

Papa Murphy's solves that problem by selling "half-baked" pizzas that you finish cooking at home. Customers can enjoy fresh-out-of-the-oven pizza right at home.

The Dynamics of Divergence

What drives divergence: consumers or companies? Actually both do. It's analogous to what happens in nature where the conditions of life (consumers) favor or disfavor the natural mutations that take place in organisms (companies).

Companies have much more control of this process than nature does because they don't have to wait for natural mutations to occur. They can deliberately introduce new brands that force-feed the process.

Unfortunately most companies have a static rather than a dynamic vision. Rather than see what could happen in the future (divergence), they see only what could be done today (convergence.)

"What if we put sit-down pizza together with take-out and home-delivery pizza? We could be bigger than Pizza Hut, Little Caesars, and Domino's combined."

Assuming a pizza chain could solve the operational problems involved (and this is a big assumption), this kind of thinking has a major flaw. The flaw is called natural selection. As time goes on, each pizza brand evolves in a different direction. Trying to stay on top of three diverging and evolving categories is difficult. (A No. 2 brand of pizza has to compete only with Pizza Hut. A "convergence" brand of pizza has to compete with Pizza Hut, Domino's Pizza, and Little Caesars.)

The pizza category is in a constant state of divergence. California Pizza Kitchen pioneered the gourmet pizza category. Sbarro pioneered the pizza-by-the-slice category. Bertucci's specializes in brick-oven pizza. Pizzeria Uno is spreading the love of deep-dish pizza Chicago-style.

Divergence in Department Stores

Years ago, department stores ruled the retail world. Every city had a department-store king. Macy's in New York, Marshall Field's in Chicago, Rich's in Atlanta. Then there were the national chains: Sears, Montgomery Ward, JCPenney.

Everyone knows traditional department stores are in trouble. And everybody thinks they know what caused that trouble. They didn't move out to the suburbs with their customers. They didn't keep up with the latest fashions. They forgot about service and focused on sales.

What department stores did wrong is trivial compared to what the competition did right. Like coffee shops, department stores were eaten alive by divergence. Every department spawned a narrowly focused national brand that rapidly moved to dominate its category.

The athletic-shoe department became Foot Locker.

The baby department became Babies "R" Us.

The bedding department became Bed Bath & Beyond.

The book department became Barnes & Noble.

The casual-clothing department became The Gap.

The consumer-electronics department became Best Buy.

The furniture department became Rooms-To-Go.

The housewares department became Crate & Barrel.

The jewelry department became Kay Jewelers.

The leather coat department became Wilsons Leather.

The lingerie department became Victoria's Secret.

The makeup department became Sephora.

The mattress department became Sleepy's.

The men's suit department became Men's Wearhouse.

The pet department became PetsMart.

The plus-size department became Lane Bryant.

The salon became Supercuts.

The shoe department became Famous Footwear.

The sports department became Sports Authority.

The young-adult department became Abercrombie & Fitch.

The toy department became Toys "R" Us.

The clearance department in the basement, of course, became Wal-Mart, the world's largest retailer.

It's interesting, too, that almost all of these department store branches were started by individual entrepreneurs, not large companies. Sam Walton started Wal-Mart with a single store in Arkansas. Donald Fisher founded The Gap with a single store in San Francisco, selling only jeans and music. Charles Lazarus started Toys "R" Us with one store in Washington, D.C.

Big companies don't usually have the patience or the vision to see opportunities in branching off. Big companies want to go after existing markets, the larger the better.

Sam Walton started with a Ben Franklin franchised dime store in Newport, Arkansas, in 1945. By 1962, Walton owned fifteen Ben Franklin stores operating under the Walton 5&10 name.

He only opened a Wal-Mart Discount City in Rogers, Arkansas, that same year because Ben Franklin management rejected his suggestion to open discount stores in small towns.

(What? Big company management misses an opportunity to own what will turn out to be the most successful retail brand in history? Sure, it happens all the time.)

Divergence in Companies

What today is called outsourcing has been a corporate trend for decades. It's surprising how many company activities are actually handled by outside specialists, creating many opportunities for building brands.

Advertising (Young & Rubicam), accounting (Pricewaterhouse-Coopers), payroll (ADP), computer operations (Electronic Data Systems), computer software development and installation (Accenture), tax preparation (H&R Block), copy and mail (Ikon), and money transfers (Brinks).

Whenever an outsourced function becomes a big enough business, there are further opportunities for divergence. In the payroll function for example, Paychex became a billion-dollar business by focusing on small companies. (Paychex has 490,000 customers.)

A typical company today might also outsource its maintenance service, janitorial service, security service, catering service, gardening service, plant and flower service, and many other services. "Do what you do best and let others do the rest" is the motto of many modern corporations.

Manufacturing, once thought to be the heart of a company's

operations, is the latest corporate activity to experience outsourcing. Nike is the obvious example, but the practice is widespread. Well over half of all products are not made by the company whose brand name is on the package.

In the high-tech field, Flextronics, a Singapore company with $13 billion in annual revenue, has become a well-known brand. With factories on five continents, Flextronics makes products for Alcatel, Dell, Ericsson, Hewlett-Packard, Microsoft, Siemens, and others.

Across industries in general, when someone says, "Where shall we have this product made?" the first thought is a brand called "China." In the computer programming area, the first thought is a brand called "India."

The ultimate in outsourcing is outsourcing your own employees. Administaff is one of hundreds of companies that lease employees to American corporations. Called "professional employer organizations," these outsourcing concerns are a fast-growing segment of the U.S. economy.

Divergence in Medicine and Law

No field of human endeavor illustrates the principle of divergence more than the medical profession.

The human body hasn't changed much in thousands of years, but the people that treat human illnesses have. A medical doctor used to be a "doctor." Today the profession has diverged into twenty-four major specialties: allergy and immunology, anesthesiology, colon and rectal surgery, dermatology, emergency medicine, family practice, internal medicine, medical genetics, neurological surgery, nuclear medicine, obstetrics and gynecology, ophthalmology, orthopedic surgery, otolaryngology, pathology, pediatrics, physical medicine and rehabilitation, plastic surgery, preventive medicine, psychiatry and neurology, radiology, surgery, thoracic surgery, urology.

That's only half the story. Most of these specialists have diverged into subspecialties. Internal medicine now has sixteen subspecialties: adolescent medicine, cardiovascular disease, clinical and laboratory immunology, clinical cardiac electrophysiology, critical care medicine, endocrinology, gastroenterology, geriatric medicine, hematology, infectious disease, interventional cardiology, medical oncology, nephrology, pulmonary disease, rheumatology, and sports medicine.

Lawyers have followed the same path. Everybody's a specialist. Check the yellow pages and you'll find categories like these: administrative agencies and governmental law, admiralty, antitrust and trade regulations, appellate practice, aviation law, bankruptcy and debtor relief, civil rights, collections, computer law, construction law, consumer law, corporation and business law, creditors' rights and commercial law, criminal law, disability law, divorce and family law, elder law, employment discrimination, employment law, entertainment and sports law, environmental law and natural resources, franchise law, immigration and custom law, international and foreign law, juvenile law, labor law, malpractice and professional negligence, mediation services, patent and trademark and copyright, pension and employee benefits, personal injury and wrongful death, real estate law, securities law, social security law, taxation, wills and estate planning, workers' compensation.

If convergence were the driving force in the legal and medical professions, physicians would be getting law degrees so they could save money by handling their own medical malpractice suits.

Divergence in Distribution Channels

Another phenomenon is channel divergence. Over time multiple channels develop for selling a product or service. A skillful marketing person can sometimes create a brand by creating not a new product, but a new distribution channel. Dell in direct sales of personal computers. Costco in warehouse clubs. Amway in multilevel marketing.

Hanes was the No. 1 brand of panty hose sold through the department store channel. But women weren't shopping department stores very often, so Hanes decided to launch a supermarket brand. They chose the name L'eggs, which has become the leading panty-hose brand in the country. Not a new product, but a new distribution channel along with a new name.

Paul Mitchell has become the leading hair-care brand sold through one hundred thousand hair salons. The largest privately owned hair-care firm, John Paul Mitchell Systems does an estimated $600 million in sales a year.

In the medical field, many prescription drugs are creating a "direct to consumer" quasi-channel. (Botox is a typical example.) By promoting their drugs directly to consumers, pharmaceutical companies are creating powerful brands. Sure, the M.D. makes the final decision, but he or she can easily be swayed by consumer preference.

Another example of branding by channel is AmeriScan, which offers high-tech medical scans directly to consumers. With twelve scanning centers already open (and more on the drawing boards), AmeriScan hopes someday soon to have a national chain that offers both CT (formerly CAT) scans and MRI scans, as well as EBT (electronic beam tomography) workups. It fits the general trend of consumers taking from doctors more responsibility for their health.

Why not? Are you a smoker concerned about lung cancer? Get a low-dose CT scan and find out. (Even better, give up smoking.)

Divergence in Homes

Look around your house and you'll see divergence at work. In every room there are opportunities to divide and conquer.

Take the basement. If you can heat the air to make a home comfortable in the wintertime, why can't you do the opposite in the summertime? Enter the air conditioner.

Did the air conditioner converge with the furnace? No, it became a separate appliance. And now there are two opportunities to create brands and dominate categories.

Take the kitchen. Did the stove combine with the refrigerator? Of course not. And now we have woodstoves, gas stoves, electric stoves, flattop stoves, and many different kinds of stoves to come. Nor did the microwave oven combine with the regular oven. It became a separate category dominated by brands unrelated to stove brands.

Take the refrigerator. Instead of its combining with another appliance, many people have two refrigerators. One regular refrigerator and one freezer. (At the high end the brand is invariably Sub-Zero.) You might also find a wine refrigerator (EuroCave).

Many kitchens are loaded with a range of appliances. Dishwashers, toasters, coffeemakers, espresso machines, electric mixers, blenders, electric waffle makers, ice cream machines, electric ice shavers, electric bread makers, juicers, electric knives, food processors, air purifiers, electric fans, etc.

Sure, once in a while a convergence device is introduced that captures the imagination and a wave of publicity. In 1973, for example, Carl G. Sontheimer introduced the Cuisinart, a sort of glorified blender whose multiple attachments allowed it to cut, slice, knead, chop, dice, grate, grind, or even blend. Here was the ultimate convergence product, a Swiss Army knife for the kitchen.

One example doesn't prove a trend. While the Cuisinart (and its imitators) continues to sell today, the total market for such products is small. As a matter of fact, Cuisinarts, Inc. went bankrupt in 1989.

Take the vacuum cleaner. Years ago every family had an upright vacuum (Hoover). Today you will find lightweight (Oreck), canister, handheld, wet/dry, and even whole-house cleaning systems.

You'll also find the Swiffer, which works like a mop, except that it has a trigger on the handle to spray cleaner on your floors. (One way to create a unique brand name is to take the key attribute "swifter" and change one or more letters.)

Then there's the Roomba, a $200 robotic vacuum cleaner that uses intelligent-navigation technology to clean your floors while you sleep, run errands, or just sit and relax.

Take lighting. The GE brand was built by its introduction of the first incandescent lightbulb. Today we have neon, halogen, and fluorescent bulbs. Coming soon is the light-emitting diode (LED), which has huge advantages in many tasks. In traffic lights they consume 80 percent less electricity and last up to ten times as long.

Will someone build an LED brand? Possibly, but chances are that the future will belong to line extensions of the big three lighting brands: GE, Sylvania, and Philips. Big companies hate to launch new brands when they can do line extensions of their famous names.

Divergence in Hotels

A hotel used to be a hotel. Now you can spend the night in a regular hotel (Hilton), a suite hotel (Embassy Suites), a motel (Holiday Inn), an extended-stay motel (Extended Stay America). With more choices to come.

Furthermore, you could spend the night in an expensive hotel (Four Seasons), a moderate-priced hotel (Marriott), or an inexpensive hotel (Hampton Inns).

You could sleep on an inner-spring mattress (Sealy Posturepedic), an air mattress (Select Comfort), a foam mattress (Tempur-Pedic), or a waterbed. At the high end, there's the Dux mattress, which has 2,000 to 4,980 innersprings compared with 300 to 1,000 springs for a regular mattress.

Oddly enough, it's often easier to establish a brand at the high end than at the low end. A high-end brand just naturally attracts publicity. Rolls-Royce, for example, is a well-known brand although they spend little on promotion and sell very few cars.

On the other hand, you can often make more money at the low end. Wal-Mart is the best example.

Divergence in Food

The average cow would be shocked to learn how many varieties of milk can be formulated from one spigot. Whole, 2%, 1.5%, 1%, skim, heavy cream, light cream, whipping cream, half-and-half, buttermilk, lactose-free milk (Lactaid), shelf-stable milk (Parmalat), and organic milk (Horizon).

The latest milk-divergence product is soymilk. Sales last year were $277 million, up 51 percent from the previous year. Silk, the brand that dominates the category with 80 percent of the market, is probably the best new brand name created in the last decade. By telescoping the words *soy* and *milk*, the brand's owners created a new name that was unique and yet also managed to connote the category. Quite a feat for a brand name with only four letters.

Have there been convergence milk products? Well, chocolate milk is one. Like virtually all convergence products, chocolate milk exhibits three characteristics: (1) It captures the consumer's imagination, especially if that consumer is six years old. (2) It represents a small segment of the milk market. Skim milk outsells chocolate milk ten to one. (3) Its primary benefit is convenience. You don't have to mix the chocolate syrup with the milk. Note, however, you give up the taste benefit of being able to adjust the amount of syrup in the glass, which is why Hershey's chocolate syrup is a big brand and chocolate milk is not.

TiVo, the Swiss Army knife, the cellphone/PDA/camera, and chocolate milk are all the same. They combine the "wow" factor with convenience and small sales. Convergence will never die in spite of its lack of success in the marketplace. The wow factor will keep it alive and well for decades to come.

Skim milk, which ranks at the bottom of the wow scale, is a good example of the discipline of divergence. You can make more money by taking something (cream) out of a product (milk) than you can by adding something (chocolate syrup) to the same product.

Everywhere you look in a supermarket, you see categories exploding. More varieties, more sizes, more price levels. In orange juice, for example, there are almost as many varieties as there are of milk. Regular, concentrate, no-pulp, extrapulp, calcium, double vitamin C, low-acid, low-sugar, even cholesterol-reducing orange juice (Minute Maid Heart Wise). In a major marketing coup, Tropicana became the No. 1 brand of orange juice by creating a new category called "not from concentrate."

In mustard, there is classic yellow (French's), brown (Gulden's), and Dijon (Grey Poupon).

Every new idea creates an opportunity for a new brand. Fat-free (SnackWell's), healthy (Healthy Choice), frozen (Birds Eye), organic (Horizon, Muir), low-carb (Atkins, Keto).

In food distribution, you are also beginning to see signs of a major divergence between traditional food and a new category that might be called natural, organic, or healthy food.

The dominant brand in the latter category is Whole Foods Market. With 140 stores in twenty-five states, Whole Foods is the world's No. 1 natural-food chain. Last year sales grew 17 percent, while sales of the three largest conventional supermarket chains (Kroger, Albertson's, and Safeway) collectively were down 2 percent.

Whole Foods is a brand to watch as America continues to eat healthier.

Addition vs. Subtraction

Addition (convergence) is the glamorous side of marketing, but subtraction (divergence) is the moneymaking side.

Another subtraction milk product is butter (Land O Lakes.) Take out the cream and make butter. Then sell the rest as skim milk.

There's also gourmet butter with a higher fat content (Plugra). And soy butter or margarine (I Can't Believe It's Not Butter!).

Ice cream has taken a similar path. There's half-fat, low-fat, nonfat, and sugar-free ice cream. As well as "double fat" ice cream (Häagen-Dazs, Ben & Jerry's). Not to mention frozen yogurt in regular, low-fat, and nonfat.

One of the more unusual subtraction products is crustless bread, introduced in Spain in 1999 and now sold in the United States as IronKids Crustless. Because the crust absorbs moisture from the white part of the bread, crustless bread stays softer longer. In Spain, the bread is promoted as "100 percent tender."

Think Category First and Brand Second

Unless you can define a new brand in terms of a new category, the new brand is unlikely to be successful. The most popular fruit in America is the banana, yet for most people a banana is a banana.

In banana-growing countries, however, there are different types of bananas. One of the most popular is the "little gold" or *orito* in Spanish. *Oritos* are sold in American supermarkets under various brand names including Chiquita and Bonita, but they're widely perceived as baby or immature bananas.

Why would you buy a baby banana, at a high per-pound price, when you can get the real thing for less money? You wouldn't unless you perceived the little one as a different category.

Central Americans like *oritos* because they have a more intense flavor than their big brothers. We believe you could drive the *orito* banana in a different direction with the general theme "twice the flavor, half the calories." Using a new brand name, of course.

Salt used to be salt. Now we have sea salt, kosher salt, popcorn salt, and no-salt salt (potassium chloride rather than sodium chloride).

Gum used to be gum. Now we have bubble gum (Bubble Yum), mint-flavored gum (Doublemint), sugarless gum (Trident), teeth-whitening gum (Trident White), nicotine gum (Nicorette), teeth-friendly gum (Freedent), fruit-flavored gum (Juicy Fruit), long-lasting-flavor gum (Extra), breath-freshening gum (Dentyne).

Wrigley's continues to dominate the gum category, with more than half the U.S. market, because they are quick to launch new brands to exploit a diverging category.

In the ever-expanding tree of brands, each new branch can cause divergence in other branches. The microwave oven, for example, has created opportunities to build new food brands. The latest is quick-serve meat. Some current choices include six-minute beef pot roast, five-minute pineapple-glazed ham, five-minute pork tenderloin in teriyaki sauce, and nine-minute meat loaf.

Divergence in Beverages

Water used to be what came out when you turned on the faucet. The only varieties were New York water, Chicago water, Los Angeles water, etc. Nowadays a host of bottled brands are on the market. Nestlé alone markets five brands: Poland Spring, Arrowhead, Deer Park, Ozarka, and Zephyrhills.

When the water washes away, the leading brands are likely to be those that have climbed out on separate limbs. Regular water (Aquafina), expensive water (Evian), carbonated water (Perrier), fitness water (Propel), calcium water (AquaCal), nicotine water (Nico), caffeinated water (Water Joe), and fluorinated baby water (Nursery).

Beer used to be beer. Today we have regular beer (Budweiser), light beer (Lite), low-carb beer (Ultra), dark beer (Newcastle), draft beer (MGD), ice beer (Icehouse), expensive imported beer (Heineken), expensive domestic beer (Michelob), cheap beer (Busch), microbrewed beer (Samuel Adams), steam beer (Anchor), wheat beer (Hefeweizen), Mexican beer (Corona), German beer (Beck's), Canadian beer (Labatt's), Japanese beer (Asahi), Australian beer (Foster's), Italian beer (Peroni), Chinese beer (Tsingtao), Belgiam beer (Stella Artois), Irish beer (Harp), nonalcoholic beer (Clausthaler), and many other types. Even extreme beer, which contains as much as 25 percent alcohol and costs as much as $100 a bottle (Samuel Adams Utopias).

Then there's stout (Guinness) and ale (Bass). Even pale ale (Sierra Nevada).

There has been an explosion of new beverage categories. New

Age drinks like Clearly Canadian. Natural drinks like Snapple. Sports drinks like Gatorade. Teenage drinks like Mountain Dew. Energy drinks like Red Bull.

Successful companies create a new brand to dominate each emerging category. Anheuser-Busch used to be focused on just one type of beer, regular Budweiser. If they had not launched Michelob and Busch, the company would have missed out on two important market segments. Today, Michelob is the largest-selling expensive domestic beer. Budweiser is the largest-selling regular domestic beer. And Busch is the largest-selling inexpensive domestic beer.

Once in a while a convergence beverage becomes an "in" drink, but it doesn't usually last long. Growing up, the popular soft drink at the skating rink was the rainbow soda. It was a combination of all the drinks, cola, lemon-lime, and orange. It might taste great, but it violates a law of nature and somehow seems offensive. (Perception is everything.)

Meanwhile down at the clubs the popular hard drink was Long Island iced tea (vodka, tequila, rum, gin, triple sec, sweet-and-sour mix, and Coke). "Mixing liquors, never sicker" was a popular refrain the morning after too many Long Island iced teas.

In general, however, combining categories is a recipe for disaster as well as a hangover. Would a liquor brand that was half gin and half vodka (ginka) be successful? (The best of both worlds.)

Would a drink that was half coffee and half tea (coftea) be successful?

Coffee and tea are two powerful limbs on the beverage tree and are never going to converge. Instead, coffee has diverged into categories like instant coffee (Nescafé), premium coffee (Colombian), freeze-dried coffee (Taster's Choice), flavored (Millhouse), and espresso (Illy).

Divergence in Trends

Many managers are obsessed with following the latest trend, when the truth is that trends often diverge and go off in two different directions at once. High-fat and low-fat. Gourmet and inexpensive. Oversize and miniature. In automobiles, for example, the trend is toward big SUVs like the Cadillac Escalade, at the same time one of the hottest cars on the market is the Mini Cooper.

A better strategy is to start your own trend by taking the category in a different direction. Often this means going against traditional wisdom.

In food, for example, bigger is better. "Do you want to supersize that?" is a common question at McDonald's. Nobody says, "Do you want to miniaturize your order?"

Yet miniature Oreos and miniature Snickers have been successful as has Palm (a miniature computer) and Game Boy (a miniature video gaming device). "Miniature" is one of those concepts that can help you dream up new divergence categories.

The miniature pocket watch became the wristwatch. The miniature camera became the Leica, the world's first 35mm camera. The miniature radio became the Sony, the world's first transistorized radio. The miniature mainframe computer became the PC. The miniature laser printer (a device once used only with mainframe computers) became the Hewlett-Packard LaserJet printer, the breakthrough product that built the H-P dynasty.

But this concept works best when it is used to create new categories, not when it is used to imply "immature" or baby versions of grown-up products. They're not baby carrots; they're Belgium carrots. They're not baby oranges; they're zipper-skin Clementines.

What Creates These New Market Segments?

In nature, the passage of time and the struggle for life create new species.

In marketing, the passage of time creates only opportunities, it doesn't create new categories. Companies create new categories by their marketing efforts.

That's why a company that devotes all its efforts to "satisfying its customers" is a company headed for trouble. Consumers don't know what they want until they are given a choice.

When a beer drinker walked into a saloon in the Roaring Twenties, he asked for a beer. And the bartender poured him a draft beer. It's highly unlikely that any beer drinker asked for a bottled beer until Schlitz, Pabst, Miller, and Anheuser-Busch started marketing bottled beer nationally.

The brewers created the categories, not the beer drinkers.

And it pays to be first. The first national brand of beer was Budweiser, and by a wide margin it's still the leading brand today.

It's marketing that creates opportunities for introducing new categories. It's not new categories that create opportunities for marketing programs to flourish.

Yet most companies are passive bystanders in marketing's "survival of the fittest." They think they will win by producing great products and surrounding those great products with great customer service.

Not true. The winners are those companies that introduce new brands that create new categories. The Gatorades, not the Power-Ades. The Mountain Dews, not the Mello Yellows. The Dr Peppers, not the Mr. Pibbs.

Many otherwise sophisticated companies introduce new brands

with lavish advertising budgets and completely forget about the issue of the category. What category is Pepsi One, a new cola drink introduced by PepsiCo with an advertising budget in excess of $100 million? And how does Pepsi One differ from PepsiCo's existing diet cola drink, Diet Pepsi?

Even the name has no meaning. You might think that Pepsi One is a diet cola with one calorie, but it's not. It's a diet cola with no calories. Pepsi No would have been a more descriptive name.

Currently, Diet Pepsi outsells Pepsi One by more than ten to one. Not that Diet Pepsi is doing particularly well. It trails Diet Coke by 42 percent.

The Role of Fashion

What accounts for erratic growth? One branch of a limb will suddenly spurt, while another branch of the same limb will wither and sometimes die. Often the driving force is fashion.

What drives fashion? It's the constant search for the new and different. As somebody once said, "Anything definitely in is already on its way out." Fashion even operates in such categories as hard liquor.

After World War II, the beverage of choice was whiskey, especially rye whiskey. "Rye and soda" was a typical bar call. Successive generations preferred Scotch whisky, then gin, then vodka, and today the fastest-growing hard liquor is tequila and the No. 1 brand of tequila is Jose Cuervo. (The most popular mixed drink in America is the margarita.)

Does anyone doubt that divergence will continue to drive the liquor industry? And that tomorrow there will be a new contender for tequila and a new opportunity to build a strong brand like Jose Cuervo? We don't.

Like a good surfer, a good brand manager has to get out in front of the wave and let the category drive the brand. You wait too long, and instead of driving the brand, the wave crushes it.

No beverage has diverged as much as wine. There are hundreds of categories, thousands of brands, and hundreds of thousands of different vintages. Some of the categories include Beaujolais, Bordeaux, Burgundy, cabernet, champagne, chardonnay, merlot, pinot, Riesling, sauvignon blanc, Shiraz, and zinfandel.

The leading wine publication, *Wine Spectator*, has a Web site that reviews more than 110,000 individual wines.

Fashion also drives wine consumption. Bordeaux and chardonnay used to be the hot wines. Today it's merlot and Shiraz.

Yesterday it was France. Today it's Australia.

In wine, in liquor, in almost every beverage, there is a lot of divergence, but little convergence. The French practice of blending grape varieties is losing out to varietal wines that are 100 percent chardonnay, 100 percent merlot, 100 percent Shiraz, etc. It's a category issue. People want to know which category they are drinking, not just which brand.

You see the same trend in Scotch whisky, from blends to single malts like Glenfiddich.

Divergence in Clothing

Fashion also drives the clothing business. Like age, fashion is cruel. You might be a jet-setter in your youth, but sooner or later you will grow old and lose your glamour. You might even have to use a walker and wear hearing aids.

The same thing is true for fashion brands. Someday you might even need to put the brand to sleep.

Calvin Klein was a big, powerful, fashionable brand. But Calvin lost his prestige to Ralph Lauren. And Ralph Lauren is in danger of losing his prestige to Tommy Hilfiger. And Tommy Hilfiger is in danger of losing his prestige to the latest hot brand, Sean John.

Clothing that is not fashionable is difficult to sell. On the other hand, fashionable clothing is not only easy to sell but can be sold for high prices.

Why would anyone spend $600 for a pair of Manolo Blahniks or Jimmy Choos that are impractical, uncomfortable, difficult to walk in, and could cause serious damage to your feet?

Because they are fashionable. "Cleavage for toes."

At the opposite end of the spectrum is the super-comfortable UGG boot made in Australia. Kate Hudson, Sarah Jessica Parker, Cameron Diaz, and Oprah Winfrey have been seen wearing them.

In clothing the essence of branding is not just creating a new category, but creating a new category that is fashionable.

Nike became the brand of choice and replaced Keds. But it wasn't enough for Nike to create a new category (athletic shoes instead of sneakers). Nike also had to make the new category fashionable.

What makes a brand fashionable? In a word, celebrities. Anytime a brand is seen worn by a number of celebrities, it automatically has credentials. The brand becomes fashionable.

What color do most celebrities wear? Black. What has become the most fashionable color? Black. What color is the most expensive credit card in the world, the American Express Centurion card, the card that requires $150,000 in annual spending plus a $1,000 fee? Black.

What color is the best-selling expensive Scotch whisky? Black. (Johnnie Walker Black Label.)

Will black continue to be the most fashionable color? Of course not. When everyone starts wearing black, celebrities will be on to the next thing. (Pink is starting to look popular, especially for women.)

You Win by Introducing New Brands

This year's fashion is next year's also-ran. You win in the world of fashion not by changing your brand to adapt to today's fashion, but by introducing new brands that create new categories.

Instead of line-extending his brand into a host of new categories, Ralph Lauren should think about creating a new brand to capture tomorrow's consumers who will be looking for the next big thing.

Ditto Levi Strauss. While sales have fallen from $7.1 billion in 1996 to $4.1 billion in 2002, Levi Strauss has been busy extending its core brands beyond the Levi's 501, 505, and Silvertab brands.

Now you can buy Levi's Vintage at Neiman-Marcus for $200 a pair. Levi's Premium at Barneys for $110 a pair. Levi's Type 1 at Kohl's for $85 a pair. Levi's Red Tab at Macy's for $35 a pair. And Levi Strauss Signature at Wal-Mart for $23 a pair.

As the category fragments, Levi is losing out to Diesel and Replay at the high end, Tommy Hilfiger and Fubu at the midprice level, and Wrangler and Old Navy at the low end.

One of the major fashion drivers is the revolt of the next generation. When kids see their parents wear Levi's, they immediately look for other brands.

Conclusion: Levi Strauss needs a new brand to reach the younger generation.

New Brands, New Companies

It's amazing how many times a new brand pioneering a new category is created, not by an existing company, but by a new company. In the clothing field the latest example is Under Armour.

A decade ago, Kevin Plank was a University of Maryland running back distracted by the athlete's curse of sweat-saturated underwear. He searched for something lighter, cooler, and dryer and came up with athletic underwear.

Today, his business, Under Armour, is one of the country's fastest-growing private companies, with sales exceeding $120 million a year.

Big companies are usually late jumping into new categories like athletic underwear. Nike has introduced the Pro Compression line and Reebok the Play Dry line. But who will win the athletic underwear war?

Our bet is on Under Armour, the pioneer of the new category. (See chapter 11, "Survival of the firstest.")

Divergence in Toiletries

It used to be that a toothbrush and some toothpaste were all you needed to maintain good oral health. Now you have mouthwash (Listerine), plaque-reducing mouthwash (Plax), dental floss (Johnson & Johnson), flat dental floss (Glide), gum stimulators (Butler), gum brushes (Sulca), water brushes (Water Pik), electric toothbrushes (Sonicare), battery-operated electric toothbrushes (SpinBrush). Even baby toothbrushes (Soft Grip).

Then there are the teeth-whitening products, like Crest Whitestrips, as well as professional teeth-whitening systems (BriteSmile).

Perhaps no category illustrates divergence more than shaving. There's dry shaving (Norelco) and wet shaving (Gillette) as well as the disposable wet-shaving razor (Bic). Then there's the double-blade razor (Trac II), the adjustable double-blade razor (Atra), the spring-mounted double-blade razor (Sensor), the triple-blade razor (Mach 3), and the quadruple-blade razor (Quattro).

In vision correction, successive branches have included eyeglasses, bifocals, progressive lenses (Varilux), contact lenses (Bausch & Lomb), and laser surgery (Lasik).

Divergence in Recreation

In every sport, there are opportunities to branch out and create a new category and a new brand.

In roller skating, the wheels can be realigned to create the in-line skate (Rollerblade). In skiing, the number of skis can be cut in half to create the snowboard (Burton).

In tennis, the racquet can be made larger (Prince). In golf, the driver can be made larger (Callaway Big Bertha).

Callaway became the leading golf club company. Prince became the leading tennis racquet company. Burton became the leading snowboard company. Rollerblade became the leading in-line skate company. And all of these brands were created by entrepreneurs, not by big companies.

Not convinced yet? Read on.

Divergence in Music

Sixty years ago, everybody listened to *Your Hit Parade*, which featured Frank Sinatra and the top ten hits of the week.

Once when Frank was a guest at the White House, Franklin D. Roosevelt sidled over to him and whispered, "If I promise not to tell anyone, will you tell me what song will be number one on the *Hit Parade* this week?"

How times have changed. Today, *Billboard*, the bible of the music business, has eighteen separate hit lists: adult contemporary, adult top 40, bluegrass, classical, classical crossover, contemporary jazz, country, dance, electronic, hip-hop, jazz, Latin pop, mainstream rock, modern rock, movie sound tracks, New Age, regional Mexican, and tropical/salsa.

And each of the *Billboard* eighteen hit lists has a separate leader: Santana, Matchbox Twenty, Alison Krauss & Union Station, Andrea Bocelli, Josh Groban, Norah Jones, Toby Keith, Daniel Bedingfield, Louie Devito, 50 Cent, Regina Carter, Marco Antonio Solis, Audioslave, Trapt, *The Matrix Reloaded*, Yanni, Los Bukis/Los Temerarios, and Ibrahim Ferrer. (If you can recognize all of these eighteen music stars, you either work for *Billboard* magazine or you're an idiot savant.)

Today, radio is highly fragmented, with the top music format (rap) accounting for only 27 percent of airplay. Is it likely that George Bush would invite 50 Cent to the White House and ask him what song will be number one on *Billboard*'s hip-hop list next week?

Markets follow the same path as music. They fragment into segments, and each segment is a separate, distinct entity. Each segment has its own reason for existence. And each segment has its own leader, which is rarely the same as the leader of the original category.

Music players have also diverged. From the audiocassette player (Walkman) to the CD player to the MP3 player (iPod).

Divergence in Dogs

In dogs, the number of breeds continues to multiply. Experts estimate that there are about seven hundred to eight hundred separate and distinct breeds of dogs. Federation Cynologique International, the world canine organization, recognizes 329 breeds divided into ten different groups.

The American Kennel Club currently recognizes 150 breeds.

The latest five breeds, which have all been added since 2000, are the Nova Scotia Duck Tolling Retriever, the German Pinscher, the Toy Fox Terrier, the Polish Lowland Sheepdog, and the Spinone Italiano.

Six more breeds have been named to an interim stage and will become eligible to show in the near future. Plott owners and Glen of Imaal Terrier enthusiasts, your day in the show ring will come soon.

Divergence in Countries

In countries, will the United States ever converge with our friends to the north to form "AmeriCan," a merger that makes a lot more sense than Daimler and Chrysler? Don't hold your breath. The opposite is happening.

Yugoslavia painfully broke up into five countries: Croatia, Slovenia, Bosnia and Herzegovina, Serbia and Montenegro, and the Former Yugoslavian Republic of Macedonia. (Greece claims the "Macedonia" brand name so there's some question about what name the Former Yugoslavian Republic of Macedonia will ultimately take.)

Potentially there's a sixth country (Kosovo) that was originally part of the former Yugoslavia, but currently Kosovo is administered by the United Nations, pending a final decision on its status.

In 1776, shortly before the Colonies became a separate nation, there were about 35 empires, kingdoms, countries, and states in the world. By World War II, the number had doubled. By 1970, there were more than 130 countries. Today the UN has 191 countries as members, the latest being Timor-Leste, the former East Timor.

Divergence in Religion

In contrast to the ancient practice of worshiping many gods, "monotheism" is considered a great step forward in religion.

Today, we might not worship many gods, but we do worship in many different religions. Historically three of the world's great faiths are branches off the same limb: Judaism, Christianity, and Islam. In turn, each of these branches have diverged repeatedly. Judaism into Conservative, Reform, and Orthodox. Christianity into Roman Catholic, Eastern Orthodox, and Protestant. Islam into Sunni and Shiite.

The process never stops. Currently the 79 million members of the Anglican Communion are in danger of diverging over the issue of gay bishops. Even the monolithic Roman Catholic Church has a small splinter movement called Traditionalist Catholicism, partially bankrolled by Mel Gibson.

In the Far East, the great tree of religion includes such branches as Hinduism, Buddhism, Jainism, Parsiism, Confucianism, Taoism, and Shintoism.

Divergence Strengthens, Not Weakens

You might think that vigorous divergence would weaken a tree, but it's actually the opposite. Whenever you see many branches (and many brands) that have diverged from a single category, you can be sure that the category is strong and dynamic and is likely to be around for a while.

Many branches (and brands) will lead to nowhere and die off, but the tree itself will remain exceptionally healthy. The computer tree with its many limbs and branches all emanating from the trunk (mainframe computer) is a good example of dynamic growth.

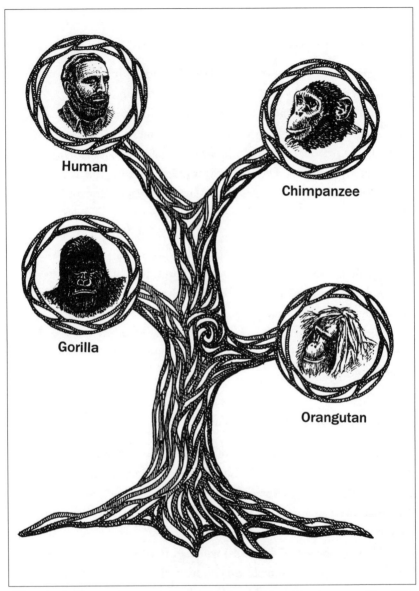

THE HOMINOID TREE INCLUDES THE ORANGUTAN, THE GORILLA, AND OUR NEAREST RELATIVE, THE CHIMPANZEE.

Chapter 10

The Mystery of the
Missing Links

ONE OF THE KNOCKS ON EVOLUTION is the absence in the fossil records of "missing links." If man is descended from the ape, where are the half-man/half-ape fossils? Paleontologists haven't found any.

Nor are they likely to find any. The missing link will always be missing.

Solving this mystery was one of Charles Darwin's most brilliant deductions. The only illustration in *The Origin of Species* diagrammed the natural tendency of species to move apart after many thousands of generations, leaving wide gaps between individual species.

And no missing links.

The genealogical line did not run from today's ape to today's man. Rather today's man is descended from yesterday's man through thousands of generations, each of which was changed by natural selection. And today's ape is descended from yesterday's ape through thousands of generations.

Today's personal computer is not descended from the typewriter. The first personal computer didn't have a keyboard, didn't have a printer, didn't work like a typewriter, and didn't look like a typewriter.

The reason for the failure of many companies and many brands is that *Homo sapiens* can overrule nature, at least in the short run. *Homo sapiens* in the business world can do things that would never occur in nature. *Homo sapiens* can introduce missing links.

And they do. Every day, in almost every industry you can name, companies are busy introducing missing links. They might live for a while, but missing links are almost certain to die in the long run. They violate a fundamental law of nature.

The Word Processor

Half-typewriter/half-personal-computer, the word processor enjoyed a brief moment in the spotlight. It made Wang Laboratories, founded by Au Wang with $600 in savings, the dominant brand in the category. By 1985, Wang was a $2.4 billion company.

Seven years later, Wang filed for bankruptcy, another victim of the missing-link myth.

Before its bankruptcy, Wang Laboratories tried to save the situation by moving into personal computers. Nothing wrong with that, except they tried to move into PCs with the Wang name, which was closely identified with word processors.

A name in the mind is like a hole in the ground. You can deepen a hole, you can widen a hole, but the one thing you can't do with a hole is move it.

Once a brand name becomes strongly identified with a category in the mind, the brand can't easily be moved.

The dynamics of divergence suggest a way out of this dilemma. Since you know that related categories are going to constantly move apart, the best way to dominate two different branches is with two different names.

Wang should have left the Wang name on its word-processing branch and invented a new name for its personal computer branch.

In the early days of any emerging industry, you see repeated examples of the same folly. Many companies jump in to provide the missing link between yesterday and tomorrow. Their motto: the best of both worlds.

Early transoceanic steamships also had sails. At first, the hybrid combinations were big winners. They were faster than pure sailing ships and more economical than pure steamships. In retrospect, it's easy to see what happened. Sailing ships and steamships diverged in different directions, and the hybrid was pulled apart and sank.

The sailing ship became a toy for the rich and famous, and the steamship became so economical to operate that the sails were nothing more than an expensive anachronism.

The Propjet

Many early jet-engined aircraft were propjets (now called turbo-props). Early on, the propjet was an attractive alternative to both propeller planes and pure jets, especially for smaller aircraft. The propjet combined the high cruising speed of a jet with the slow-speed stability of a propeller plane.

That was early on. Today's small, thirty-to-a-hundred-seat regional jets are rapidly replacing the turboprop because they are faster, more comfortable, and quieter.

Furthermore, jets can fly higher than turboprops and avoid the turbulence found at lower altitudes.

Still, America's major airlines operate some seven-hundred turboprops, which they probably wish they hadn't bought.

It's hard to avoid the problem of the mushy middle. In the beginning, a new technology starts slowly and is burdened with problems. The halfway approach seems the safest and most productive. And many times it is, but a halfway strategy is almost always a loser in the long term.

Take the motion picture industry. Today, big-budget films are shot on film and then converted into a big digital file for adjustment of color, contrast, and the addition of digital effects. Afterward, the digital file is recorded back on film and then duplicated for showing in movie theaters.

Is there any doubt that someday soon all movies will be shot in digital, manipulated in digital, and distributed in digital?

Not to us.

Facsimile

Of course, the "long term" might be a long term indeed. Take the facsimile, for example. After decades of growth, we're beginning to see the end of the road for fax.

The problem? Fax is a mushy-middle product that combines the physical aspects of a letter with the transmission speed of an email message. The letter is likely to be around for generations to come, and there's no question that email is here to stay. But fax? Its days are numbered. (Western Union's Mailgram, another halfway service, has already met the same fate.)

In the last four years, from 1998 to 2002, the number of pages faxed fell by more than 50 percent.

What put fax on the ropes? Email evolution. Today email is cheaper, faster, more accurate, and more flexible than facsimile. The day of the turboprop is ending and so is the day of the fax.

Genigraphics (originally a service of General Electric) and a number of other companies were founded to turn computer-generated type into photographic slides. A nice idea until Power-Point and the low-cost video projector put the photographic slide out of business.

DVDs by Mail

Another halfway brand is Netflix. Instead of renting DVDs at Blockbuster, the consumer can use the Internet to order discs directly from Netflix, saving time and money. It's a step up the evolutionary ladder.

Netflix has grown rapidly and now has more than a million subscribers. But sending electronic data (in the form of a DVD) by mail in a digital era seems like a step backward. Someday Netflix will meet the same fate as fax.

Companies are comfortable with halfway brands because they fit with management's perception of itself. Or as General Electric used to say, "Progress is our most important product." The idea that a company's products and services are constantly evolving in a better, faster, cheaper direction is a comforting thought.

Companies are uncomfortable with divergence because it represents a break with the past. Instead of better, faster, cheaper, many technological forks in the road are marked "different, slower, and more expensive."

You can easily predict what will happen to the DVD-by-mail business. Sooner or later, we are going to have DVDs by the Internet, and Netflix is going to be left out in the cold.

The Problem at Kodak

There's no question that digital photography (a separate branch) is rapidly replacing analog or chemical photography, which is Kodak's mother lode. This year more digital cameras will be bought than analog cameras. It could be years, it could be decades, but there's no question that Kodak's photographic film and paper business will eventually disappear.

Kodak is trying to do what Wang failed to do. That is, move its name into a different category. Ironically, the very strength of the Kodak brand (one of the most recognized and respected brands in the world) makes this move difficult to accomplish. (The deeper the hole, the harder it is to move.)

Kodak tried to bridge the gap between traditional and digital photography with its Advantix Advanced Photo System cameras and film. The company spent more than $1 billion to develop and bring Advantix to market in 1996.

The 24mm Advanced Photo System (or APS) was actually developed by five companies, including Kodak, Canon, and Fuji. Its features include the ability to shoot regular and panoramic shots on one roll and the inclusion of technology designed to improve lighting. The system, which costs 15 percent more than conventional film, never caught on with consumers, who either stayed with the higher quality of 35mm film and cameras or jumped the divide and went digital. APS represents the mushy middle, a no-man's-land where survival is difficult.

Even worse is Kodak's attempt to merge chemical and digital photography into one overall category called infoimaging. (Have you ever heard an actual consumer say, "What we need around here is some infoimaging"?)

"Infoimaging," said a recent Kodak advertisement, "is perhaps the most promising convergence of technologies since the Internet itself, and we welcome other partners to the task of realizing its potential."

Convergence of technologies? That's a sure sign that infoimaging is going to fade out.

The Problem at Polaroid

Here is a brand (Polaroid) tightly tied to a category (instant photography) that is seriously declining. With the rise of the one-hour-photo shops the mess and expense of Polaroid prints weren't worth the bother when you could get an entire roll of film developed and printed in sixty minutes.

So Polaroid tried to move its brand name into conventional photographic film (Kodak's territory) and a number of other categories including medical imaging products, digital scanners, and digital photoprinters. Result: Polaroid Corporation went bankrupt in 2001.

What did in the Polaroid brand? Evolution in film processing.

The DVD/VCR Player

Retail stores are loaded with many "addition" products that might make sense in the short term. Take the combination DVD/VCR player. There's no question that some form of DVD is making the VCR format obsolete.

The trouble is, most people already have a videocassette recorder. Instead of a combination device, they are much more likely to buy a single-function DVD player. Then when DVD replaces VCR, they'll just throw away their old VCRs.

It's DVD in the long run, but in the short run, consumers need something to play their VCR cassettes on. So it might make sense for a few consumers to buy a combination DVD/VCR player.

But it might not make sense for a company to flit from one short-term product to another. You can't build a brand that way. It often takes decades to associate a new brand with a new category. (The world's most successful brands are those that sell the same stuff with the same strategy for an extended time. Dom Pérignon champagne, Mercedes-Benz automobiles, and Rolex watches are three good examples.)

If hot chocolate becomes the next "in" drink, should Starbucks switch from coffee to hot chocolate? Only at its own peril.

Chasing the latest fad is only one of the many branding mistakes a company can make. Even worse is branching out the brand rather than branding the branch.

The Problem at Macintosh

What's a Macintosh? It's a personal computer as well as a personal-computer operating system.

Does any other PC manufacturer try to use the same brand name on two branches (machines and operating systems)? Dell markets machines, but not operating systems. Microsoft markets operating systems, but not machines. IBM tried to market both its OS/2 operating system and its personal computer machines. It was not successful with either.

Macintosh is mired in the mushy middle trying to hang on to two branches at once. No personal computer has received more favorable reviews than Macintosh, yet the brand has only 3 percent of the market.

Cars, Wine, and Warehouse Clubs

And what are car buyers to make of the Chrysler Crossfire, the $35,000 sports car with a Mercedes engine and a Chrysler body? In the mind, which branch do you put this beauty on? The one marked "expensive German car" or the one marked "cheap American car"?

(Doesn't anyone remember the Porsche 914? The sports car

with the Volkswagen engine and the Porsche body. It was shunned by Porsche enthusiasts because it was a cheap sports car and by Volkswagen enthusiasts because it was an expensive sports car.)

Also consider wine. There are two basic kinds of wine: red wine and white wine. There's also rose wine, the best of both vineyards. How much rose, the wine in the mushy middle, do you suppose is sold? Not very much.

A local supermarket chain is feeling the competition from the warehouse stores (Costco and Sam's Club) so they are running an advertising campaign that puts them right in the middle. The theme: "Supermarket nice. Warehouse price."

Logically the campaign makes sense, but mentally, which branch do you put the chain on?

There are no missing links in nature, and there are no truly successful brands in the mushy middle either.

AT EACH STAGE OF GROWTH, THE FIRST SEEDLING TO GERMINATE IS
TALLER AND STRONGER. SO, TOO, WITH BRANDS.

Chapter 11

Survival of the
Firstest

TWO SEEDS FALL ONTO THE FOREST FLOOR. Maybe it was the angle one seed hit the ground, maybe it was the soil underneath that seed, but for some reason one seed germinates first and the other seed a day or two later.

At each stage of growth, the first seedling is taller, stronger, more resistant to drought. As time passes, the first seedling grows up to become a gigantic tree, blocking the sunlight from reaching the second seedling. Eventually the second tree-in-the-making withers and dies.

Survival of the fittest? To be sure. But how did the first seedling become the fittest seedling? In the forest or in the marketplace, the battle is usually won by the first contestant to occupy the space.

No Free Ride

Being first doesn't automatically mean your brand will become the leader in a new category. It only gives you a license to do so. If you're first, your brand starts off as the leader since no other brands are trying to occupy the same branch.

Here's where evolution comes in. Your brand needs to evolve to maintain its leadership. In this respect, you need to be protective of your brand and be especially vigilant when competitors threaten your position.

Sales, however, don't matter nearly as much as perception. To become successful, your brand needs to establish the perception of leadership in the minds of consumers.

What Works in Movies

The motion picture industry has figured out how the game is played. If a movie doesn't open with a big weekend, it's not going to become a blockbuster. A big opening weekend, especially if the film is No. 1 in ticket receipts, almost guarantees that the film will be successful.

Sleeper hits, which build by word of mouth, like *My Big Fat Greek Wedding*, are a rarity in Hollywood today. Most films are gone in a few weeks, heading straight to video if they don't have a big first weekend.

Sales don't matter. It's the publicity generated by sales that builds the buzz for the brand. People want to see what other people are seeing. A motion picture that opens with a big splash creates the perception that it's a "must-see" movie, especially among the younger crowd who make up the majority of the movie market.

The Matrix Reloaded sold $42.5 million worth of tickets on its opening day, a new record. Naturally this new record generated loads of publicity.

Every trade has its tricks. One of the tricks of the movie trade is to magnify the first-weekend numbers by opening the picture in as many theaters as possible. An ordinary movie might open on a thousand or fewer screens. *Matrix* opened on 3,603 screens, more than 10 percent of all the movie theater screens in America.

Even if you know you're not going to like a blockbuster movie, you have to see it to be able to talk about it with your friends.

What Works in Music

"If a record doesn't do well the opening week," said Ron Baldwin, a music manager and producer, "people say it's dead." Music labels fight for exposure on four fronts: radio airplay, video exposure, media coverage, and placement at retail stores.

To promote her new album *American Life*, Madonna did an interview on NBC's *Dateline*, a special on MTV, a feature role on the sitcom *Will and Grace*, and an appearance on *Live with Regis and Kelly*.

It worked. With 241,000 copies sold in its first week, *American Life* opened at No. 1 on the charts. It was not a fluke. Of the top ten albums of last year, eight had first-week sales of 220,000 or higher. If you don't win the first week, the odds are against you.

What Works in Books

If a book doesn't make the best-seller lists in its first few weeks, the book will never make the best-seller lists. Bookstores display their top-selling books up front and also discount them. The rest of their books are buried on the shelves at full price. Win early or lose out is the general rule in publishing.

The key, of course, is advance publicity. You have to use publicity to create demand before the book goes on sale. J. K. Rowling's fifth book in the Harry Potter series, *The Order of the Phoenix*, created a tidal wave of publicity in advance of its on-sale date. Fans dressed in costumes showed up at midnight bookstore parties.

No book has ever received as much advance publicity as Hillary Clinton's *Living History*. The results were predictable. The book sold more than a million copies the first month. You win early or you don't win at all.

After a book, a music CD, or a movie makes the best-seller lists or hits the top of the charts, the standard strategy is to try to keep it there by advertising that fact. "America's #1 Movie" is a typical headline.

"Firstness," or leadership, strikes a powerful emotional nerve in the consumer's mind. "If everyone else thinks *Harry Potter and the Order of the Phoenix* is a terrific book, it must be a terrific book, regardless of what I might personally think."

Fortune Favors the First

Majority rules, especially when it involves perceptions. Heinz ketchup, Hellmann's mayonnaise, Thomas' English muffins, Philadelphia cream cheese, Budweiser beer, and many other leader brands are powerful brands not because they are better than competitive brands (although they might be), but because they are widely perceived to be the leader brands in their categories.

Firstness creates leadership. If your brand is the only brand in the category, your brand must be the leader. And when competition arrives, leadership creates the perception of betterness for your brand.

The first brand in the mind can survive a long time and still maintain its leadership. Coca-Cola has been the No. 1 cola brand for 118 years. GE has been the No. 1. lightbulb brand for 102 years. Kleenex has been the No. 1. tissue brand for 80 years.

Two things work in favor of the first brand into the mind. First is the perception that the leading brand must be "better." It's axiomatic that the best product or service wins in the marketplace. Since the first brand into the mind is automatically the leader (there are no other brands), the first brand will tend to maintain its leadership. (It blocks the sunlight from competing brands.)

Second is the perception that the first brand is the original. Every other brand is an imitation of the original. "The real thing" applies only to Coca-Cola, not to me-too brands like Pepsi-Cola and Royal Crown cola.

Even if Pepsi did outsell Coca-Cola someday (an unlikely occurrence), Pepsi-Cola would never be perceived as the real thing.

First Mover in the Mind

Business books often denigrate what they call "the first-mover advantage" and they're right. There is no advantage in being the first mover in the marketplace unless you can use that opportunity to also become "the first mover in the mind."

The great tree of life is a physical analogy. The great tree of brands is a mental analogy. Branding occurs only in the mind and has no physical reality. Being first in the marketplace is a physical first and does not necessarily lead to a mental first.

- Duryea built the first automobile in America, but the brand never got into the consumer's mind.
- Du Mont built the first television set in America, but the brand never got into the consumer's mind.
- Hurley built the first washing machine in America, but the brand never got into the consumer's mind.

Edmund Hillary (along with his Sherpa guide Tenzing Norgay) was the first person to climb Mount Everest. Fifty years after his famous feat, Sir Edmund is still widely known around the world, while the more than 1,650 people who have made the trek after him are virtual unknowns, as are most of 175 people who have died on the mountain.

Were any of these people better rock climbers than Hillary? Sure. Did any of these people climb faster than Hillary? Undoubtedly. But it doesn't matter. Being better seldom tops being first.

On May 23, 2001, Erik Weihenmayer reached the summit of Mount Everest, the first blind person to do so. Will Erik become famous like Sir Edmund? Not a chance.

On May 16, 2002, fifty-four people reached the summit of Mount Everest on a single day. Will any of these fifty-four people become famous like Sir Edmund? Not a chance.

When you're first in the mind, your brand creates a powerful emotional connection with consumers. In contrast, when you're first in the marketplace, your brand is just another brand.

Losing Its Leadership Doesn't Destroy a Brand

Even *if* the first brand into the mind loses its leadership, the brand doesn't lose its emotional connection with consumers.

Mikimoto isn't the leading brand of cultured pearls, but it's widely known (and admired) because it's the "originator of cultured pearls." Apple (and its Macintosh descendants) maintains an emotional connection with personal computer users in a way that Dell, Compaq, Hewlett-Packard, and other brands do not. Why? Apple was the first personal computer brand into the mind.

Hertz isn't the leading rent-a-car brand anymore (Enterprise is), but Hertz still resonates with car-rental customers in a way that Avis, National, and other brands do not.

Harvard, the first college founded in America, is still widely believed to be the "best" college in America, even though it's not the largest, nor does it usually win the popularity contests run by the media, most notably *U.S. News & World Report.*

The Fortune 500 is still perceived to be the gold standard in corporate rankings, even though larger, more successful publications are publishing lists of their own (the Business Week 1000 and Forbes 500). All corporations brag about their position on the Fortune 500 list, but few corporations ever mention *Business Week* or *Forbes.* Why is this so?

In 1955, *Fortune* published its first list, ranking the five-hundred largest industrial corporations in America by sales volume. *Fortune* was first.

Fortune favors the first.

Imprinting a Brand

Branding is like imprinting, the process whereby a young animal learns to bond with its mother. A gosling, for example, will follow the first moving object it sees after hatching. As a result, it can easily become imprinted on another species, or even an inanimate object, if one happens to be moving.

In a similar way, brands become imprinted in the consumer's mind. The first brand in a new category usually makes a strong impression. Kleenex in tissue. Scotch in cellophane tape. Kodak in film photography. Red Bull in energy drinks. Survival of the firstest.

Creating a new category and then imprinting your brand on that category is the essence of success. The first goose to wag its tail in front of the newborn goslings is sure to capture their hearts and minds. The first brand to wag its tail in front of a newborn category is sure to capture the hearts and minds of potential consumers.

While the concept of establishing a leader brand is simple, the execution is difficult. Too many companies fall into the convergence trap. "We can be the first to put the cellphone together with the handheld computer."

With thousands of categories out there, there are literally millions of possible combinations that could in turn yield an equal number of unexploited opportunities.

True in theory, but not in practice. The "catdog" approach has wasted billions of research and development dollars.

Breakthrough Products Are Rare

The second approach is the breakthrough product approach. The airplane, the helicopter, the jet engine, the microwave oven, the computer, the microprocessor, the cellphone, and other revolutionary products were obvious successes. But the odds of striking it rich by inventing a breakthrough product are extremely long.

Consider IBM, a company that has been spending $5 billion a year on research and development. What breakthrough product has IBM launched in the last decade? Refinements of existing products, to be sure. But breakthrough products? None that we can think of.

In many ways a breakthrough product is an accident of history. The time was right for the development to occur. At the same time the Wright brothers were getting airborne at Kitty Hawk, Ferdinand Ferber, Ernest Archdeacon, Gabriel Voisin, Robert Esnault-Pelterie, Leon Levavasseur, and Alberto Santos-Dumont were experimenting with heavier-than-air flight in Europe.

Less than three years after Orville and Wilbur achieved their initial success, Santos-Dumont made the first recognized airplane flight in Europe.

The airplane was an idea whose time had come. If the Wright brothers hadn't got their invention off the ground, somebody else would surely have.

Breakthrough products capture the public's imagination, but they play only a minor role in branding. More money can be made more easily and more quickly with mundane products that are effectively marketed.

Food, clothing, housing, transportation, and entertainment account for the vast majority of consumer spending. Breakthrough products like cellphones, laptop computers, handheld computers, digital cameras, and Segway human transporters represent a small portion of a typical family's monthly expenses.

"Create a New Category You Can Be First In"

This has been our marketing mantra for decades. The supermarkets, the drugstores, the department stores, the discount stores, are filled with brands built by this powerful strategy. So is the Internet. Some examples:

- Amazon.com, the first online bookstore
- Band-Aid, the first adhesive bandage
- California Closets, the first closet organizer
- Callaway Big Bertha, the first oversize golf driver
- Carrier, the first air conditioner
- Charles Schwab, the first discount stock brokerage firm
- CNN, the first cable news network
- Dell, the first direct seller of personal computers
- Domino's, the first home-delivery pizza chain
- Dr. Scholl's, the first foot-care product
- Duracell, the first alkaline battery
- ESPN, the first cable sports network
- Evian, the first expensive bottled water
- Footjoy, the first golf shoe

- Gore-Tex, the first breathable waterproof cloth
- Heineken, the first imported beer
- Hoover, the first upright vacuum cleaner
- Jell-O, the first gelatin dessert
- Kentucky Fried Chicken, the first fast-food chicken chain
- Kleenex, the first pocket tissue
- *National Enquirer,* the first supermarket tabloid
- Nike, the first athletic shoe
- Oracle, the first database company
- Pampers, the first disposable baby diaper
- *Playboy,* the first men's magazine
- Polaroid, the first instant camera
- PowerBar, the first energy bar
- Q-tips, the first cotton swab
- Reynolds Wrap, the first aluminum foil
- Samuel Adams, the first microbrewed beer
- Saran Wrap, the first plastic food wrap
- Swatch, the first fashion watch
- Sun Microsystems, the first UNIX workstation
- Tide, the first detergent
- *Time,* the first weekly newsmagazine
- Vise-Grip, the first locking pliers
- WD-40, the first superlubricant
- Xerox, the first plain-paper copier

These brands (and many, many others) were built by creating the perception that they were first in a new category. It's not necessary to actually be first, it's only necessary to create the perception that your brand was first.

("Saying it" and creating the perception of being first are two different things, of course. This is an issue we discuss in detail in chapter 14.)

Firstness vs. Fitness

The biggest issue in marketing today involves the difference between "firstness" and "fitness." The Darwinian concept of "survival of the fittest" is accepted in most companies as the essence of marketing. "We have to convince prospects that our brand is the best." That is, the fittest.

"Survival of the firstest" does not have nearly as much acceptance among top management. "Who cares who's first? Consumers only care who's better."

And they're right. Consumers don't care who's first. They only care who's better. That's why they buy Kleenex tissues, Heinz ketchup, Band-Aids, and Q-tips. "Because they're better."

But is it product quality or perception of product quality that guides the consumer's decision? The evidence strongly suggests that perception plays the major role.

"Why do you buy Heinz ketchup?"

"Because it's the best."

"Have you ever tried Hunt's ketchup?"

"No, I haven't. I would never buy Hunt's because everybody knows that Heinz is the best ketchup."

The Perception of Leadership

When your brand is the first brand in a new category, it's widely perceived as the original and the pioneer. When other brands invade your territory, they are widely perceived as me-too copycats.

This perception of leadership (in both senses of the word, pioneer and largest-selling) creates a strong feeling that your brand must be the best.

It gets worse for the competition. In an effort to boost sales, second-tier brands often cut prices. What does a lower price say to consumers? "Hunt's ketchup must not be as good as Heinz."

In well-established categories, it is almost impossible for a second or third brand to find a clear-cut physical difference between its brand and the leader. And even if a laggard brand does find such a difference, what's to stop the leading brand from just copying the idea?

We call this tactic "blocking" and recommend it for every leading brand. In essence, blocking is nothing but evolution, or gradual change, at work.

As a result, most categories consist of very similar products with one leading brand having a dominant share. Survival of the firstest.

The real issue in marketing is not creating a brand. The real issue in marketing is creating a new category and then using your new brand name to dominate that category.

No Use Crying over Spilled Milk

Once the opportunity to create a category has passed you by, you might as well forget about it and look for other opportunities. Yet some companies never learn:

- Coca-Cola missed the caffeinated, carbonated citrus category (pioneered by Mountain Dew), so they tried to get into the game with Mello Yello. That didn't work, so they tried Surge, which didn't work either.
- Coca-Cola missed the spicy cola category (pioneered by Dr Pepper), so they tried to get into the game with Mr. Pibb. That didn't work either.
- Coca-Cola missed the natural beverage category (pioneered by Snapple), so they tried to get into the game with Fruitopia which never went anywhere.

- Coca-Coca missed the energy drink category (pioneered by Red Bull), so they tried to get into the game with KMX. Not only was KMX fourteen years too late, but it's also saddled with a weak name. (*Red Bull* connotes energy by conjuring up the image of waving a red flag in front of a charging bull. *KMX* sounds like an additive for a motor oil.)
- Coca-Cola missed the sports drink category (pioneered by Gatorade), so they tried to get into the game with Power-Ade, which hangs in there as a weak No. 2 brand.

Pepsi-Cola, on the other hand, gave up on its me-too sports drink brand (All Sport) and spent $13 billion to buy the real thing (Gatorade along with its corporate parent, Quaker Oats).

PowerAde, KMX, Fruitopia, Mr. Pibb, Surge, and Mello Yellow represent six misguided attempts on the part of the Coca-Cola Company to create new brands when they should have focused on creating new categories.

If the world's leading soft-drink company and owner of the most valuable single brand in the world (Coca-Cola) has consistently been unsuccessful in building new brands, why should you think your company can succeed using similar strategies?

You Don't Build Brands. You Create Categories

In truth, you don't build brands at all. You exploit divergence to create a new category, and the expansion of that new category allows your brand to flourish.

What built the IBM brand? Was it a massive marketing program communicating the benefits of doing business with Big Blue? Or was it the fact that International Business Machines dominated the mainframe category?

Would Fortune 500 companies still be using adding machines if IBM had not run a massive mainframe marketing program? No. The computer was an idea whose time had come. (Someone once said that the way to establish yourself as a leader is to find a parade starting to form and then run in front of the crowd with a flag.)

What built the Dell brand? Was it a massive marketing program communicating the benefits of doing business with Dell? Or was it that Dell pioneered a new way to buy personal computers? (By phone.)

Or, for that matter, what built the Coca-Cola brand? Was it a massive marketing program communicating the benefits of drinking Coke? Or was it that Coca-Cola pioneered the cola category?

If creating a new category is the essence of brand building, then it pays to spend some time thinking about where new categories come from.

Where Do New Categories Come From?

Invariably by divergence of existing categories. Over time, the computer category diverged, and today we have many different types of computers and many different brands. Does anyone doubt that there will be more categories to come?

But where did the mainframe computer come from? you might be thinking.

Well, there was a category called calculators. Then the category diverged and we had mechanical calculators and electronic calculators.

In reality the mainframe computer is an electronic calculator with a million-dollar name. Strategically it's often wise to avoid the logical name for a new category and instead give the new category a sexy new name. The problem with the name *electronic calculator* is that it locks the perception of the new category into the limits imposed by the physical constraints of a mechanical calculator.

Many years ago, we worked with Hewlett-Packard on marketing strategy for a personal calculator (code name: Qwert). What's it going to cost? we asked. Thirteen thousand dollars was the reply. Anything that costs $13,000 is a computer, we replied, not a calculator.

And where did the calculator category come from? Well, first you had fingers which gave rise to the decimal system.

Convergence Would Destroy Brand Building

Convergence (should it ever happen) would destroy brand building. How can you create a new category by combining two existing categories? What do you call a combination cellphone/handheld computer? A cellhand? That doesn't make sense.

Furthermore, if categories do combine (and we strongly believe they do not), then the surviving brand names are likely to come from one side or the other. No new brands would have a chance.

If convergence were the driving force in business, over time we would expect to see fewer categories, fewer brands, less competition. Is this a realistic view of the future? We think not.

It's certainly not a realistic view of the past. For hundreds of years, the future has always brought more categories, more brands, more competition. What possible reason is there to believe that the future will be any different from the past?

Marketing Is a Battle of Categories

Marketing is not a battle of brands; it's a battle of categories. Winners are those companies that can invent and dominate new categories. (Think Dell, Intel, Microsoft.) Losers are those companies that get blindsided by new categories created by their competitors. (Think Western Union, Polaroid, Wang.)

Every year companies throw billions of dollars in the general direction of innovation. Many more dollars are spent on innovation than on marketing. Much of that money is wasted on convergence concepts.

If divergence has been the wave of the past (and it has), then we conclude that divergence is also the wave of the future. This is an escalating situation.

The more categories there are, the more opportunities there are for categories to diverge, and therefore the more opportunities there are for creating new categories and new brands.

The Hardest Thing to See Is a Trend

Have you ever stood on a beach watching the waves come in, trying to decide whether the tide was coming in or going out? It's not easy.

In day-to-day life, you see signs of both convergence and divergence. Some concepts are coming together and some are concepts breaking apart. Where's the trend?

In the early evolution of an industry, economics often favor convergence, but that usually changes as the industry grows up.

Convergence in the Airline Industry

In the thirties, passenger airlines decided they could make extra money by also carrying freight. Their planes were flying the routes anyway, so marginal costs were low and they could charge high prices for fast deliveries. So every major airline set up an air cargo division. It was like found money.

Not for long. The air cargo plum lasted only long enough for entrepreneurs to figure out a way of launching all-cargo airlines.

The first air cargo company to take off was Emery Air Freight, which was founded in 1946. By leasing extra space on scheduled airlines, Emery rapidly became the air cargo leader. Later, of course, Emery lost its leadership to the more narrowly focused Federal Express, the first "overnight" package-delivery company.

Today the three big airlines (American, United, and Delta) carry relatively little cargo. Last year cargo revenues for the big three were $1.7 billion or just 3.6 percent of their total revenues of $46.7 billion. (FedEx alone carried $15.3 billion in air cargo last year.)

Maybe that $1.7 billion was just "frosting on the cake." If so, either the frosting or the cake is in serious trouble. Together the big three airlines lost $8 billion last year.

Well, you might be thinking, the entire airline industry is in trouble, in part because of 9/11 and a decline in passengers. True, but how come Southwest Airlines continues to make money?

(Southwest Airlines alone is worth more than three times as much on the stock market as American, United, and Delta combined. And FedEx alone is worth more than five times as much on the stock market as the big three airlines.)

Divergence in the Airline Industry

Why are Southwest and FedEx successful? In a word, divergence. Each picked off one of the services offered by the major airlines and built a company around that single service. Overnight air cargo in the case of FedEx. Coach passengers in the case of Southwest.

Much has been written about the culture and the cost-cutting at Southwest, as if these things alone could make the difference in airline profitability. How would you, for example, apply Southwest culture to the three classes of service on a big airline?

Imagine a training session for flight attendants at United Airlines. "Okay, folks. Here's the drill. You say hello to the coach passengers. You shake hands with the business-class passengers, and you give a big hug to the first-class passengers." Southwest culture in the undemocratic environment of a United flight is simply going to fall flat.

As time goes on, categories diverge. Knowing that divergence always happens can help you make the right decision at the right time. Assuming the opposite can cause major long-term problems.

Initially, airline service was expensive. Planes were small, maintenance costs were high, and flight-personnel-to-passenger ratios were extremely high. Because only upper-income people could afford to fly, the airlines created a luxury service with gourmet food, fine wines, and attentive hostesses.

Larger planes that were less expensive to operate (especially the jets) created an opportunity to appeal to a broader market. Do we give up our high-tariff customers to appeal to the mass market?

Of course not. Whenever an airline came to a fork in the sky, they took both forks.

- Do we serve coach passengers or first-class passengers? Let's do both.
- Do we handle passengers or freight? Let's do both.
- Do we fly to business destinations or do we fly to tourist destinations? Let's do both.
- Do we operate domestic routes or international routes? Let's do both.

Execution Is Not a Strategy

Southwest Airlines, and its clones AirTran and JetBlue, execute well because they are serving a new airline branch called "low-cost coach service."

A good strategy allows a company to execute well. On the

other hand, excellent execution is impossible for a company with a poor strategy. It's a cause-and-effect relationship. Good strategy is the cause. Excellent execution is the effect.

Southwest became the first low-cost, point-to-point shuttle airline. Once that strategy was set, CEO Herb Kelleher pushed the envelope. No meals, no reserved seats, no interairline baggage exchange, no animals. To minimize training and maintenance costs, Southwest flies only one type of airplane, the Boeing 737.

While Southwest was gearing up to take over the business, you would think that the major players would have paid attention and changed their strategies. But they didn't.

UAL, the holding company for United Airlines, bought a car-rental company (Hertz) and two hotel companies (Hilton and Westin) and in 1987 changed its name to Allegis Corp. From now on, the corporation would be a *travel* company, not an airline company.

Within months of the name change, the Allegis chairman lost the allegiance of his board members and resigned. (American Airlines tried to do the same with its Americana hotel chain.)

What's a travel company anyway? What branch of the transportation tree is labeled "travel"?

Responding to Southwest, Twenty-three Years Later

It wasn't until 1994, twenty-three years after the first Southwest flight, that one of the major players in the airline industry finally responded to the threat posed by its no-frills competitor. That was the year United Airlines launched the Shuttle by United.

What's a United? Hanging the same brand name on two different branches is not the way to build a brand, especially in competition with a powerful brand like Southwest. The Shuttle by United didn't keep its parent company from going bankrupt.

Would it be possible to break off the front of the plane and launch a first-class-only airline? We think so, but so far no one has put the right combination together.

Midwest Express had the right planes, the right seating, the right food, and the right service, but still went bankrupt in the aftermath of 9/11. Midwest had two problems: the name and the route structure.

The name *Midwest Express* sounds like a regional trucking firm. Furthermore, why would you want to start a first-class airline in the Midwest? You need to start that kind of an airline in a place with a high percentage of egomaniacs. Our choice would have been New York or Los Angeles.

But it's only a name. Right. It's only a name like Starbucks, Red Bull, and Rolex are only names. What if these three companies had used different brand names? Would Coffee Connection, EnerGee, or UltraSwiss have become big, powerful, worldwide brands?

Don't count on it. The branding experience is intimately locked into the name itself. An inappropriate, mundane name will only work in a category with little or no competition. (Wal-Mart, for example, is the leader in a category whose major competitors Kmart and Target have equally mundane names.)

It wasn't until 2003, which was thirty-two years after the first Southwest flight, that one of the major carriers launched a low-cost, low-fare subsidiary with a unique name. Song, from the folks at Delta Airlines.

Will Song become a hit? Perhaps, but it's going to be difficult to compete with Southwest Airlines, a competitor that has almost a third-of-a-century head start.

Will Ted, United's new low-cost airline, become a big success?

Too little, too late. That's the story of many companies who wait until a new market gets established before launching their new brands.

In 2001, for example, United Airlines formed a subsidiary to offer fractional ownership of business jets. Unfortunately for United, NetJets, a Berkshire Hathaway Company, pioneered the category fifteen years earlier and continues to dominate it.

Two Psychological Barriers

Why didn't United launch a fractional-ownership subsidiary two decades earlier? And get a big jump on competition? Two psychological barriers keep companies from making this kind of move.

First is the absence of a market. "What! You want us to launch a brand into a category that has no sales? Even if we get one hundred percent of the market, there's still no market."

To be first, that's exactly what you need to do. Launch a brand into a naught market. Psychologically that's difficult to do.

Second is the targeting of a slice of an existing category (the divergence concept) that may itself not be very profitable. "What! You want us to launch a coffee shop brand that just sells coffee when traditional coffee shops that sell everything are marginally profitable at best?"

Even Starbucks stumbled when it took its coffee shop concept overseas. To date, Starbucks' 1,532 overseas stores, which represent 23 percent of its stores, account for only 9 percent of its sales. Even worse, they are a net money loser.

In America, Starbucks was the first European-style coffeehouse. In Europe, Starbucks is just another coffee-shop brand. The coffee is the same in a Starbucks in Milwaukee or in a Starbucks in Milan, but what's missing in Milan is the glamour, the mystique, the romance of being first in an exciting new category.

Starbucks in Milan is just another coffee shop.

Yet McDonald's used exactly the same strategy as Starbucks

and was even more successful in Europe, where sales per unit are 12 percent higher than they are in the U.S.

The difference is that McDonald's was first. It was the first hamburger chain in America and also the first hamburger chain in Europe and in most countries of the world.

The Part Is Greater than the Whole

We live by mottos like "The whole is greater than the sum of the parts." It's difficult to accept the idea that the part can be greater than the whole.

Would you rather own the United States Postal Service, which consistently loses money, or United Parcel Service, which focuses only on the package-delivery segment of postal service? The part is much more profitable than the whole.

Would you rather own *People* magazine, which used to be a section of *Time* magazine and has since become one of the most profitable publications in the world, or would you rather own *Time*, which is only marginally profitable?

Microsoft, whose major products are software components for personal computers, makes several times as much money every year as all the personal computer manufacturers combined. "Fools," wrote Hesiod circa 800 BC, "they do not even know how much more is the half than the whole."

In building a brand for the long run, in every category you can name, the half is much more than the whole. A brand that tries to appeal to every major market segment is doomed to become a minor brand . . . in the long run.

In the short run, it's different. Until a competitor seizes the opportunity to launch a divergence attack, the "all things for everybody" brand is going to do all right.

THE SECOND SEEDLING TO GERMINATE HAS A MUCH BETTER CHANCE OF
SUCCESS IF IT FALLS SOME DISTANCE AWAY FROM THE FIRST ONE.

Chapter 12

Survival of the
Secondest

THREE SEEDS FALL ONTO THE FOREST FLOOR. Two land close together, the other lands some distance away.

In the struggle for life, the two seeds that are close together will fight an epic battle until one dominates the other. From that point on, it will be survival of the firstest.

But suppose your brand was not first, suppose your brand has no chance of being first, suppose your seed is the one that fell some distance from the leader.

You're in exactly the right position to survive. Your brand will benefit from another principle derived from Darwin. Survival of the secondest.

An Acorn Doesn't Fall Far from the Oak Tree

True, which is why most acorns don't survive in the forest. An acorn needs enough sunlight to germinate and grow. Any brand that tries to grow too close to a leader is likely to suffocate and die.

A few acorns will fall some distance away. These are the ones that have a chance to grow up and become oak trees.

In nature, this is the force that eventually leads to the creation of a new species. In business, this is the force that leads to the success of many No. 2 brands despite the presence of powerful leadership brands. Target in competition with Wal-Mart. Scope in competition with Listerine. Lowe's in competition with Home Depot.

In nature, it's easy to see why survival demands a certain separation of species. Why a monkey takes to the trees to escape the bigger primates on the ground. Why a giraffe uses its long neck to find food that its shorter competitors cannot reach. In the long run, each species occupies a different niche on the great tree of life.

The second-largest city in America is not Boston, Philadelphia, Baltimore, or any other city close to No. 1 New York. The second-largest city in America is Los Angeles, about as far away from New York as you can get without leaving the country.

Consider, too, the plight of cities that live in the shadow of a larger, more dynamic metropolis. Newark is a typical example, but there's also Fort Worth, overshadowed by Dallas. St. Paul, overshadowed by Minneapolis. Oakland, overshadowed by San Francisco. Trenton, overshadowed by Philadelphia.

Be the Opposite of the Leader

In business, you can generalize the survival of the secondest concept with the principle "Be the opposite of the leader."

It doesn't matter what the leader's strategy is, whether it makes sense or not, it's always better to be the opposite of the leader in some fundamental way than it is to emulate the leader.

Maybe it's genetic, maybe it's a certain perverseness of the human spirit, whatever the reason, there's always an opportunity to get into the mind as a strong No. 2 brand.

Why is it that the younger generation rebels against the older generation? In music, in clothes, in food, in automobiles.

The driving force of human nature seem to be going off in two different directions: the desire to conform and the desire to be different. Most people balance these two conflicting forces by conforming in certain areas and being different in other areas.

It's the interplay of these two forces that creates opportunities for leading brands to maintain their leadership (survival of the firstest) and for the development of strong No. 2 brands (survival of the secondest).

Fortunately conformity is a stronger force than nonconformity, but both are necessary for a dynamic society. Conformity creates stability in a society, and nonconformity creates periodic upheavals that bring new ideas and concepts into the culture.

There is no one way to build a brand. There are two ways. Either be first and establish your brand as the leader. Or be second and establish your brand as the opposite of the leader.

No Right Way and No Wrong Way

Too many businesspeople allow their emotions to cloud their judgments. There is no right way and no wrong way to build a brand. There is vanilla ice cream and there is chocolate ice cream. Some people like vanilla. Some people like chocolate.

In politics, you can see the same two forces at work. Each political party is almost a mirror image of the other. The Democratic Party is widely perceived to be pro-consumer, pro-lower-income people, pro-choice, pro-big-government. The Republican Party is widely perceived to be pro-business, pro-upper-income people, pro-life, pro-small-government.

Given these dynamics, where is there room for a third political party? If the two leading brands in any category (in politics or in business) are properly positioned, there is little room for a strong No. 3 brand. (We often call this the Royal Crown problem.)

In business, the interplay between conformity (the leading brand) and nonconformity (the No. 2 brand) creates serious problems for brands that are trapped in the middle. (Kmart, for example.) Nor is this dichotomy often understood by either the leading brand or its major competitor.

In their desire to enlarge their market, leading brands often use strategies more appropriate to No. 2 brands. "What's mine is mine and what's yours is mine, too." Carried to an extreme, this strategy can destroy a brand. It's commonly called the all-things-for-everybody trap and the best example is Chevrolet.

What's a Chevrolet? It's a large, small, cheap, expensive car or truck. Any wonder that Chevrolet has lost its automobile leadership to Ford. (Ford is also falling into the same trap, but that's another story.)

The Danger of Trying to Emulate the Leader

No. 2 brands often fall into the opposite trap, trying to emulate the leader. The best example is Burger King.

- McDonald's expanded into breakfast; Burger King expanded into breakfast.
- McDonald's added chicken nuggets; Burger King added chicken tenders.
- McDonald's created Ronald McDonald; Burger King created the Magical Burger King.
- McDonald's added a kiddie menu and a playground; Burger King added a kiddie menu and a playground.

The only thing Burger King hasn't been able to emulate is Mc-Donald's revenues. The average Burger King in the United States does 33 percent less business than the average McDonald's.

It's hard to make money when you copy everything your major competitor does and you wind up selling a third less food.

But Burger King keeps trying. They keep replacing generals faster than the Germans did on the Eastern Front. Burger King has had nine chief executives in the last thirteen years. Eight marketing leaders in the last eight years. And five advertising agencies in the last four years.

It takes courage to be the opposite of the leader. The leader is successful; they must know what they're doing. Sure, they do, but in a perfect world, what works for the leader won't work for a No. 2 brand.

The world isn't perfect. If Burger King could find communities with no McDonald's restaurants, a copycat strategy would work fine. Unfortunately, McDonald's has 31,108 locations in 120 countries, which leaves few holes for Burger King to fill.

In Strength There Is Weakness

McDonald's is widely perceived as a kiddie paradise. The No. 1 destination for every kid between the ages of two and six. (We suspect the popularity of that nursery rhyme "Old MacDonald had a farm, ee i ee i oh" has something to do with the brand's recognition among the kiddie crowd.)

Where is the weakness of McDonald's strong appeal to the younger folks? Potentially, this strength could turn off the older crowd. Especially the preteen and teenage kids who might not want to eat their hamburgers with the kiddies in the playground.

"Grow up. Grow up to the flame-broiled taste of Burger King" is the strategy we once recommended to Burger King management, nine or ten CEOs ago.

It may be too late for Burger King to adopt an antikid, anti-McDonald's strategy. Getting rid of the playgrounds alone might be an impossible task given the control franchisees have over operations.

In a sense, Burger King is trapped in the mushy middle between McDonald's appeal to kids and Wendy's appeal to adults. Burger King doesn't have much room to maneuver.

It's not to say that No. 2 brands like Burger King don't have a strategy. They do. (1) Emulate the leader, and (2) do it better. The problem is, these strategies are self-defeating.

The Do-It-Better Trap

Many companies (and brands) have found a way to "do it better." What they haven't solved is the mental problem. How do you persuade consumers that your brand is better than the leader's brand?

- If you built a better watch, how would you persuade consumers that your brand is better than Rolex?
- If you build a better appliance battery, how would you persuade consumers that your brand is better than Duracell?
- If you made a better cola, how would you persuade consumers that your brand is better than Coke? Blind taste-tests have demonstrated that both Pepsi-Cola and Royal Crown cola taste better than Coca-Cola, yet most people still prefer to drink Coke.

Did Fuji overtake Kodak in photographic film? Did Goodrich overtake Goodyear in tires? Did Avis overtake Hertz in rent-a-cars?

Did Reebok overtake Nike in athletic shoes? Did Wisk overtake Tide in detergents?

We can think of examples where No. 2 brands overtook a leader, but none where two conditions were met: (1) the leader was strongly entrenched in the mind, and (2) the No. 2 brand used a "we do it better" strategy.

Doing It Different

Invariably when a leader is overthrown, it's because the No. 2 brand used a "do it different" strategy.

Enterprise became the leading rental-car brand not by overtaking Hertz at airport terminals, but by setting up car-rental facilities in suburban locations and focusing on the "insurance replacement" market. In other words, Enterprise did what a would-be No. 2 brand should do. Set up a mental distance between it and the leader. (In Enterprise's case, it was a physical distance, too.)

Today, Enterprise racks up $6.9 billion in annual revenues compared with $5 billion for Hertz. But guess what? Hertz is still widely perceived as the leader in rent-a-cars.

Perception is a long-lasting phenomenon. You can lose your sales leadership and still maintain your brand leadership in the mind as the Hertz example demonstrates. Perception is an immensely valuable attribute. We fully expect Hertz to regain its revenue leadership at some point in the future. Its task is simplified because it doesn't have to also regain its perceptual leadership.

Perception is sticky. For a short time in 1997 and 1998, Colgate outsold Crest toothpaste, but did Crest lose its leadership perception? No, it did not. Crest was still widely perceived as the leading toothpaste brand in America.

Doing It Different at Lowe's

In the home-improvement warehouse category, Lowe's demonstrates the same principle. Home Depot is the big gorilla in the category. Home Depot started first, pioneering the category, and now has 1,650 stores in comparison with 930 stores for Lowe's.

With its large, cavernous warehouses stacked to the rafters with merchandise, Home Depot is the Wal-Mart of the home-improvement category. And Lowe's is the Target.

Home Depot appeals to men; Lowe's appeal to women. Home Depot is huge, crowded, dark, and dingy; Lowe's is large with wide aisles, neat shelves, and bright lights. Lowe's is a good example of a brilliant No. 2 brand strategy. Be the opposite.

Doing It Different at BMW

Perhaps the best example of what a No. 2 brand should do is BMW. The company is in the unfortunate position of having to compete with Mercedes-Benz, perhaps the most prestigious car brand in the world.

How do you compete with a brand like Mercedes-Benz? It's not easy, but the principle is quite clear. You become the opposite. Mercedes is known for big, powerful, luxurious cars with an emphasis on a smooth ride and comfortable seats. Even Mercedes sports cars like the SL500 are not exactly nimble machines.

So BMW positioned itself as the opposite of Mercedes. "The ultimate driving machine" has been the brand's longtime advertising slogan. But it's more than just a slogan. BMW designs cars that are smaller, lighter, and more fun to drive than the big Mercedes.

As a result, BMW outsells Mercedes (in units sold) in the United States and in many other countries around the world.

BMW is probably the best example of staking out a position that's the opposite of the leader's and then sticking with that position over an extended time. In BMW's case, it has stuck with its "driving" strategy for more than thirty years. If it ain't broke, don't fix it.

Doing It Different at Reebok

Don't change it either. Reebok became the No. 2 brand of athletic shoe by being the opposite of Nike. In the 1980s, while Nike was a male-focused, sports-oriented brand with superstar Michael Jordan as its spokesperson. Reebok with its leather uppers was the stylish, comfortable aerobics shoe that appealed to women.

That didn't last long. Reebok has since copied Nike's strategy, using endorsements from jocks like Allen Iverson and Kenyon Martin. Today, Reebok is no longer the No. 2 brand of athletic shoes.

In 1991, Reebok sold $2.2 billion in athletic shoes, taking a respectable second place to Nike's $2.7 billion. By last year, however, Reebok sold only $1.6 billion behind Nike's $5.8 billion and Adidas's $2.8 billion.

Recently, Reebok has changed its strategy. The onetime aerobics queen has tapped into the lucrative hip-hop market to fuel a comeback. In just over a year, the shoemaker has inked deals with hip-hop stars 50 Cent, Shakira, Fabolous, Eve, and Jay-Z.

Will it work? It's too early to tell, but a hip-hop strategy has the advantage of doing it different than Nike.

Doing It Different at Phoenix

What's the largest private university in America? Many people probably don't know that America's largest private university is the University of Phoenix with 157,800 students.

The University of Phoenix is not in the same category as Harvard, Princeton, Yale, or Stanford. It has no campuses, no sports teams, no endowments. Yet at a time when most private schools are losing money, the University of Phoenix generates annual profits of $200 million on revenues of $1.2 billion.

Of all the marketing opportunities in the world today, education offers the most potential. Except for a handful of universities and graduate schools (Wharton, Kellogg, MIT, Thunderbird, and Babson, to name a few) most educational institutions are flunking Marketing 101.

Most colleges, universities, and graduate schools don't do it different. As a result, they don't stand for anything. Consequently they don't build strong brands.

Rock/Scissors/Paper

Remember that kid's game rock/scissors/paper? (Rock breaks scissors. Scissors cuts paper. Paper covers rock.)

What's the best strategy in a game of rock/scissors/paper?

It all depends on what strategy your opponent has selected. Your best strategy is to be the opposite. The University of Phoenix took this approach in almost everything it did.

- Instead of appealing to the traditional eighteen-to-twenty-two-year-old market, the University of Phoenix appeals to working adults. Average age: thirty-five years.
- Instead of using full-time teachers and tenured professors, the University of Phoenix uses working professionals hired part-time. Out of a faculty of more than 9,000 people, only about 250 are full-time.
- Instead of building expensive campuses, the University of

Phoenix leases relatively inexpensive office space for its classrooms.

Often, a manager is the victim of his or her own expertise. A common reaction to an idea like the one used by the University of Phoenix is "That's not the way it's done in our industry."

"That's not the way it's done" is usually a good indication that an idea has merit. Don't ask, does the idea make sense? Ask whether the idea is the opposite of the leader's strategy.

Doing It Different at Scope

All mouthwash brands tasted bad, including Listerine, the first mouthwash and the leading brand. "The taste you hate, twice a day," said Listerine ads.

Many competitive brands tried to take Listerine's leadership away, including Micrin from Johnson & Johnson, which spent $15 million advertising the brand in 1962, an enormous amount in those days.

No luck. The only brand that has made progress against Listerine is Scope, the good-tasting mouthwash. Today Scope is a strong No. 2 brand in the category.

Does good taste make sense in a product designed to kill the germs that cause bad breath? Maybe not, but the concept is the opposite of the leader's and therefore deserves serious consideration. (Repositioning Listerine users as having "medicine breath" helped build the Scope brand, too.)

The No. 3 brand of mouthwash (Plax) escaped the Royal Crown trap by setting up a new category. Plax is the first plaque-fighting mouthwash. (Plax/plaque. A simple, easy-to-remember, and effective brand name.)

Doing It Different in Beer

In some categories, it's hard to see the forest for the trees. Take beer, for example. Product proliferation in the beer business makes it difficult to see the battle for the No. 1 and No. 2 positions. Some supermarkets carry between fifty and one hundred different beer brands.

In the jockeying for beer positions, two trends are apparent. One is the trend to light beer.

The largest-selling beer in America is not Budweiser, it's Bud Light, which recently passed its full-calorie sibling. As far as beer leadership is concerned, the game is over and Bud Light has won. Bud Light outsells the next two light beers, Coors Light and Miller Lite, combined.

The second trend is the gradual decline of the longtime No. 2 brand Miller Lite.

The first brand of light beer, Miller Lite lost its leadership to Bud Light and has since fallen behind Coors Light. Total sales of all Coors brands are likely to pass the Miller menagerie sometime in the future.

What's killing Miller are its numerous line extensions. In addition to Miller Lite, the brewer also sells Miller High Life, Miller High Life Light, Miller Genuine Draft, and Miller Genuine Draft Light.

And let's not forget the many other brands that have been launched with the Miller name over the years, including such clearcut losers as Miller Clear, Miller Ultra Lite, Miller Regular, Miller Reserve, Miller Reserve Light, and Miller Reserve Amber Ale.

It's difficult to be the alternative to the leader. It's almost impossible to be a family of alternatives to the leader. Miller needs to put all of its resources behind one brand . . . and that one brand is obviously Miller Lite.

But how does Miller Lite become the opposite of Bud Light? Except for being the "hot" brand, Bud Light is an anonymous product with little identity except perhaps for its Midwestern roots.

In reality, Coors Light has a natural "reversal" idea that it let slip through its fingers. Instead of being a Midwestern beer, Coors is brewed in Golden, Colorado, with "Rocky Mountain springwater." Now that the brand is no longer brewed exclusively in Golden, that idea is out the window, although the perception lingers on.

What Should Miller Do?

Perceptions do linger. Two of the perceptions associated with the Miller brand are "Tastes great, less filling" and "Miller Time." Miller should select one of these two ideas to promote its Miller Lite brand.

But which one?

"Tastes great, less filling" is a generic idea that applies to any light beer. If you like beer, then all light beers taste great and are less filling. Furthermore, the slogan didn't build the brand. The brand built the slogan. It was the roaring success of Lite beer, the first light beer into the mind, that made people remember the slogan.

The reverse is true for the Miller Time idea. In an era when the traditional No. 2 brand (Schlitz) was declining, Miller Brewing relaunched Miller High Life with a "reward for a hard day's work" theme. Television ads showed farmers, factory workers, and construction men heading to the bar after a hard day on the job. At five o'clock, it was "Miller Time."

Miller sales took off. By 1979, Miller High Life's market share was only 21 percent behind Budweiser. Miller was the strong No. 2 beer brand.

As a matter of fact, the two Miller beers combined, Miller High Life and Miller Lite, actually outsold Budweiser in the years 1978–80. Miller was on a roll.

Then the effects of line extension struck. Miller Lite went up and Miller High Life went down, the classic symptoms of line-extension disease. From a high of 23.6 million barrels in 1979, Miller High Life sunk to 5.3 million barrels last year.

From time to time, Miller Brewing, now SABMiller, has attempted to revive its Miller Time slogan, but the execution has been pathetic.

There are verbal slogans and there are action slogans. "The real thing" is a verbal slogan. Consumers instantly get the idea that Coca-Cola is the original and the other brands are imitations.

"Miller Time" is an action slogan. It has little meaning without the actions that take place before the slogan is uttered. A television commercial needs the buildup of a hard day's work to make the emotional connection with the reward, having a beer at five o'clock.

Is it too late to clean up the mess at Miller? Will Miller go the way of Schlitz? By coincidence, Schlitz Light was the second light beer on the market, a line-extension move that failed to halt the decline of the Schlitz brand.

Only time will tell.

Searching for the Big New Idea

The question often arises in situations like Miller, why should we limit ourselves to what's already in the mind? Surely there must be a new idea out there someplace that will turn the brand around.

Wishful thinking. When a brand has been on the market as long as Miller has (148 years), when a brand has been advertised as heavily as Miller has (currently $459 million a year), it's wishful thinking to believe you can find a new idea that will move the needle. An old idea with a new twist? Maybe. But a totally new idea? No.

"Miller, the smooth beer."

What? Miller has been brewing beer for fifteen decades and somebody just noticed that it's a smooth beer? The slogan sounds phony.

G.I. Joe vs. Barbie

Suppose you wanted to develop a doll to compete with Mattel's Barbie. It's tough because kid toys are often standards wars. There was Barbie and there was no No. 2 brand.

So toy company Hasbro took the doll concept to the extreme. Instead of a better Barbie for girls, the company developed a doll for boys called G.I. Joe.

Would boys play with dolls? No problem, Hasbro called its new product an "action figure."

G.I. Joe stormed the toy market in 1964 the way its namesake stormed the beaches at Normandy twenty years earlier. Some 375 million have been sold to date.

Bratz vs. Barbie

At her peak in 1997, Barbie sales reached $1.9 billion, or more than 90 percent of the fashion-doll market. Recently, however, her share has dropped to 70 percent.

Bratz is the reason. While Barbie appeals to girls three to seven years old, Bratz targets tweens, or eight-to-twelve-year-old girls. Introduced in 2001 by MGA Entertainment, Bratz dolls are strikingly different. With their oversize heads, pursed lips, and cartoon eyes, Bratz dolls project an image of fun, while Barbie dolls are sweet and serious. Bratz sales this year are expected to be more than half a billion dollars.

A common lament among companies and individuals is that

we're too late. We missed the big opportunities in television, computers, the Internet. Yet every development creates endless opportunities for No. 2 brands and for new branches. And it's surprising how long these opportunities will remain open, just waiting for an entrepreneur to pounce.

Forty-three years elapsed between the launch of Barbie and the introduction of Bratz, the most viable alternative to the Mattel monopoly. Forty-three years to come up with an effective No. 2 strategy.

Don't lament the lack of opportunity. Just look around and you'll see opportunities in every direction.

Macho Managers Beware

"There is no room for second place," said Vince Lombardi. "There is only one place in my game, and that's first place."

In the world of football, maybe, but in the world of business there's plenty of room for second place. One of the biggest mistakes a company can make is trying to overtake the leader when it should have been trying to carve out a secure No. 2 spot.

Beware. Corporate culture doesn't take kindly to managers who are willing to settle for second. It's not macho. In the words of a Nike Olympics commercial, "You don't win silver; you lose gold."

The essence of a good marketing strategy is knowing when you can win and when you can't. And if you can't, settle for silver rather than knocking yourself out going for gold.

The Problems of High Tech

In beer and other consumer products, the problem of establishing the No. 2 position is relatively simple. Sometimes even a trivial difference is enough to cement a second brand's position. In high tech, however, the problem of establishing a second brand is more difficult.

In high-technology products, there is always the issue of de facto standards. Macintosh OS might be a better personal-computer operating system than Windows, but no one is going to switch to the Apple product if everyone else in the company is using the Microsoft product.

With 95 percent of the market, Windows is the de facto standard for personal-computer operating systems. There's nobody in second place.

You can argue all you want about Apple's engineering excellence, Apple's cutting-edge designs, Apple's striking colors, and Steve Jobs's publicity coups, but facts are facts. There's something wrong with Apple's strategy.

The iPod might be a brilliant product with brilliant PR, but it does nothing to solve Apple's problem, which is Microsoft. Currently Apple has just 2.6 percent of the worldwide market for personal-computer operating systems, just ahead of Linux at 2.3 percent.

A Standards War Is Different

In a standards war, it's all or nothing at all. If every bar and restaurant in America could carry only one brand of beer, Budweiser's market share would double overnight. Second place is no place in a standards war.

This is not a hypothetical situation. In the cola category, for example, there is definitely a one-cola-brand-per-restaurant standard. As you might have expected, the leading brand (Coca-Cola) has a much greater share of the winner-take-all restaurant market than it does in supermarkets and convenience stores, where it faces Pepsi-Cola competition. (Coca-Cola has 68 percent of the domestic fountain business versus only 22 percent for Pepsi.)

Selling a personal computer operating system (and in Apple's case, the computer to run it) is like selling a cola brand in a one-cola-per-restaurant market. It's not good enough to be in second place because there is no second place.

With the lion's share of the worldwide PC operating system market, Microsoft is an incredibly strong position. An old joke illustrates the company's power.

"How many Microsoft programmers does it take to screw in a lightbulb?"

"None. They just declare darkness to be the standard."

What can you do when you are up against a company like Microsoft? You need to segment the market. You need to write off half or more of the market and concentrate your efforts on the remaining segment. In competition with Budweiser, you would obviously write off the low-end bars and restaurants and concentrate on the high-end segment.

What Should Apple Have Done?

We would have given up on the general business market, a war that Apple has lost anyway, and focused on the graphics market, a war that Apple has already won. Art directors, designers, architects, and other graphics professionals for the most part use nothing but Macintosh machines.

But here's the twist. We would have taken those Macintosh machines and also promoted them to a segment of the business community who are heavy graphics users. Millions of executives are running around the country in any given week making PowerPoint presentations. (Microsoft estimates that there are 30 million PowerPoint slide shows a day.)

But not the current crop of Macintosh machines, which are kissing cousins of Wintel machines. Rather, the 2004 Macintosh computers should have been the end result of two decades of a graphics focus. In other words, evolution along a branch marked "graphic" computers rather than evolution along a branch marked "general business" computers.

You can't win a standards war with a better product; you need a better strategy. (Think Sony Betamax.)

When Apple introduced the Macintosh computer in 1984 (remember its Super Bowl commercial entitled "1984"?), it was widely hailed as a major improvement over the IBM PC. Especially the GUI, or graphics user interface.

No matter. By the time 1984 rolled around, it was too late for a better product.

But it's never too late for a better strategy.

Before pruning.

After pruning.

TO KEEP A PLANT HEALTHY, PRUNE. TO KEEP A COMPANY (AND A BRAND) HEALTHY, CORPORATE GARDENERS SHOULD DO THE SAME.

Chapter 13

The Power of
Pruning

AS EVERY GARDENER KNOWS, the way to keep a plant vigorous is by pruning.

Why is it that corporate gardeners have trouble accepting this principle? Growth in all directions weakens a plant and it also weakens a corporation.

Every hour, every day, every week, every month, the typical company expands into more products, more industries, more distribution channels, more price points. Like organic growth, corporate growth is mostly invisible. You can't see the grass grow. You can't see a company grow.

Unrestrained Growth at Sears

Take Sears Roebuck. Most people think Sears Roebuck is a good place to buy appliances and maybe clothing. Check your yellow pages and you'll find that Sears is also into a lot of other businesses. Some examples:

- Sears Auto Centers
- Sears Carpet & Upholstery Cleaning
- Sears Dry Cleaning & Shoe Repair
- Sears Driving School
- Sears Electrical Repairs
- Sears Eyeglass & Contact Lens Center
- Sears Fencing
- Sears Hearing Aid Center
- Sears Painting
- Sears Plumbing, Drain & Sewer Cleaning
- Sears Pool Management Consultants
- Sears Portrait Studio
- Sears Rent-A-Car
- Sears Termite & Pest Control

Sure, many of these side deals are franchised operations, but they still require management time and attention. Furthermore, they detract from the power of the Sears brand. When you stand for everything, you stand for nothing.

Years ago, Sears boasted of being "The Cheapest Supply House on Earth." Obviously that's no longer true.

Cheap is only one of the many ways to build a retail brand. Unfortunately Sears lost its cheap concept to Wal-Mart and failed to replace the core concept with an alternative.

What's a Sears? We don't know, do you?

What could a Sears be? We would prune the soft goods and focus the retailer on hard goods, specifically home appliances, where Sears is No. 1 with a 39 percent market share.

Look at appliances from a competitive point of view. Lowe's is No. 2 and Home Depot is No. 3, and both retailers are catching up to Sears. Does Lowe's or Home Depot sell clothing or jewelry?

The Limits of Growth

It's management that ultimately limits the optimum size of a corporation. How can you manage a business you don't understand?

You can't. Furthermore, if you can understand your business today, you are unlikely to understand your business tomorrow, thanks to evolution and divergence.

If Alfred P. Sloan came back from the grave to run General Motors today, he would be at a loss to understand the array of vehicles and market segments the company is currently pursuing.

- Take the vision correction business. It used to be that you went to an optometrist, who tested your eyes and prescribed a pair of glasses. Today we have many different types of eyeglasses, including those with progressive lenses. We also have contact lenses (regular and disposable) as well as laser surgery. As a category evolves and diverges, a company has to decide which paths to take and which paths to ignore.
- Take the video recording business. First we had the video-cassette, then the laser disc. Today we also have digital video disc or DVD as well as DVD+RW, DVD-RW, and DVD-ROM.
- Take baby car-seats. They now come in four varieties: infant seats, rear-facing infant seats, front-facing toddler seats, and booster seats. Having a child means going through at least three different kinds of car seats. Used to be the kid just sat on your lap.

  And the simple stroller has evolved into categories such as carriages, full-size strollers, midsize strollers, all-terrain strollers, lightweight strollers, umbrella strollers, joggers, doubles and triples, and frames (which infant seats attach to).

In the long run things always get more complicated and more difficult to manage. In the long run the only solution is pruning.

The Law of the Closet

Every day every closet in America gets messier and messier. The only solution to the closet problem is to restructure and prune regularly.

Among physicists, the law of the closet is known as the second law of thermodynamics. In a closed system, entropy (or the degree of disorder) always increases. In other words, things always become more disordered.

It's the slow, insidious nature of the process that leads corporate executives astray. Day to day, it's difficult to see divergence at work. (No one has seen divergence operate in nature either.) You can only see the effects of divergence if you look backward in time. Unfortunately by then it's usually too late.

In the garden, you hear the word *pruning* a lot. In the boardroom, almost never. The buzzword in the boardroom is *expansion*. How do we expand our business to increase sales and profits?

One way is by merger or acquisition. The great M&A wave washed over corporate America in the last half of the 1990s. Except for the investment banking industry, mergers and acquisitions have been a loser's game. One estimate put the loss due to mergers in the years 1995 to 2000 at $1 trillion of share-owner value.

Good Mergers and Bad Mergers

From a strategic point of view, mergers aren't necessarily bad. When a company buys a direct competitor, two things happen that are both good. The company increases its market share and the company reduces its competition.

When a company buys another company in a different industry, two things happen that are both bad. The brand is weakened because it now stands for a wider range of products or services, and management is weakened because its span of control is stretched thinner.

Unfortunately it's the latter mergers that win the plaudits of many M&A people. Mergers that increase a company's product line are generally considered to be a "good fit." (Think AOL Time Warner.)

Since *expansion* is the current buzzword, a good fit might be between an automobile company that makes expensive cars and an automobile company that makes inexpensive cars. That way each company can expand its market. So Daimler-Benz Aktiengesellschaft merges with Chrysler Corporation to form DaimlerChrysler.

What a disaster!

Since the November 1998 merger, shares of DaimlerChrysler have fallen by about half.

Another merger that has won favorable press, but has yet to produce much in the way of results, is the Hewlett-Packard/Compaq combination. On September 4, 2001, the day before the deal was announced, the two companies combined had a market capitalization of $66 billion.

Today Hewlett-Packard is worth $76 billion, thanks to a booming stock market. But the jury is still out on whether the merger will turn out to be a positive or a negative for stockholders.

And look at the travails of AT&T. Computers were going to converge with communications, so AT&T bought a computer company (NCR), which it spun off five years later, losing a reported $6 billion. To become a one-stop telecom provider, AT&T bought Mc-Caw Cellular, then the No. 1 U.S. cellphone operator.

The acquisitions continued. Cable was going to converge with telecommunications, so AT&T bought Tele-Communications Inc and a couple of other cable companies that briefly turned AT&T into the country's largest cable system operator.

All for naught. Because of increasing pressure from Wall Street, AT&T spun off its cellular business and sold its cable business to Comcast.

Normally, as categories diverge, companies should spin off divisions. This is good for the division and good for the company. It's also consistent with the laws of nature. The sum of the parts is greater than the whole.

The Upgrading Myth

Another myth that has created a good deal of harm to corporate America is the "upgrading" myth. That is, the need to define a company's business in the most grandiose way possible. Why did AT&T buy all those cable companies? Because AT&T wasn't in the "telephone" business, it was in the "communications" business.

What's a communications business? Telephone, television, cable TV, satellite TV, Internet, newspapers, magazines, radio, advertising, and public relations are all facets of the communications business.

Should one company be in all those businesses? When you broaden your definition of what business you're in, you are swimming against the divergence tide. As time goes on, you should think about narrowing the definition of your business.

Narrowing your definition (and pruning your company) runs counter to conventional wisdom. It also runs counter to the advice given in perhaps the most famous article ever to appear in any management publication anywhere in the world.

Blinded by "Marketing Myopia"

In the July/August 1960 issue of the *Harvard Business Review*, Theodore Levitt wrote an article that would influence thousands of corporate managers for decades to come.

Entitled "Marketing Myopia," the article indicted "short-sighted management" for defining their industry too narrowly. His classic example was the railroad industry:

"The railroads did not stop growing because the need for passenger and freight transportation declined. That grew. The railroads are in trouble today not because the need was filled by others (cars, trucks, airplanes, even telephones), but because it was *not* filled by the railroads themselves. They let others take customers away from them because they assumed themselves to be in the railroad business rather than in the transportation business."

Granted, the railroad business was a lousy business to be in. But do you know of any company that has been successful in the "transportation" business?

We have successful airline companies, air cargo companies, shipping companies, trucking companies, taxi companies, container companies, bus companies, cruise ship companies, and even some successful railroads. But we don't know of any successful "transportation" company. Transportation is a convergence concept in an era where the laws of nature favor divergence.

And the railroads that continue to be successful went in the opposite direction from that recommended by Ted Levitt. They got out of the passenger business and focused on freight.

Actually, the major theme of Mr. Levitt's article was not railroads at all, but the oil industry. Levitt indicted the industry for considering itself to be in the oil business rather than the energy business. "I believe that within twenty-five years," predicted Mr. Levitt, "the oil industry may find itself in much the same position of retrospective glory that the railroads are now in."

The Oil Business vs. The Energy Business

Have you noticed that the oil industry is doing just fine?

Forty-four years after the publication of "Marketing Myopia," do you know of any company that could legitimately define itself as being in the energy business?

There are oil companies, oil pipeline companies, electric utilities, gas utilities, coal companies, and many other types of companies in one aspect or another of the energy business. But no company could call itself Global Energy Corporation and mean it.

Well, maybe there is one. In 1985, InterNorth bought Houston Natural Gas to create the country's largest natural gas pipeline system. With Kenneth Lay as CEO and a new name (Enron), the company transformed itself from a gas pipeline operator to the world's largest energy trader.

And we all know how that strategy worked out.

Sad to say, the most sought-after managers in corporate America are not those who espouse divergence, downsizing, and focus. The most sought-after managers are the Ken Lays of this world, the visionary big thinkers who are always on the hunt for their next acquisition.

Do you want to fly up where the egos soar or dive down where the dough is?

Upgrading at United Parcel Service

The propensity for pomposity is deeply embedded in the corporate psyche. A senior marketing person at United Parcel Service once asked Al what he thought of the company's new trademark.

"I like it," said Al, "but what UPS really needs is a motivating idea or rallying cry, Something like 'UPS delivers more parcels to more people in more places than any other parcel delivery company in the world.'"

"UPS," said the senior marketing person, "is not in the parcel delivery business."

"Huh. That comes as a big surprise to me. We're a customer and I always thought that UPS was in the parcel delivery business."

"No. UPS is in the logistics business."

He wasn't joking. UPS is repainting some eighty-eight thousand vehicles with its new theme: "Synchronizing the World of Commerce." (Sounds like UPS might be thinking of going into the watch business.)

Ditto FedEx. When the company's chief information officer was asked to describe its business, he replied, "We're in the business of engineering time."

Meanwhile Ryder, one of UPS's minor competitors, is doing the same thing. Ryder's theme: "Logistics and transportation solutions worldwide."

Upgrading Language and Downgrading Meaning

"We're not in the beer business," said Coors's executive vice president of marketing. "We're in the social mood amelioration business."

An impediment to clear thinking is this constant upgrading of the language. No aspect of life is left untouched by the upgrade police.

- Doctors are now physicians.
- Lawyers are now attorneys-at-law.
- Policemen and policewomen are now law enforcement officers.
- Maintenance people are now physical plant managers.
- Janitors are now custodial engineers.
- Garbage collectors are now sanitary engineers.
- Business strategies are now business models.
- Numbers are now metrics.
- Accounting firms are now professional service firms.
- Purchasing departments are now procurement departments.
- Personnel departments are now human relations departments.
- Fireworks are now pyrotechnics.
- Jails are now correctional facilities.

"Anyone setting off pyrotechnics will be taken into custody by a law enforcement officer and sent to a correctional facility."

What's a Financial Services Company?

One of the enduring business buzzwords is *financial services*. Many companies want to be leaders in a category they define as financial services. But is that the way people think?

- If you want to buy banking services, you go to a bank like Citibank.

- If you want to buy insurance, you go to an insurance company like Prudential.
- If you want to buy stocks, bonds, or mutual funds, you go to a brokerage firm like Merrill Lynch.

"Let's go to a financial services company to get our finances serviced" is not the way people talk. People talk in terms of specifics, not generalities.

(According to a survey by the TowerGroup, the typical household in America has twelve to fifteen financial products. Credit cards, checking accounts, saving accounts, mortgages, life insurance, automobile insurance, home insurance, etc. And these financial products are supplied by *five* different institutions.)

As a matter of fact, it's easier to go from the specific to the general than vice versa. People know that a drugstore sells a lot more things than just drugs. Toiletries, candy, soft drinks, stationery, photo supplies, etc.

Should a drugstore (pardon us, pharmacy) describe itself as a "personal services" store? We think not.

"Market" and "Marketing Communications"

Boston Chicken was a huge hit when it first opened its doors. It was the first fast-food restaurant chain to focus on rotisserie chicken for the take-home dinner market. But then it added turkey, meat loaf, ham, and other items to the menu and changed its name to Boston Market.

Everybody knows what a chicken dinner is, but what's a "market" dinner? No wonder the company went bankrupt.

You probably know many famous advertising agencies and many famous PR agencies, but how many famous "marketing communications" agencies do you know?

Name one.

Clients of these blown-up agencies usually see these grandiose names as harmless puffery. If your ad agency calls itself an integrated marketing communications agency, who really cares? You still think of them as your "ad agency," call them your "ad agency," and refer them to others as your "ad agency."

Marketing communications has no future as a category name.

A Multiplatform Media Brand

You might be surprised to learn that the largest-circulation newspaper in America is "no longer a newspaper," according to President-Publisher Tom Curley. It's a "multiplatform media brand." Harmless enough as long as readers and advertisers still think of *USA Today* as a national newspaper.

It usually doesn't hurt an old, established brand like *USA Today* to inflate its category, but it does hurt a new brand that tries to break into a mythical category called multiplatform media brand.

Take Talk Media, a division of Miramax, itself part of the Walt Disney Company. The driving force behind the new venture was Tina Brown, former editor of *Vanity Fair* and *The New Yorker* as well as British magazine *Tatler*.

Tina's goal was huge. She wanted to link the world of magazines and books with the film and TV industries. The first link in the multiplatform media chain was *Talk* magazine.

In spite of a torrent of favorable publicity, *Talk* magazine managed to lose $54 million in its first two years, so Miramax shut it down and Tina took her talents elsewhere.

Another multimedia disappointment is DreamWorks SKG. Founded nearly a decade ago by Director Steven Spielberg, animation executive Jeffrey Katzenberg, and music mogul David Geffen,

DreamWorks hoped to become a powerhouse in music, television, and film.

The dream has faded. The movie business isn't doing particularly well. With the exception of *Spin City*, its TV shows have never really taken off. And recently DreamWorks sold its music division for about $100 million.

In spite of all the hype about "multimedia," it's hard to think of one new brand that has established itself as a multimedia brand.

It's the old reality/perception conundrum. Life is real, but what counts in business, what counts in life, is not reality, but perception of reality. Just because General Motors has company cafeterias for some of its employees doesn't make GM a transportation and restaurant company. Just because *USA Today* has a money-losing Web site doesn't make it a multiplatform media brand.

A Full-Service Media Company

A prime example of the dangers of blowing up your category is Primedia. In 1999, Tom Rogers was hired away from NBC by the buyout firm Kohlberg Kravis Roberts to expand Primedia from a hodgepodge of magazines and directories into a full-service media company that embraced the Internet.

At the time, Henry Kravis of Kohlberg Kravis said, "Today, what is really needed for us is to become a full-service media company; that means not just print, not just television, not just the Internet, but we need to take the assets that we have and really go into the new technologies."

Months after Mr. Rogers was hired, Primedia stock hit a high of $34 a share. Current price: $2.60.

"Part of the reason that Primedia's stock price never recovered," according to the *New York Times*, "was that Mr. Rogers never disavowed his strategy of converging print and digital properties, analysts said."

Today Tom Rogers has resigned and Kohlberg Kravis Roberts is paring Primedia back to a profitable set of hobbyist magazine like *Guns & Ammo*, *National Hog Farmer*, and *Truckin'*.

Down-to-earth. That's what works best in marketing.

Multimedia Everything

A vivid example of the failure of multimedia to amount to anything is Vivendi Universal and its former CEO Jean-Marie Messier. According to the *New York Times*, "He lived in a $17.5-million apartment on Park Avenue, flew around the world in a fleet of private jets and spoke of 'synergies' and 'convergence' with zeal."

In just six years, Messier managed to turn Vivendi (originally a French water utility) into a worldwide media conglomerate with the acquisition of MCA Records, Universal Studios, USA Networks, plus various publishers, theme parks, video-game producers, and Internet companies on both sides of the Atlantic.

According to *Business Week*, the game plan went like this: "For a while, many media execs dreamed that by snatching up Web start-ups, Net and wireless-distribution systems, and cable-TV companies, they could create a new world. It was to be a utopia in which every kind of media—from movies to games to music—could be delivered to anyone, anytime, and anywhere via every imaginable gizmo and gadget."

Today, Messier is gone and Vivendi, after losing some $70 billion in market value, is being watered down and sold. Financially forced pruning.

It's been our experience that almost any company in any industry could be stronger and financially healthier by selling, spinning off, or discontinuing some of its operations.

Less is more, but "less" is extremely difficult to sell in the boardroom where the focus is usually on "more." More mergers, more acquisitions, more distribution channels, more line extensions, more activities that will take advantage of the equity in the brand.

The destructive effects of unchanneled growth are hard to see, especially when they take place over decades.

The Sad Situation at Sony

Take the Sony Corporation, for example. If you did a survey, you would probably find that Sony is the world's most admired electronics brand. Way ahead of whatever brand might be in second place.

Terrific for owners of Sony products. But how about owners of Sony stock? Does the company make any money? The sad fact is no. Net profits after taxes at the Sony Corporation are small. Very small.

In the last ten years, Sony Corporation had revenues of $519.2 billion. But net profits after taxes were only $4 billion. That's eight-tenths of one percent of sales. It's hard paying off your bank loans, not to mention paying dividends to investors, with that kind of return.

Of course, this is Japan, so who pays off their bank loans anyway? Not when the Bank of Japan has cut its benchmark short-term rate effectively to zero.

Like most Japanese companies, Sony is heavily line-extended. Sony puts its brand name on television sets, videocassette recorders, digital cameras, personal computers, cellphones, semiconductors, camcorders, DVD players, MP3 players, stereos, broadcast video equipment, batteries, and a host of other products.

Yet Sony's most profitable product is the PlayStation video-game player, a brand that makes minimum use of the Sony name. (As powerful as the Sony brand might be, PlayStation is an even better brand name for a video-game player because it stands for something in the prospect's mind.)

Compare Sony with Dell

Sony makes personal computers and a lot of other products. Dell just makes personal computers (until recently when they added printers). In the last ten years, Dell had sales of $140.3 billion and net income after taxes of $8.5 billion, or a net profit margin after taxes of 6.1 percent versus 0.8 percent for Sony.

That's not fair, you might be thinking, to compare Dell with Sony. You picked a company (Dell) that is exceptionally profitable.

Actually that's not true. Dell is in a highly competitive business where profit margins are thin. As a result, Dell's 6.1 percent profit margin is not particularly spectacular, but it is above average.

In the last ten years, net profit margins at the average Fortune 500 company were 4.7 percent of sales. (If you leave out the last two years, the percentage jumps to 5.7 percent.)

Many American companies have done a lot better. Microsoft: 31.7 percent. Intel: 21.6 percent. Coca-Cola: 16.5 percent. Sony at 0.8 percent net income after taxes is just not playing in the big leagues.

We have preached against the perils of line extension ever since the publication of the *Positioning* book some two decades ago. And every time we do, someone always says, "What about the Japanese? They do the exact opposite of what you are recommending and they are extremely successful."

Are they?

The Japanese Track Record

In the last ten years, Hitachi had revenues of $708 billion and managed to lose $722 million. NEC had revenues of $397 billion and lost $1.3 billion. Fujitsu had revenues of $382 billion and lost $1.6

billion. Toshiba had revenues of $463 billion and a net profit margin of just 0.15 percent.

Large, unfocused companies make little after-tax profits. And if you don't make money, you can't pay off your bank loans. And if you can't pay off your bank loans, the banks are in trouble.

And if the banks are in trouble, a country's economy is in trouble. And if a country's economy is in trouble, the country's political system is in trouble.

The top of the Japanese economic system is weak because the base is weak. Japanese companies, for the most part, make everything except money.

Why is it so difficult for large, unfocused Japanese companies to make money? It can't be product quality. Most Japanese companies have a worldwide reputation for high quality. A reputation that, for the most part, they deserve.

Our conclusion is that line extension inhibits branding. When a company makes and markets a broad range of products under one name, it is extremely difficult to build that name into a powerful brand.

Don't any Japanese companies make money? The companies whose brands are relatively focused do much better. Sharp (1.8 percent), Toyota (3.1 percent), Honda (3.3 percent), and Canon (3.8 percent).

We have followed the financials of Japanese companies for years. We find that the average large Japanese company has a net profit margin after taxes of about 1 percent compared with the average large American company at 5 percent.

The Track Record at IBM

Early success builds confidence as well as profits. No company has had as much early success in the computer industry as IBM. At one point IBM accounted for 80 percent of the revenues of the computer industry. With this type of track record, it was a foregone conclusion that IBM would try to dominate every hardware and software branch of the computer tree.

As time went on, money, resources, and talent poured into the computer industry from all sides, creating hordes of competitors. Instead of covering every segment, IBM would have been well advised to prune its operations rather than expand them.

IBM has been extensively criticized for its "mainframe mentality." That is, not moving into personal computers fast enough. But maybe IBM should not have moved into personal computers at all, a product category the company has made no money in.

The high-water point in IBM's scheme to dominate and control the computer industry was the March 17, 1987, announcement of Systems Applications Architecture (SAA), a collection of software interfaces, conventions, and protocols that would allow software written for one of IBM's three groups of computers (mainframe, midrange, and personal) to run not only on that group, but on the other two groups as well.

This was a grand scheme to put a layer of software frosting on one big integrated computer cake. Estimated by one observer to cost $10 billion, SAA was a scheme that only a gigantic company like IBM could undertake.

One of the key SAA components was the notion of a "common view." All three product lines (with their many variations) would have a common user interface. It's analogous to having a common user interface (the dashboard) for planes, automobiles, and boats, on the basis that they are just "different forms of transportation."

By the early 1990s, IBM was deeply in the red and SAA was clearly going nowhere. (Grandiose schemes never die; they just fade away.) CEO John Akers was thrown out and Lou Gerstner was hired from RJR Nabisco.

"What's your vision for IBM?" Lou Gerstner was asked. His famous answer: "The last thing IBM needs right now is a vision." We think he was right. One of the things that got IBM in trouble was an overarching vision called SAA.

History repeats itself. What IBM tried in the eighties and nineties with SAA is exactly the same strategy Microsoft is trying today. Lock everything together in one big software ball.

The Demise of the Generalist

In a rapidly expanding industry (think divergence) you are asking for trouble if you create a vision that covers all aspects of the market. Better to be selective and pick segments of the market you can dominate.

Today IBM accounts for about 11 percent of the economic activity of the computer and allied industries, but it's a much healthier company than it was during its days of rapid growth.

If you go back in history, you'll find that the first retail outlets in America were "general" stores that sold everything from groceries to clothing to household items to furniture.

Groceries and clothing were the first categories to branch off, causing many general stores to become "dry goods" stores. Except in isolated communities, the general stores and dry goods stores are gone, replaced by more specialized establishments.

There are no general computer companies left either. Even IBM is turning itself into a global IT outsourcing and consulting company. (Today, services and software account for 61 percent of IBM's revenues.)

As Lou Gerstner wrote in his book, *Who Says Elephants Can't Dance?*, "As I look back on my IBM life, there is no question that a good portion of our success was due to all of the deals we *didn't* do."

Spin-offs and Pruning

Instead of acquiring Compaq Computer (a deal Gerstner turned down), perhaps Hewlett-Packard should have been looking for ways to streamline its operations (perhaps by spinning off its printer business) rather than by complicating them.

Spin-offs are like pruning a plant. How do you make sure a plant stays healthy? You prune it frequently.

How do you make sure a company stays healthy? You prune it frequently by spinning off divisions that have grown apart from the core business, as they are bound to do in a diverging environment.

The question of brand names often makes spin-offs difficult. When Andersen Consulting attempted to break apart from the tax and audit operations of Arthur Andersen, the hang-up was the name of the new entity. It was obvious that both companies couldn't continue to use the same name. (Today it's unlikely that anybody would want the tarnished Andersen name.)

An arbitrator decided that Andersen Consulting could be spun off from Arthur Andersen, but it would have to use a different name. The new entity was called Accenture, and they promptly spent $150 million to try to create awareness for the company's new brand name.

Most of this money and much of the hard feelings created in the spin-off could have been avoided if Andersen Consulting had initially used a different name.

The Problem of the Name

What happens when a tree "branches" out? Each year the various limbs grow farther and farther apart.

So what happens when a category diverges? The same thing. The categories grow further and further apart. And what happens when you try to cover all categories with a single brand name?

Your brand gets stretched until it reaches the breaking point. Not good for the brand, not good for the company.

Succeed safe. Having a second brand name makes spinning off a division much easier. Could Lexus be spun off from Toyota? Sure, no problem. Could Dockers be spun off from Levi Strauss? Sure, no problem. Could DeWalt be spun off from Black & Decker? Sure, no problem.

Could Levi's Silvertab be spun off from the core Levi Strauss brand? Only with great difficulty and only with a change of name.

Recently Palm Inc. announced that it was spinning off its operating system software into a separate company, PalmSource. The new company will license the software to Palm and its competitors.

Good move if it isn't too late. Palm's software, which used to power two-thirds of all handheld computers, now claims just 57 percent. Meanwhile, Microsoft's share of the handheld computer-operating-system market has risen to 30 percent.

When you market both the hardware and the software, you make the classic mistake of competing with your customers.

The spin-off will help to reassure potential customers such as Dell, which currently licenses Microsoft's Pocket PC operating system exclusively. "Palm needed this sort of firewall," says Tony Bonadero, director of Dell's handheld division. "Now we wouldn't hesitate to use the Palm OS."

What iz it?

Zima™ ClearMalt™ is, let's see…it's lightly carbonated but not filling like beer… (even though it is brewed) and it's um, zophisticated tasting but lighter than a mixed drink, and um, eazy drinking but not so zweet (gaaaaack!) like a wine cooler; and it's clear, so you can zee through it and check out what's going on in the rest of the room even while you're drinking it (very important) and… what else? You can drink it straight or on the rockz.

So it's sort of like different from ahh… anything…ever.

© 1993 ZIMA Beverage Co. Memphis, TN

WHAT IZ IT? THAT'S THE ISSUE FOR ALL NEW BRANDS. IF YOU CAN'T DEFINE THE CATEGORY, YOUR NEW BRAND IS UNLIKELY TO BE SUCCESSFUL.

Chapter 14

Creating a Category

THE MOST DIFFICULT JOB IN MARKETING, and also the most rewarding, is creating a new category.

Consider the situation facing a company about to launch a new brand into a new category. There is no definition of what the category is all about, there is no market, there are no distribution channels, and there are no competitors to benchmark. The first brand in a new category is truly a pioneer with all the problems that a pioneer has to overcome.

The first, and the most important question of all, is what's the name of the new category. If you cannot define the new category in simple, easy-to-understand terms, the new category is unlikely to become successful.

Consider Zima, a new beverage introduced in 1992 by the Adolph Coors Company. Coors has never told us what a Zima is. As a matter of fact, Coors ran advertising bragging that the new category defies definition. Here's the entire copy from one of the first Zima ads:

"Zima ClearMalt is, let's see . . . it's lightly carbonated but not filling like beer . . . (even though it is brewed) and it's, um, zohisticated tasting but lighter than a mixed drink, and, um, easy drinking but not so zweet (gaaaaack!) like a wine cooler; and it's clear, so you can zee through it and check out what's going on in the rest of the room even while you're drinking it (very important) and . . . what else? You can drink it straight or on the rockz.

"So it's sort of like different from ahh . . . anything . . . ever."

What's a Zima? Does anybody really know?

The First Energy Drink

In contrast, consider Red Bull. The product is a lightly carbonated, highly caffeinated concoction containing liberal quantities of herbs, B-complex vitamins, and amino acids. Founder Dietrich Mateschitz based his drink on Krating Daeng, a popular health tonic he had encountered in Thailand.

A temptation that's hard to resist is to give the category an "exotic" name. Mateschitz could have bought the rights to the name Krating Daeng, for example. Or perhaps he could have called the new drink Thailand Tea.

What Mateschitz actually did was to call his Asian compound "an energy drink." As it happens, the first energy drink.

Simple names work best when defining a new branch. Not only is "energy drink" a simple name, it also benefits from an analogy with PowerBar, the first "energy bar."

Marketing can be visualized as filling a hole in the mind. If there is a category called energy bar, the prospect thinks, there must be a category called energy drink. Red Bull, of course, was the first brand to fill the empty hole in the mind called energy drink.

Energy drink works as a category name even though there is little relationship between the ingredients in a can of Red Bull and the ingredients in energy bars like PowerBar, Balance bar, Cliff bar, and Atkins Advantage bar.

Marketing people are sometimes too literal when they try to dream up a name for a new category. What matters most is not describing exactly what the benefits of the new category are, but expressing the essence of the new category in as simple a way as possible.

After all, Red Bull became a powerful brand because it is perceived as a drink that improves performance especially during times of increased stress or strain, which some people take to mean sexual performance. (*Energy* is just a way of expressing that idea in a socially acceptable way.)

Red Bull is a runaway success. Worldwide sales of Red Bull are currently $1.5 billion a year. And Dietrich Mateschitz is the richest person in Austria.

Brand Name Follows Branch Name

As form follows function, brand name follows branch name. Once you have landed on a simple name for the category, the next step is to select a unique, distinctive brand name that connotes the essence of the category.

Note that it's redundant to try to include the category name in the brand name. Each name should stand alone, being connected only by a conceptual idea, not by a repetition of words.

Red Energy would be a redundant name for an energy drink brand. Furthermore, it wastes half the name that is much better occupied by the word *Bull*.

When it comes to brand names, words, syllables, and letters are precious. You don't want to waste any of them on redundant category names. Nor do you want to use a long word when you can find a shorter one.

The best brand names are short, unique, and distinctive. Rolex, Kodak, Tide, Crest, Nike, Sony, Aleve, Coors, Dell, Google, Ford, Lexus, Hertz, Intel, Linux, Palm, Visa, Xerox, Yahoo!, Zara, to a name a few.

When to Be Different and When to Be the Same

An often-overlooked aspect of branding is packaging. There's a time to be the same as everybody else and there's a time to be different.

When you are trying to be a strong No. 2 brand in an established category, your packaging (but not your color scheme) should reflect the leader. Pepsi-Cola comes in twelve-ounce cans in six-packs and twelve-packs, which tells consumers that Pepsi is in the same category as Coca-Cola.

When you are trying to establish a new category, it's the time to be different. Almost every drink in a bar or restaurant comes in twelve-ounce cans and twelve-ounce bottles. As a new category, an energy drink needed to be different. So Red Bull comes in 8.3-ounce cans.

The smaller size helps Red Bull be perceived as a brand in a different category from Coca-Cola, Budweiser, or Sprite. Furthermore, the small size connotes the idea of potency and energy better than a larger container would.

As Red Bull built momentum, competitors jumped into the energy drink category. Many of these me-too brands tried to shoehorn the word *energy* into their brand names. Some examples: AriZona Extreme Energy, Bomba Energy, Energade, Energy Fuel, Go-Go Energy, Hansen's Energy, and Jones Energy.

So far, no one has succeeded in establishing a strong No. 2 brand in the energy drink category. What a would-be No. 2 brand has to do is to find a way to become the opposite of Red Bull while still staying in the energy drink category. Not an easy task.

Select the Simple, Not the Complicated

People often like long, complicated category names because they imply that the category itself is important and complicated. The first computer was called ENIAC, an acronym for "electronic numerical integrator and computer."

Why didn't they just call the new device a computer? Anything with miles of wiring, eighteen thousand vacuum tubes, and thousands of resistors and switches was just too complicated to be called a computer. Furthermore, ENIAC weighed thirty tons. A big machine like that needed a big name.

IRIS Technologies invented a product that was initially called the VideoTizer. Essentially a "tapeless" VCR, the VideoTizer allows users to digitize videotape content into ordinary MPEG2 video files.

Once the videotape is digitized, the user can then "catalog" the digital files to allow "instant" jumps to any of the material on the files. This feature (and many others) makes the VideoTizer an ideal presentation device for training, education, and many other applications.

In essence, the $5,000 VideoTizer can do much of the same things that a $150,000 video playback machine does for an NFL football team.

But the VideoTizer name would have severely handicapped the brand. Not only is VideoTizer a complicated name, but it puts too much emphasis on how the product works (the features) rather than what the product does (the benefits).

So IRIS decided to call the new category a "play analyzer" and to market the device to high school football coaches. As a brand name, the company selected *Landro,* which is an abbreviated version of the name of the CEO of IRIS Technologies, Jerry Salandro.

The Landro play analyzer has been a roaring success. Many high school football coaches credit their improved records to the use of this superb training tool.

You Need Two Names, Not Just One

The Landro play analyzer demonstrates another important point. Every product needs two names, not just one. A brand name and a category name.

The failure to think clearly about the relative functions of the brand name and the associated category name often cause needless confusion. Take the PalmPilot, the first . . . well, what is the category name?

Some people call the Palm an electronic organizer. Others call the Palm a handheld computer. And still others, a PDA (personal digital assistant).

All of these category names are too long and complicated. They lack the clarity and simplicity a good category name should possess.

If a personal computer that fits on your desk is called a desktop computer, and a personal computer that fits on your lap is called a laptop computer, then the logical name for a computer that fits in the palm of your hand is a palm computer.

And it's true that many people use *palm computer* generically. As in "What brand of palm computer do you recommend?"

Of course, Palm Computer preempted *Palm* as a brand name, leaving a nascent industry struggling to find an appropriate generic name. As the leading brand in an emerging industry, Palm Computer should have been just as concerned with choosing an appropriate generic name as it was in choosing an appropriate brand name.

People think generic first, brand second. (1) "I'm thirsty, I want a beer." (2) "What brand of beer should I ask for? Give me a Bud Light." Sure, maybe the thought process takes only microseconds, but a lot of evidence suggests that the brand name always arrives last in a person's thinking.

If you are promoting a brand called Zima, the thought process might be: (1) "I'm thirsty, I want a . . ." (2)"What kind of . . . should I ask for? Give me a Zima." No wonder Zima sales have taken a dive.

Coors should have given a lot more thought to the name of the category.

You Can't Short-Circuit the Process

To create a hot brand, you need to first create a hot category. Instead of calling its new brand the PalmPilot, Palm Computer would have been better off calling its new brand the Pilot palm computer. (This solution conveniently overlooks the fact that Palm lost its Pilot name in a trademark dispute with the Pilot Pen Company.)

There's another lesson to be learned from the handheld computer or PDA industry. When pioneering a new category, it's important to create enough "distance" between the emerging new category and an existing category. Nature abhors compromise. Nature favors species that are at the opposite ends of the spectrum.

In reality, the first successful handheld computer was produced by a British company, Psion PLC. The Psion was a miniature laptop with a miniature keyboard and a suite of software applications that mimicked Wintel machines. Psion didn't push the envelope the way the PalmPilot did. As a result, the Psion was perceived as a "baby" personal computer rather than a separate category.

New Category First, New Brand Second

In the rush to build a new brand, the need to first build a new category is often overlooked. In the beverage category, the current fad is the alternative malt beverage or "malternative." Currently all the big brewers have malternatives on the market, with names like Smirnoff Ice, Mike's Hard Lemonade, Bacardi Silver, Skyy Blue, Stolichnaya Citrona, Sauza Diablo, and Captain Morgan Gold.

In a recent year, these seven brands alone spent more than $300 million on advertising. While the brand names might be well-known (especially Smirnoff Ice and Mike's Hard Lemonade), the long-term success of the category is in serious doubt.

What's a malternative? Let's see, beer is a malt beverage, so a malternative must be an alternative to beer. But don't we already have an alternative to beer? Wine is an alternative to beer. So is hard liquor in all its many variations.

It's a bad sign that some people are referring to malternative beverages as beer coolers, reminding consumers of the eighties wine-cooler craze that cooled off quickly in the nineties.

Our prediction: beer coolers will go the way of wine coolers.

Chaos and Confusion in Cars

From a marketing point of view, one of the most dysfunctional industries in America is the automobile industry. Everybody makes everything and markets everything under every one of its brand names.

When your brand doesn't stand for anything, you have to compensate by increasing your marketing expenditures. The largest advertiser in America is the automobile industry.

Seven of the thirteen biggest advertisers are automobile brands: Ford, Chevrolet, Toyota, Nissan, Honda, Dodge, and Chrysler. Together these seven brands spent $4.2 billion on advertising last year.

Do you remember any individual ad for any one of these car brands? Most people can't.

When your brand doesn't stand for anything, your advertising can't stand for anything either. No wonder the automobile industry has to cut prices to move the metal.

Last year, the average General Motors incentive was $4,300. Not only does this heavy discounting erode profits, it cheapens the brands.

When everybody makes everything (a trend not limited to automobiles), everybody's costs of design, development, manufacture, distribution, and marketing go up.

When everybody makes everything, the average revenue per brand goes down because of the greater competition.

This explains why margins for expensive cars, where there are only a handful of brands, are higher than for inexpensive cars, where there are dozens of look-alike brands.

Economics 101 would seem to indicate that the entire automobile industry would be better off if each brand were focused on a single category. Average revenues would go up (because of reduced competition), and average costs would go down (because of reduced production and marketing costs). Even consumers would be better off because of reduced confusion in the marketplace.

Unfortunately, Economics 101 has been superseded in the marketplace by CRM 101. And the first law of customer relationship management is "take good care of your customers."

Did Porsche introduce an SUV (the Porsche Cayenne) to take business away from Jeep? Obviously not, since the Cayenne costs $60,000, a lot more than any other SUV on the market.

Porsche introduced the Cayenne to take care of Porsche owners who might want to buy an SUV.

The Cayenne is the first step in a process that will ultimately undermine the Porsche brand.

The Ladder of Life

Brands are the rungs on the ladder of life. As you move up the ladder, your brands mark your progress.

- When people are single and just starting out in life, they buy entry-level cars like Saturns or Kias.
- When people get promoted (along with a big raise), they don't want to buy a more expensive Saturn, they want to buy a BMW.
- When a couple gets married and has kids, they buy a Volvo.
- And in the normal course of events, when a couple gets divorced, the wife keeps the kids and the Volvo and the husband buys a Ferrari.

No one automobile brand can stand on every rung of the ladder of life. When you try to stand for all the rungs, you stand for nothing.

Let Your Customers Go

Customer loyalty is the most overrated aspect of marketing. In theory everybody wants to have loyal customers. But in practice, what does customer loyalty mean?

In practice, customer loyalty means that your customers are willing to do business with you even though they can buy the same products or services at lower prices (or better quality) somewhere else.

In the long run, your loyal customers tend to be your stupid customers. It may take a while, but when they find out they've been had, there's usually a backlash. We used to be loyal customers of Delta Airlines, but with the advent of AirTran and JetBlue, we now realize that there is a fine line between loyalty and stupidity and we have crossed it.

There's a strong analogy between the airline business and the automobile business. Each industry used to believe that they had to be all things to all people. In the aftermath of the United and US Airways bankruptcies and the financial problems at American and Delta, the airline industry no longer believes the "everything for everybody" story.

In the future, you are likely to see an evolution in air travel where brands begin to have some meaning. Southwest, AirTran, and JetBlue are leading the way at the low end. Someday, we'll see similar brands develop at the high end.

Will the automobile industry travel the same road? Eventually, yes, but it's going to take a shocking event, like a major bankruptcy, to get the industry moving in a new direction.

Let them go. Your best strategy for dealing with customers who want something new and different is to let them go to your competition. That way you keep the purity of the brand. That way you make sure your brand stands for something in the prospect's mind.

A World Filled with Worthless Brands

A brand that doesn't stand for anything is a brand that is worthless. The only brand owned by American Motors that stood for anything was Jeep. What if American Motors had renamed itself the Jeep Corporation and sold nothing but Jeeps at Jeep dealerships? Would the Jeep Corporation be a viable brand today?

We think so. There is power in building a brand on a diverging category like sport-utility vehicles and then dominating that category with your brand name, as Jeep has done. Especially if you concentrate all your talent and resources on that single category. As Jeep could have done.

When Chrysler Corporation bought American Motors, Lee Iacocca threw out all the brands except for Jeep.

What if Chrysler had renamed itself the American Motors Corporation and sold nothing but Jeeps, Chrysler minivans, and Dodge trucks? Three brands, three branches, three dominant automobile positions.

Would the former Chrysler Corporation still be a viable company today instead of a money-losing division of DaimlerChrysler? We think so.

What works best in marketing is not expanding the brand, but expanding the market. Chrysler probably hated the fact that their Jeep brand was so "limited." *Jeep*, army slang for "GP" or "general purpose" vehicle, couldn't be used on sedans or passenger cars. Which is why Chrysler called its sedan version of the Jeep an Eagle.

Being narrowly focused on the sport-utility market was a big advantage for the Jeep brand. As the SUV market grew, so did Jeep. Today Jeep sells 440,000 vehicles a year. Our guess is that Jeep is the most profitable part of Chrysler.

If not the only profitable part of Chrysler.

The Mess at McDonald's

The tide doesn't always run in your direction. Sometimes the tide runs against you. Take the mess at McDonald's.

McDonald's became a powerful global brand by riding a branch called hamburger. The signs at many McDonald's restaurants say "billions and billions served." You don't have to be told that the billions refer to hamburgers.

Over the years, McDonald's has added breakfast, chicken, fish, salads, ice cream, and an array of other items. They've gone both low (with a dollar menu) and high (with a $3.99 premium salad).

It's not working. McDonald's per-unit restaurant sales in the United States have been essentially flat the past decade.

- 1993: $1,550,000
- 1994: $1,577,000
- 1995: $1,538,000
- 1996: $1,439,000
- 1997: $1,399,400
- 1998: $1,458,500
- 1999: $1,514,400
- 2000: $1,539,200
- 2001: $1,548,200
- 2002: $1,527,300

To put these numbers in perspective, if McDonald's had just kept up with inflation since 1993, its 2002 per-unit sales would have been $1,909,290.

For better or for worse, in good times and in bad, McDonald's is a brand forever nailed on a branch marked hamburger. Instead of trying to take chicken business away from chicken chains like KFC, Church's, Popeye's, and Chick-fil-A, McDonald's should try to take hamburger business away from hamburger chains like Wendy's, Burger King, Hardee's, and Jack in the Box.

Furthermore, if beef has no future, how come steak houses like Morton's, Ruth's Chris, and Outback are doing so well? If you were running Outback Steak House, would you start advertising chicken, fish, and premium salads? We think not.

The Tide Comes In, the Tide Goes Out

There is a natural rise and fall in almost any category you can name. Today Republicans are in; tomorrow Republicans are out. Today skirts are short; tomorrow skirts are long. Today sport-utility vehicles are in; tomorrow sport-utility vehicles are out. The politician who changes parties every time his or her side loses an election is a politician who has no future.

The brand that tries to follow the day-to-day whims of consumers is a brand that has no future. Patience pays off. A better strategy is to batten down the hatches and wait for the tide to turn in your direction again.

Consider McDonald's again. There's a perception that chicken consumption has soared and beef consumption in the United States has substantially declined, but that's not true. While per capita poultry consumption jumped 20 percent in the decade of the nineties, annual consumption of beef has been essentially flat, at 96.6 pounds per person in 1990 and 97.3 pounds per person in 2000. In the same decade, U.S. population has increased 13 percent.

So the total beef market is actually up 13 percent in a decade. Why turn the clock back and make McDonald's into a coffee shop instead of a hamburger place? This makes no sense.

The truth is, the day the hamburger dies will be the day that McDonald's expires, too. We can't think of a single brand that has survived the death of its category. Sure, brands have been line-extended and gotten into other categories, but their salvation has usually been the dominant positions they maintain in their core categories.

Some Categories Will Die

This is not to say that a category will never die. Some certainly will, a prime example being cigarettes. Can the Marlboro brand be saved by moving the brand into chewing gum? We think not.

Or what about Polaroid? There's no doubt that instant photography will become extinct in the coming years. Can the Polaroid brand be saved by moving into computers? We think not.

The stronger the brand, the more difficult the brand is to move in the mind. Herein lies the paradox. If you have a weak brand, you can easily move your brand into other categories. But it's not worth doing so because the brand itself is weak.

Uniden is a weak telephone brand. One reason Uniden is weak is that it makes all types of communication devices including cellphones, cordless home phones, home networking equipment, scanners, radar detectors, CB radios, and marine electronics. Uniden also makes business products, including phones (IP-based, wireless, multiline) and networking equipment (wireless, wired, routers, and switches).

Suave is a weak toiletries brand because the Suave name is used on a wide variety of products including hair care, body washes, skin care, and antiperspirants.

There are a lot of Unidens and Suaves are in the marketplace. They don't stand for anything in particular, so they can be used on any product or service. And they will sell as long as their prices are cheap enough.

A "price" brand or "value" brand is not a brand in the traditional sense of the word. It's just a product name that is vaguely familiar, but stands for nothing in particular.

A strong brand, however, is difficult to move because the brand's strength lies in its association with its category: Xerox copiers, Kleenex tissue, and Tanqueray gin. So when these brands were line-extended to Xerox computers, Kleenex toilet tissue, and Tanqueray vodka, they were notably unsuccessful.

Some categories, like some species, are destined to die, although it is surprising how few categories totally die out. Even the typewriter hangs in there, though its days are numbered.

When a category or a species is on its way out, there's not much a company can do about it. Take the dinosaur, for example. They could have eaten healthy food and exercised regularly, and today the dinosaur would still be extinct. Conditions change. You can't fight evolution.

Save the Brand or Save the Company?

What can you do if your brand is riding a dinosaur down evolution alley? You have two choices. The first is to try to save the brand. The second is to try to save the company.

Most companies try to save the brand. Polaroid got in trouble because instant photography got in trouble. So Polaroid figured its only hope was to use its brand name on a range of other products including conventional photographic film.

Not a good idea. Polaroid means instant photography, not conventional film. Result: the company went bankrupt.

Kodak is pursuing a similar save-the-brand strategy. It is spending heavily on research and development to get into the digital photography business . . . using the Kodak brand name. So far, Kodak's position in digital photography is nowhere near its dominant position in analog or film photography.

Currently Kodak is in third place in U.S. digital camera sales with a 12 percent market share, behind both Sony and Olympus.

Brands Are Just the Means to an End

The end being the creation of consumer preference. The truth is, consumers prefer Sony digital cameras to Kodak digital cameras because Sony means "electronic" and Kodak means "film photography."

Kodak should have selected the second option: save the company. What Kodak should have done is launch a line of digital cameras under a new brand name. This has two benefits.

A second brand name for the digital line would have allowed Kodak to keep the Kodak name focused on photography. Film photography might be a dying art, but it's going to take many years before consumers throw away the millions of film cameras they already own. In the meantime, Kodak can continue to sell billions of dollars worth of film and paper under the Kodak brand name.

The second benefit would be the creation of a new brand name that would stand for digital cameras only. When a category is diverging (as digital is from analog photography), the conditions are ripe for the creation of a totally new brand name.

If a company can combine adequate resources with a unique second brand name, success is almost always assured.

New Brands Almost Always Beat Old Brands

If the category is important enough, the ultimate winner is always the new brand created exclusively for the category and not the old brand that has been stretched to fit the new category.

Personal computers turned out to be an important category. So the winner was not the old brands stretched to cover the category (IBM, Digital, Wang, and a host of others), but the new brand created especially for the category (Dell).

Cellphones turned out to be an important category, so the winner is not the old brands stretched to cover the category (Motorola, Ericsson, Sony, and a host of others), but the new brand created especially for the category (Nokia).

It's certainly true that in a lot of important categories the dominant brand is not a new brand but an old brand stretched to cover the category. Light beer and diet cola, for example. A closer look at these and other categories usually shows that no new brands were ever introduced in an attempt to preempt the categories. Or, if they were, they weren't backed by adequate resources.

Take light beer, for example. Bud Light, Coors Light, Miller Lite, Michelob Light, Schlitz Light, Corona Light, the category is loaded with stretched brands, not new brands. No wonder the leading light (Bud Light) is not a new brand.

It's also a curious fact that in a new category without new brands, there's no particular advantage in being first. The sales ranking of the three leading light beers (Bud Light, Coors Light, and Miller Lite) are in the reverse order of their dates of introduction. Miller Lite was first. Coors Light was second. Bud Light was last.

Something similar is happening in breath-freshening strips. The first brand into the category was Listerine PocketPaks oral-care strips. The product consists of twenty-four small pieces of "tape," packaged in a carrying case, which dissolve on the tongue, releasing an intense minty flavor designed to freshen breath.

Breath strips are popular, currently racking up sales of more than $250 million a year. Listerine is still the leader but is likely to be overtaken by Eclipse flash strips introduced by Wrigley's. Listerine PocketPaks oral-care strips have three strikes against them.

- *Listerine* is a mouthwash brand.
- *PocketPaks* sounds like a pocket-tissue brand.

- *Oral care* is a category name used by dentists and marketing people, not by consumers.

Eclipse is not a perfect name either, but it's better than Listerine.
(Wrigley's uses Eclipse for its breath-freshening gum.) *Flash strips*, on
the other hand, is a short, simple, easy-to-remember category name.

Our prediction: Eclipse will eclipse PocketPaks in short order.

Winning the Line-Extension War

What correlates with success in a category composed of stretched
brands only? In beer, that correlation is obviously leadership. Budweiser is the leading regular beer. Bud Light is the leading light
beer.

What this all means, of course, is that consumers perceive light
beer and regular beer to be just flavor variations. Light beer being
regular beer with added water. The two branches (light and regular
beer) have not diverged very much.

That's fine if you're Anheuser-Busch with your powerful Budweiser brand. But why would a minor player in the game (Schlitz)
use the same strategy? Bud Light makes sense, but Schlitz Light
makes no sense at all.

It's in the best interest of a minor player to introduce a new
brand to encourage the new category to diverge. In other words, you
want the new beer category to be as far away from regular beer (and
the dominant Budweiser brand) as possible.

But will consumers accept light as a separate category from
regular beer?

Winning a New-Category War

Have faith. With the right name and some tangible difference, it's always possible to force divergence. Do consumers put Evian in the same category as Aquafina? Or Aquafina in the same category as tap water?

A chemist can easily tell the difference between light beer and regular beer, but might have trouble telling the difference between Evian and tap water.

The difference you need to create is not in the glass anyway, it's in the mind of the consumer. An indication of what might have been is the rise of a brand called Natural Light. With little promotion and a weak, generic name, Natural Light has become the fourth-largest-selling light beer in America.

Suppose the brand had a better name and a larger marketing budget, what might have been accomplished?

Short brand names, especially for products bought or consumed publicly, are generally better than long brand names. Which is why a short nickname can also be a big advantage. *Bud* rather than *Miller* when ordering a beer. *Coke* rather than *Pepsi* when ordering a cola.

New Names vs. Stretched Names

One of the advantages of a new brand name (instead of a stretched brand name) is that the new name is invariably shorter. A stretched brand needs to carry the category name as well as the brand name. Bud Light. Diet Coke. Tanqueray Vodka.

Tab doesn't need to call itself Diet Tab because Tab is not a stretched brand. Tab is only a diet cola. The inherent power of a category-defining name is demonstrated by the fact that Tab was outselling Diet Pepsi-Cola by 32 percent the day the Coca-Cola Company introduced Diet Coke.

What earthly reason was there to introduce a line extension (Diet Coke) into a category in which you already had the leading brand (Tab)?

If there is a legitimate answer to this question, we don't know what it is. Perhaps Coca-Cola lacked faith that a totally new brand (Tab) could in the long run actually outsell a powerful line-extended brand like Diet Pepsi-Cola.

Yet history shows that the new brand that defines the category will almost always outsell the old brand stretched to encompass the new category. (Have faith, Coca-Cola.)

Taking a Chance on the Future

Unlike the bad guys in the *Terminator* movies, companies don't have the luxury of launching brands retroactively. Companies have to take a chance on the future. Which is why they tend to be conservative.

What if the new category doesn't develop into a big market? We'd be wasting resources if we go to the added expense of creating a new brand name, so let's just use an existing name.

"Fail safe" is a fine philosophy if the category stays small. But what if the new category takes off and becomes a gigantic success, as cellphones, personal computers, light beer, and diet cola have?

"Succeed safe" is the better philosophy. Assume that the new category is going to be enormously successful. That assumption favors the use of a new brand name, not a stretched or line-extended name. Then if the category does become big, you'll have done exactly the right thing.

Where Does Opportunity Lie?

Opportunity does not lie in brands, opportunity lies in categories. More than 2.5 million brand names are registered with the United States Patent and Trademark office. A vast majority of these brands are worth little or nothing. Yet some of these brands are worth billions of dollars. What makes a brand valuable?

- Starbucks is a billion-dollar brand because it stands for a category called "high-end coffee shop."
- Rolex is a billion-dollar brand because it stands for a category called "expensive Swiss watch."
- Red Bull is a billion-dollar brand because it stands for a category called "energy drink."
- Tide is a billion-dollar brand because it stands for a category called "detergent."
- Costco is a billion-dollar brand because it stands for a category called "warehouse club."
- Home Depot is a billion-dollar brand because it stands for a category called "home improvement warehouse."

How strong the brand is depends on how strong the branch is. If nobody wants to buy an expensive Swiss watch, then the Rolex brand isn't worth very much. If high-end coffee consumption takes a dive, then the Starbucks brand loses much of its value.

Companies should think about creating categories, not brands. If you can dream up an exciting new category and then preempt that new category with a unique new name, you have a powerful combination.

Where Do Categories Exist?

On Main Street or in the mall? In the drugstore, in the department store, or in the supermarket?

None of these places. Categories exist in the mind. You create categories in exactly the same way you create brands. By positioning the name of the category in the mind of the prospect.

Be careful of research, however. If you want to find out what categories exist in the mind, you can't necessarily rely on research to tell you.

Consumers seldom use category names to describe their feelings. When you ask consumers what kind of car they prefer, they will seldom say, "A European luxury car." Rather, they will say, "Mercedes or BMW." They might think in terms of categories, but they express categories in terms of brands.

When you ask someone what kind of beer they prefer, few people will say, "A European luxury beer." Rather they will say Heineken or Beck's. They might think categories, but they talk brands.

So naturally marketers follow the same pattern. They tend to forgot about the category and jump right into promoting the brand. Big mistake. Unless you are first in a new category, you are unlikely to capture the attention of the prospect.

Prospects see new brands in relationship to old brands. When Coca-Cola introduces the energy drink KMX, the prospect thinks, "Why should I drink KMX when Red Bull is the brand that everyone else thinks is terrific?"

When you introduce a new brand as a new category, you remove the comparison factor. The new brand now has a chance to get into the prospect's mind because another brand doesn't already occupy the category.

Pigeonholes in the Mind

The mind is like the sorting rack in a post office, which has a slot or "pigeonhole" for every name on a letter carrier's route. Every piece of mail is put into the hole corresponding to the name on the mail. If there is no hole for a new piece of mail, it's set aside in a pile called undeliverables.

So, too, with brands. The mind has a slot or pigeonhole for every category. If the pigeonhole is named "safe cars," this is the hole for a brand called Volvo.

But there's one big difference between the post office and the mind. The post office delivers almost everything. The mind does not. If there's a brand strongly established in the pigeonhole in the mind, the second brand doesn't have much of a chance unless it becomes the opposite following the strategies outlined in chapter 12.

Name a second brand that fits into the pigeonhole marked "safe cars." Name a second brand that fits into the pigeonhole marked "driving machines." That's hard to do.

So new brands want to avoid trying to get into somebody else's pigeonhole. New brands want to create their own slots or categories.

Locking the Brand into the Pigeonhole

There are categories (the pigeonholes in the mind) and there are brands (the names that fit into the pigeonholes in the mind.) The two are related in the sense that the brand name is locked into the category. Mercedes-Benz is locked into a category called imported luxury car.

You need both. You can't be just a brand. You can't be just Rolex. You need to lock Rolex into a category in the mind called luxury Swiss watch. You need to lock Swatch into a category in the mind called fashion watch.

So far, so good. Most marketers would agree that the brand has to lock into some kind of category, although the actual categories that companies try to use are sometimes impossible to put into anyone's mind.

What often happens, however, is that companies try to short-circuit the process. They try to make the category name and the brand name virtually the same. We want to be the first natural-food brand, so we'll call our brand Nature's Choice.

Not good thinking.

Two Names. Two Different Purposes

The two names, the category name and the brand name, serve two different purposes. The category name is a generic word (generally spelled with lowercase letters) that encompasses all the brands in the category. The brand name is a proper name (generally spelled with uppercase letters) that specifies your individual brand. How can one name serve both purposes?

When you hear the words *Nature's Choice*, do you hear the word *Nature's* with uppercase or lowercase letters? *Nature* or *natural* is a generic word usually expressed in lowercase letters.

Take Seattle's Best Coffee. Ask the average person, "What is Seattle's Best Coffee?" He or she invariably replies, "Starbucks." The person hears the words *best coffee* with lowercase letters.

Take the Video Warehouse. Ask the average person, "Where is the nearest Video Warehouse?" and he or she will invariably direct you to Blockbuster.

These are not trivial differences. The mind treats categories as generic words and brands as proper names. You want the brand (uppercase) to occupy the category (lowercase). You need both and you need to think of both names when you develop a marketing strategy.

Opportunities Are Constantly Created

Evolution and divergence create opportunities in almost every direction you look. The semiconductor created opportunities in computer hardware and software, which created opportunities on the Internet. That's why it's important to think category first, brand second.

It wasn't America Online, Yahoo!, Amazon, Priceline, and eBay that created the Internet. It was the Internet that created opportunities for companies to build brands like AOL, Yahoo!, Amazon, Priceline, and eBay.

Nor does the creation of a powerful, worldwide billion-dollar brand depend on complicated, high-tech, sophisticated products or systems. Simple analogies work best.

- Books: Barnes & Noble
  Books on the Internet: Amazon.com

- Auctions: Sotheby's
  Auctions on the Internet: eBay

- Customer relationship management software: Siebel
  Customer relationship management software on the Internet: Salesforce.com

The Specialist Strategy

Many brands are the fruits of inventions of some complexity. But brands need not be built that way. Nor is it always necessary to be first. Sometimes all you need to be is a specialist in a category of generalists. Nike, Adidas, and Reebok are the big generalists in athletic shoes, but a number of smaller brands have carved out a slice of the shoe market by specializing. K-Swiss in tennis shoes. Vans in skateboard shoes. Sidi in bike shoes.

Categories exist in minds, not just in markets. K-Swiss sells a lot of "tennis shoes" to people who don't play tennis. And Harley-Davidson sells a lot of motorcycle jackets to people who don't drive motorcycles. Literal-mindedness is one of the biggest impediments to good marketing thinking.

North Face, now owned by VF, is a successful clothing brand with annual sales in the neighborhood of $250 million. But how many people climb mountains for a hobby? Not many. Furthermore, how many people have climbed the North Face of Mt. Everest? Very few, certainly not enough to support a clothing brand.

There are a lot more surfers than mountain climbers, but still not enough to support a surfer brand like Quicksilver, a clothing company that did $705 million in sales last year. And there are a lot more boat people than surfers, but not enough to support Nautica, a clothing brand that was recently bought by VF Corporation for $586 million.

Less is usually more. The world's largest fitness chain is not a unisex operation. It's Curves, a women's-only fitness chain. (*Entrepreneur* magazine selected Curves, as the world's second-best franchise, second only to Subway.)

Clarity Beats Cleverness

The folks at Dr Pepper/Seven-Up turned a bottle of 7 UP upside down and came up with a brand called dn L. (Turn this page upside down to get the joke.) Then they reversed everything about the brand.

- 7 UP is clear; dn L is green.
- 7 UP has no caffeine; dn L is caffeinated.
- 7 UP is lemon-lime flavored; dn L is a blend of fruit flavors.

What Dr Pepper/Seven-Up needs to turn upside down is not the bottle, but 7 UP's sales curve. The brand has lost market share every year for the last five years in a row. They need to figure out how to be the opposite of market leader, Sprite.

And what pigeonhole in the mind will dn L fit into?

And in what pigeonhole in the mind will the beer drinker put the new Anheuser World Select beer? Furthermore, what do you ask for when you want to order one? "I'd like an Anheuser World Select."

It's a whole lot easier to say, "Give me a Bud."

Adding Attributes as the Brand Ages

Once established in a category, brands pick up additional attributes as time passes. BMW established itself as the first "driving machine," then picked up the added attribute as the car for young urban professionals (yuppies).

Starbucks might be perceived as a hip place for the corporate crowd, but the core concept of the brand is high-end coffee. Take away its high-end coffee leadership and Starbucks becomes just another me-too brand.

A Kodak executive once insisted that the Kodak brand didn't stand for photographic film, it stood for trust. People might trust Kodak to produce good photographic film, but not much else. Take away its film leadership and Kodak becomes just another me-too photographic brand.

Even the most complex situations can be handled by following simple principles. In the game of golf, keep your head down and your left arm straight.

In the game of business, think category first and brand second.

Big & comfortable.

Driving.

Masculine.

Feminine.

Older people.

Younger people.

EVERY BRAND NEEDS AN ENEMY. BMW, LOWE'S AND PEPSI-COLA
ESTABLISHED THEIRS AND THEN BECAME THE OPPOSITE.

Chapter 15

Establishing an
Enemy

ESTABLISHING AN ENEMY is almost as important as creating a new category. No category will be successful unless it has an enemy. No new brand will be successful unless it also has an enemy.

The world is filled with inventions that never go anywhere because they don't have enemies. They are just interesting concepts that never find a place in the consumer's mind.

Solving a Problem Is Not Enough

Most people don't think in terms of problems, they think in terms of categories. "I need a better job, a better house, a better car, a higher salary."

Ask the average person to name their most pressing problem, and they will have to think long and hard before answering, "Aaaahhhh . . . my spouse?"

What problem did the automobile solve? People were happy with their horses. (Even today, some people would like to turn back the clock and get rid of the noise, the expense, the traffic jams, and all the other problems caused by the car.)

At the point of divergence is the identity of the enemy. To establish a new category, it's helpful to identify the enemy category by name, then try to force the new category to branch out as much as possible from the existing category.

The first automobile was positioned as a "horseless carriage." An open vehicle, it looked like a carriage and drove like a carriage. In other words, the enemy of the automobile was the horse.

Evolution rapidly changed the appearance of the automobile, while the horse-drawn carriages you see in New York's Central Park stayed pretty much the same.

Note the absence of hybrids. There were no horse-drawn carriages with an auxiliary engine in case the horse got tired. Today's automotive hybrids (which we predict will ultimately prove to be transition products) use electric batteries in case the gasoline engine gets tired.

Establishing a New Category Is Not Enough

You build brands by establishing a new category in the mind, then making sure your brand is the first brand to occupy that new category. But that's not enough to insure marketing success.

That strategy overlooks an important point. Why would a consumer want to put a new category into his or her mind? The truth is, the average person has enough mental junk to last several lifetimes.

If given a choice, most people would rather clear out the crap that already exists in their minds. They don't need or want to remember the hundreds of categories and thousands of brands that already clutter up their mind.

You need to ask yourself, why would a consumer want to take the time to put my new category into his or her mind?

The best way to put a new category into the mind is to use the new category to attack an old category. It's like clothing and fashion. The best way to put a new fashion brand into a mind is to make the old fashion brand obsolete.

A New Category Needs an Enemy

It's easier to see how this strategy works if you study the past. Whiskey used to be the largest-selling distilled spirit in America. Then a new category called gin came along. How did gin get to be a big category? Gin treated whiskey as the enemy. Whiskey was old-fashioned and gin was the latest "in" drink.

Every new category enters a mind by positioning itself against an existing category. By treating an existing category as its enemy.

Take the diet cola category. The enemy of diet cola is regular cola, yet that puts the leading brand (Diet Coca-Cola) in a difficult position. Diet Coke should be attacking regular cola by running advertisements that say, in essence, "150 calories, for what?"

In other words, Diet Coke should put regular cola in the same category as smoking cigarettes or driving without a seat belt. They're all bad for you.

That's difficult to do psychologically if Coca-Cola is part of your brand name, another reason why the Coca-Cola Company should have used Tab or some other name for its diet cola product.

The numbers illustrate the relative lack of success of the current approach used by both Coca-Cola and PepsiCo. Even though obesity is the number one health problem in America, regular colas outsell diet colas by more than two to one. That's a shame.

Diet Coke has two strikes against it. The *Diet* half of the name stigmatizes the brand as "not very good tasting." The *Coke* half of the name keeps the company from using its most potent marketing tool, attacking the cola category.

In the high-tech field a new product or system is considered worthless without a "killer application." Take the Internet, which was something of a high-tech curiosity until the killer app came along. That application was email.

Email's enemy is easy to define. It's regular mail and facsimile. Especially facsimile.

Facsimile wiped out Telex and TWX. And now email is wiping out facsimile.

Category Competition

Darwin's description of the endless struggle for life and the survival of the fittest is a good metaphor for what happens in branding wars. But instead of "dog eat dog," it's "dog eat cat" as each category, each branch, struggles to dominate nearby branches.

When American Home Products (now Wyeth) introduced Advil ibuprofen in 1984, who was the enemy? Tylenol and aspirin.

So Advil messages showed pictures of all three major pain relievers and then labeled each with its date of introduction: aspirin, 1899; Tylenol, 1955; Advil, 1984. Then to reinforce the idea that Advil was the newest (and presumably the best) pain reliever, Advil advertising used the theme "advanced medicine for pain."

When McNeil Nutritionals introduced a no-calorie sweetener called Splenda, who was the enemy?

The enemy obviously was NutraSweet, the first artificial sweetener without an unpleasant aftertaste. In an era where "natural" food is becoming more and more important, the obvious angle of attack against NutraSweet is the artificial ingredient.

So Splenda was positioned as "made from sugar so it tastes like sugar."

At retail, Splenda has a market share about equal to that of its two competitors—Equal (aspartame) and Sweet'N Low (saccharin)—combined.

Competition is good for the category and good for the brand. Yet companies often downplay competition in favor of cooperation. In a multibrand company, they try to create a family of friends rather than a family of enemies.

In this connection they often use a corporate or megabrand name on the friends in the family. Coca-Cola, Gillette, Kraft, Hanes, Kellogg's, General Mills, and many other companies are wedded to a megabrand strategy.

Bad strategy. Let your brands, or rather the categories your brands represent, fight it out with each other as well as with competitive brands and categories.

Credit Cards vs. Debit Cards

The latest victims of faulty competitive strategy and faulty brand names are Visa U.S.A. and MasterCard International. So far, it has cost the two credit card companies $3 billion with possibly more financial penalties to come.

The categories are credit cards (charges paid monthly or by installments) and debit cards (deducted directly from a bank account). It would be hard to find two categories that are more competitive. Credit cards are the enemy of debit cards. And vice versa.

So what did Visa and MasterCard do? They put the same names on both cards. Visa on credit cards and Visa on debit cards. And the same for MasterCard.

To compound the problem, both card companies force their retailers to "honor all cards." In other words, if a retailer accepts a Visa credit card, the retailer must also accept a Visa debit card.

Then they put the debit card charges through the same

signature-based system as the credit card charges, forcing the retailer to pay five to ten times as much in fees as it would if the customer had used one of the alternative debit card networks such as Star, Pulse, or NYCE, which use a personal identification number, or PIN-based system.

In the biggest antitrust settlement in history, Visa U.S.A. agreed to pay $2 billion and MasterCard International $1 billion to a group of retailers led by Wal-Mart. Their contention: "honor all cards" was an illegal tie-in scheme.

Why not launch a second "debit" brand to complement the Visa or MasterCard "credit" brands? It's the chicken-and-egg problem, explained one Visa executive. Visa would have had to start a new brand from scratch, one not yet issued by any bank or honored by any merchant. "But why would we possibly have done that?"

We can think of three billion reasons. But more important than the short-term financial losses at Visa and MasterCard are the long-term implications of their "honor all cards" strategy. By integrating its debit with its credit card system, Visa (as well as MasterCard) is locked into a slower, less secure, and more expensive way of processing debit-card charges.

Actually MasterCard did try a second-brand strategy, launching a PIN product called Maestro. But Maestro was losing out to the Visa signature debit card, so MasterCard reversed course and came up with their own signature debit card.

Too bad. If they had had a little more faith in their strategy, today MasterCard would be a billion dollars richer with a big lead in PIN-based debit cards over its Visa competition.

Like many marketing problems, the debit card situation is complicated. How do you design a product that has benefits for all the players in the game—consumers, retailers, banks, and the card network itself? It's not easy.

Here is where the power of conceptual thinking comes in. You may not know how, when, or where divergence will take place, but you can be sure it will. Two different products, credit cards and debit cards, will ultimately diverge, and there's nothing one company can do about it. Trying to keep them locked together under the same brand name is futile.

Stockbrokerage vs. Investment Banking

The current turmoil in the securities industry is another example of divergence at work. Recently ten Wall Street firms paid $1.4 billion to settle government charges that the firms routinely issued overly optimistic stock research to curry favor with corporate clients and win their investment-banking business.

It wasn't much of a secret to the average investor. ("I am shocked, *shocked* to find that gambling is going on in here!")

Sandy Weill, chief executive of Citigroup, is now required to have a lawyer present if he wishes to confer with his firm's stock analysts about the companies they cover.

Citigroup and the nine other companies that participated in the settlement face two mutually impossible tasks:

- Maximize the price of stock issued by its investment bank clients.
- Minimize the cost of stock purchased by its retail clients.

One firm obviously can't do both. That's a conflict of interests. Logic suggests that the investment banking business be spun off from the stockbrokerage business, but it will never happen as long as powerful players benefit from the conflict of interests.

Managing a megacompany headed in multiple directions is impossible. A person with one watch always knows what time it is. A person with two watches is never quite sure.

The best way to make sure your company is headed in the right direction is to first establish an enemy. Then set your sights on your enemy and make sure every move you make undermines the position of that enemy.

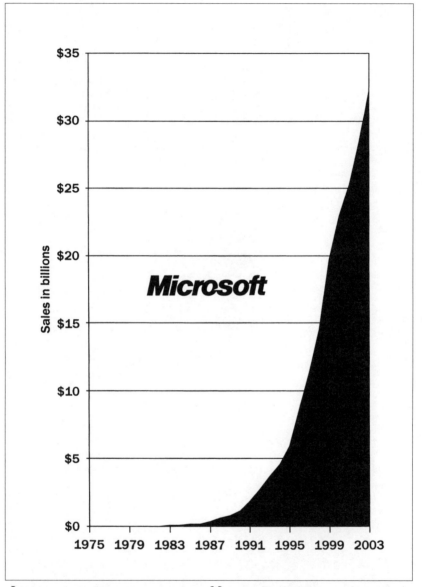

LIKE MOST SUCCESSFUL COMPANIES, MICROSOFT TOOK OFF VERY SLOWLY.
IT WAS TEN YEARS BEFORE THE BRAND EXCEEDED $100 MILLION IN SALES.

Chapter 16

Launching the Brand

PARVIS E GLANDIBUS QUERCUS. Tall oaks from little acorns grow.

The biggest, most powerful world-class brands start from little ideas. If you try to force-feed your new brand or your new company with massive resources including a massive advertising budget, you are unlikely to be successful.

Time and Patience Are Your Allies

You can kill a plant with too much water and too much fertilizer. You can kill a brand the same way.

The strongest and longest-lasting brands are created by divergence of an existing category. But this divergence is a slow process. Television was invented in 1927, but was not commercialized until after World War II. A company formed to launch a television brand in the 1930s would have gone bankrupt.

Perhaps no revolutionary product grew as fast as the personal computer. The first personal computer was introduced in 1975, the same year Bill Gates dropped out of Harvard to go to Albuquerque, New Mexico, to write a basic software program for the Altair computer.

Microsoft, the company Gates founded, is today the second most valuable company in the world, worth $304 billion on the stock market.

Things weren't always so rosy. On February 3, 1976, Bill Gates wrote an open letter to Altair users complaining about software piracy. Published in the Homebrew Computer Club newsletter, Gates's letter stated, "The amount of royalties we have received from sales to hobbyists makes the time spent on Altair BASIC worth less than $2 an hour."

Most people who found themselves working for less than $2 an hour would have looked for some other line of work. Not Bill Gates. His faith in the future of software paid off in a big way.

Branching takes time. It even takes a while for a new category to be recognized as a new category. One of Bill Gates's early problems was the perception that software wasn't worth anything. So owners just copied the software needed to operate their computers from friends. (Less than 10 percent of Altair owners bought Microsoft's software.)

How do you launch a brand anyway? There are two theories.

Theory A vs. Theory B

Theory A (for "airplane") is the airplane launch. Your brand rolls slowly down the runway for thousands of feet, and then after a massive effort your brand slowly lifts off the tarmac. After the brand is airborne for a while, it starts to accelerate into its cruising altitude.

Theory B (for "big bang") is the rocket-ship launch. Your brand takes off like a rocket and then coasts into orbit.

Advertising favors the rocket-ship launch because ad programs are traditionally launched with a big bang. That's the only way to create enough attention to get above the noise level.

PR has no choice. It has to use an airplane launch. PR programs are invariably rolled out over an extended period. That's the only way that PR can deal with the needs of the media, which are focused on scoops and exclusives.

What about the Real World?

Does a new brand take off like a rocket ship? Or does it take off like an airplane?

Take a typical new brand in the beverage industry. This brand took four years to break $10 million in annual sales and another five years to reach $100 million.

The brand is Red Bull, a brand built primarily by PR and a brand that took off like an airplane, not like a rocket ship.

Take a software brand that took even longer to get off the runway than Red Bull. This brand took ten years to reach $100 million in annual sales.

The brand, or course, is Microsoft, a brand that took off like an airplane, not like a rocket ship.

Take another example, a retail brand. This brand took fourteen years to break $100 million in annual sales. Today the brand does $198 billion in annual sales and has become the world's largest retailer.

The brand, of course, is Wal-Mart, a brand that took off like an airplane, not like a rocket ship.

The turning point for new products comes when slow initial sales suddenly accelerate toward the mass market. According to a recent research report, this averages six years after launch in America.

The largest, most powerful brands, the brands that have stood the test of time, are the brands that have taken off slowly, like an airplane. The brands that take off rapidly like a rocket ship usually turn out to be fads. Here today, gone tomorrow. The hula hoop, Bartles & Jaymes wine cooler, Crystal Pepsi, and many others.

Initially, consumers loved Crystal Pepsi. They voted it "Best New Grocery Product of 1992" according to AcuPOLL, an independent nationwide survey of sixteen thousand new grocery products. Crystal Pepsi also won critical acclaim as one of the best new products of 1992 by *Time* magazine. And the *Washington Post* ranked it among what's "in" for 1993.

Three months after its national introduction, Crystal Pepsi had a market share of 2.4 percent.

A year later the product was gone.

What about Nature?

Nature offers many examples of the superiority of slow growth. Small dogs outlive large dogs. Slow-growing hardwood trees outlive fast-growing softwood trees.

The oldest living tree is not some giant sequoia, it's a bristlecone pine that stands just fifty-five feet tall. Its estimated age is 4,767 years, which means that this particular bristlecone has been growing at the rate of fourteen-hundredths of an inch a year. (Fingernails grow a lot faster than that, around one and a half inches a year.)

Concrete is stronger if it cures slowly rather than rapidly. In hot weather contractors will spray water on freshly laid sidewalks to cool the concrete and slow down the curing time.

Rapid growth weakens rather than strengthens. That's true for a brand as well as for a plant or an animal.

The tallest person who ever lived was Robert Wadlow, who was eight feet eleven inches. Unfortunately he didn't live very long. Wadlow died at the age of twenty-two.

Experts now believe that autism in children is caused by rapid brain growth. A recent study of forty-eight autistic preschoolers found that the kids' heads had been smaller than average at birth but had grown explosively during infancy. On average, they went from the twenty-fifth percentile to the eighty-fourth percentile in about a year's time.

And what is cancer? Rapid and abnormal cell growth.

This is not to say that you don't want your new brand to grow as rapidly as possible. As in nature, the odds favor the brand that can stick its head above its neighbors' and get more than its share of nutrients. You want your new brand to dominate its category, and to do so you need to push its growth.

Be patient, though. Divergence takes time. People are suspicious of the new and different. A typical reaction: "I'll wait and see if this new concept turns out to be worthwhile." You need to sell the category as well as the brand.

Satellite radio has taken off slowly. After more than two years of heavy promotion, XM Satellite Radio, the market leader, has only 1.4 million subscribers. That sounds like a lot, but it's less than one percent of the 200 million cars on the road in America.

Furthermore, to sign up those 1.4 million subscribers, XM Satellite spent $100 million on advertising the first year and $60 million the second.

They should have saved their money and waited for the turning point. Let the brand build slowly using primarily PR techniques. Then when the turning point arrives, jump in with a massive advertising program.

Two Problems: Credibility and Convention

The launch of a new brand that defines a new category has two problems.

Credibility is the first. A new concept is just not believable, especially when presented in an advertisement. If Viagra had been launched with an advertising campaign ("The pill that can cure impotence"), it would probably have gone nowhere.

Advertising is like spam. (In fact, spam is advertising, although not all advertising is spam.) Advertising has little credibility. To be effective, advertising needs the credibility that only third parties can provide. Third parties being friends, neighbors, relatives, and especially the media.

That's why the most effective marketing program for launching a new brand starts with a PR campaign, which drives word of mouth, which creates credibility for the brand. Only after a brand has achieved a measure of credibility can a company afford to spend its resources on an advertising program.

After credibility, the second problem is "convention." People want to buy what is "conventional." In other words, people want to buy what other people are buying. In general, they don't want to be seen as unconventional.

Of course, if this conclusion were totally true, it would be almost impossible to get a new concept off the ground, whether it's light beer or living together before marriage. Fortunately, a small cadre of consumers consider themselves unconventional and are not only willing but sometimes eager to try something new.

So the trick to launching a new brand is to make a connection with unconventional people, or the people whom marketers have called innovators or early adopters. That's why the process takes time.

It takes a while for a new concept to work its way up the convention ladder. From totally unconventional at the bottom to totally conventional at the top.

Other Complicating Factors

Everybody is conventional and everybody is unconventional. That is, people might dress conventionally, but are willing to try any new restaurant that opens in their neighborhood. On the other hand, you have the computer nerd who might buy any new gadget the high-tech industry offers, but lives on pizza, hamburgers, and Mountain Dew Code Red.

The younger generation also plays a role in this process. It's natural for each generation to create its own identity by rebelling against the previous generation. This rebellion often takes the form of changes in music, clothing, hairstyles, food, beverages, etc.

Many brands have been built by creating the perception that they represent the younger generation. Examples include BMW, Mini Cooper, Pepsi-Cola, Mountain Dew, Red Bull, Tommy Hilfiger, The Gap, and Abercrombie & Fitch.

Nor can the role of mutation be overlooked. Parents who expect their sons or daughters to be carbon copies of themselves are always surprised. It's mutation and natural selection that assures that the next generation is not only rebellious, but also different.

Launching a new brand involves solving several problems. How do you move rapidly in a process that's inherently slow? How do you create credibility for a new brand (and a new category) that has no credibility?

Both problems are interconnected. The best way to deal with both issues is a public relations strategy called the leak. You release information about the new brand before it's ready to be launched. The more radical the concept, the longer the gestation period.

Brand building, especially of the new-category variety, is not easy. You may have the best product in the world, you may have the best marketing strategy in the world, you may have the best names (for the new category and the new brand), and you may have all the resources you need.

But you'll never be successful unless you get into the prospect's mind first.

So How Do You Get into a Mind?

For most marketing people, the conventional answer is advertising. We hire an advertising agency, we set an advertising budget, we prepare advertising plans (preferably with a big broadcast-television allotment), we shoot the commercials, and we launch the program.

Then we sit back and wait for the results. In most cases, the results are a big disappointment. In truth, advertising is not a good way to launch a brand. Advertising has a role and function, but it's in brand maintenance, not in brand building.

This is the era of public relations. Today you build brands with PR, not advertising. Today advertising must take a secondary role.

In fact, brands like Starbucks, Wal-Mart, Palm, Viagra, and Red Bull were built with virtually no advertising at all.

Advertising lacks credibility, the crucial ingredient in brand building. Only PR can supply the credibility that allows your brand to get into consumers' minds.

Furthermore, the big bang approach advocated by advertising people doesn't work either. You need a slow buildup by PR. Advertising should be used only to maintain brands once they have been established . . . by publicity.

When your brand can make news, it has a chance to generate publicity. And the best way to make news is simple. Announce a new category and not just a new product. The news media wants to talk about what's new, what's first, and what's hot. They definitely don't want to talk about what's better. That makes them look like a shill for an individual brand.

Furthermore, what others say about your brand is much more powerful than what you say about it yourself. That's why publicity in general is more powerful than advertising.

And why over the past two decades, public relations has eclipsed advertising as the most powerful force in branding.

Revolutionary Concepts Are Even Slower

The more revolutionary the concept, the slower the concept is likely to take off. In this sense, long-term potential and short-term growth are inversely proportional.

Take a new product introduced in January 2001 by Kimberly-Clark. According to the corporation's press release, "It is the most significant category innovation since toilet paper first appeared in roll form in 1890."

The innovation? "Cottonelle Fresh Rollwipes, America's first and only disposable, premoistened wipe on a roll."

In its press release, Kimberly-Clark said that the U.S. toilet paper market was $4.8 billion a year and that they expected first-year Fresh Rollwipes sales to reach at least $150 million (a modest 3 percent of the market), and $500 million annually within six years.

So Kimberly-Clark confidently launched the Fresh Rollwipes brand with a $35-million advertising campaign that carried the slogan "sometimes wetter is better" and featured shots from behind of people splashing in water.

But instead of $150 million in sales, the brand delivered only about a third of that amount. Today the brand hangs in there, but Kimberly-Clark executives said sales are so weak they are not financially material.

"This is not the best time to be introducing a new product," said President/COO Thomas Falk in a conference call with analysts. "So far, it looks like it's going to take longer for the category to develop than we originally thought."

Fresh Rollwipes are a classic example of a brand with long-term potential (a $4.8-billion market) and slow growth in the short term. Sometimes you need to believe your press release.

If Fresh Rollwipes are "the most significant category innovation since toilet paper first appeared in roll form," then the company should have expected the brand to start slowly. Furthermore, the more revolutionary the concept, the less a role advertising should play.

You Can't Just Replace Advertising with PR

Launching a brand with public relations and launching a brand with advertising are two totally different things. When you launch a brand with PR, you have to change almost everything you do.

Letting go of what you learned in Advertising 101 is not easy. Advertising and marketing are so entwined inside the minds of managers that many won't consider the possibility of launching a new brand without advertising.

And not just a modest advertising program, either. Big-bang thinking is so ingrained in managers' minds that the launch is invariably described as "the biggest advertising program we have ever run."

We strongly recommend that all new brands be introduced with PR only, a launch that invariably involves seven steps.

Step 1: The Leak

Newsletters and Internet sites are favorite outlets.

The media loves inside stories that describe events that are going to happen. Especially when it's an exclusive. In other words, a scoop.

That's the way the Segway was launched. Almost eleven months before its formal introduction, the product was leaked to Inside.com. Codenamed Ginger, the new product was described as more significant than the World Wide Web.

Eleven months later, the Segway was formally introduced on ABC's *Good Morning America*, where Diane Sawyer and Charles Gibson gave it a spin. Naturally the Segway made all the evening news shows as well as most of the nation's newspapers.

You waste an enormous resource if you don't leak details of your new product or service to the media. What do people like to talk about? Rumors, gossip, inside information. It's the same with the media.

Advertising is the opposite. An advertising program is normally launched like a military attack. It's usually kept a top secret until the day the first ad runs.

Step 2: The Slow Buildup

A PR program slowly unfolds like a flower blooming. A company has to allot enough time for a PR program to develop momentum. That's why a PR launch often starts months before the details of a new product or service are firmly fixed.

Big-bang thinking is out. Unless you have an earth-shattering invention, you have to start slowly and hope the media coverage will gradually expand. (If you do have an earth-shattering invention, you probably don't need PR at all. The word will get out regardless of what you do.)

Fortunately this slow buildup is consistent with the way most consumers learn about new products and services. A news item here, a mention from a friend there, and pretty soon you are convinced you have known about the product forever.

Advertising is the opposite. An advertising program often starts with a Super Bowl ad.

Since consumers tend to ignore advertising messages, a new ad program has to be big and bold enough to get above the "noise level." The easiest thing to hide in America is a million dollars' worth of advertising. If you divide the million into small chunks and spend the money in many different media, your messages will disappear into an advertising black hole.

Step 3: The Recruitment of Allies

Why go it alone when you can get others to help communicate your message?

The slow buildup of a PR program allows enough time to recruit allies to your cause. Furthermore, the publicity will often attract volunteers.

Who are your natural allies? "The enemy of my enemy is my friend." When we wrote *The Fall of Advertising* book, we asked ourselves who might be the enemy of such a book.

The obvious enemy is the advertising conglomerate, the ones who control the bulk of advertising expenditures in the United States. Who might be the enemy of these ad conglomerates? It's the independent PR firms that have been losing business to the PR subsidiaries of these ad conglomerates.

So we sent advance copies of our book to the 124 largest independent PR firms in the country and followed up with copies of media stories about the book.

These mailings generated a lot of response along the lines of "We'll buy copies to send to clients and prospects, we'll invite you to make speeches at industry meetings, we'll write letters to the editors of trade publications, etc."

Advertising is the opposite. An advertising program has a difficult time recruiting allies. There are two problems: time and money.

With a big-bang launch, there usually isn't enough time to line up supporters. Also, advertising alliances usually fall apart over the question of who pays for what.

Step 4: The Bottom-Up Rollout

You have to crawl before you walk, and you have to walk before you run. The media work the same way. You need to start small, perhaps with a mention in a newsletter, then move on to the trade press. From the trade press, you might move up the ladder to one of the general business publications. Eventually you might see your new product or service on the *NBC Nightly News*.

Each rung of the ladder adds credibility to your brand. If you approach NBC directly, you might get an instant turndown. If they see your new product or service mentioned in *Time* magazine, however, they might call you.

As you move up the media ladder, your brand creates its own momentum.

Advertising is the opposite. An advertising program is more likely to start with network TV. Again, the idea is to launch the campaign with a big bang and follow up with smaller "reminder" advertisements.

Step 5: The Modification of the Product

Feedback is an important element in a PR launch. By launching the public relations program ahead of the actual product introduction, there is enough time to modify the product before it goes on sale. This can be a major advantage.

Advertising is the opposite. Once an advertising program is launched, a company is committed. There is little feedback and no time to change the product or service before it is introduced to consumers.

Apple launched the Newton MessagePad, the world's first handheld computer, with a big press conference at the Consumer Electronics Show in Chicago.

Apple followed the press announcement with a traditional big-bang advertising campaign including TV commercials that proclaimed with breathless prose, "Newton is digital. Newton is personal. Newton is magic. Newton is as simple as a piece of paper. Newton is intelligent. Newton learns about you, understands you. Newton is news."

Because of its flawed handwriting-recognition software, the product received scathing reviews. Especially devastating was a full week of Garry Trudeau's cartoon strip *Doonesbury* mocking the Newton. "I am writing a test sentence" came out "Siam fighting atomic sentry."

A prospect tested a Newton by writing "My name is Curtis." *Business Week* reported the event with the headline "My Norse 15 Critics," which is how the Newton interpreted the prospect's message.

Too much hype is self-defeating. You are asking the media to take your product down a peg. Better to launch a brand in a modest way by asking friends and allies to offer their suggestions. Then modify the product to meet the needs of the marketplace.

Palm Computing took the Newton idea and simplified it. They dropped the telecommunications function and the elaborate handwriting-recognition software in favor of a stylized "all-cap" system called Graffiti. The PalmPilot went on to be an enormous success.

When dealing with media, humility beats hype all the time. If you ask for advice and counsel, you are likely to get a wealth of ideas you can use.

Step 6: The Modification of the Message

When you launch a new product, you usually find that you have a range of attributes that you could attach to the brand.

Which one attribute should you focus on?

This is the sort of question that can stir up endless hours of debate in the boardroom. Too often the question is ducked and the brand is launched with a smorgasbord of attributes (which is what happened with the Newton). Or a decision is made that turns out to be wrong. There's a certain lack of objectivity on the top floor.

The media can be helpful. Which attribute does a reporter or an editor think is most important? After all, the media looks at a new product from the consumer's point of view.

Their opinions are not only helpful but are likely to prove extremely convincing to prospects. They hold the reins of consumer opinion. You cross them at your own peril.

Volvo spent years advertising durability. Yet the media fell in love with the safety aspects of Volvo cars. They carried stories about Volvo's invention of the three-point lap-and-shoulder seat belt, the collapsible steering column, front and rear crumple zones, etc.

Volvo finally threw in its durability towel and switched its advertising to safety. Volvo sales took off.

Forget focus groups. Why pay consumers for advice when the media will give it to you for free? Furthermore, the media will back up their advice with stories that will plant your ideas in the prospect's mind.

Should you ever go against media advice? Sure, but when you do, you'd better have a good reason to do so.

Advertising is the opposite. Once launched, an advertising program is cast in stone. It's difficult, expensive, and embarrassing to try to change strategies and messages in the middle of an advertising campaign.

Step 7: The Soft Launch

How long should the PR phase of a new product program take? It depends on a lot of factors. That's why we recommend a "soft" launch.

The new product or service should be launched only after the PR program has run its course. The product will be introduced when it is ready. In other words, when the media coverage runs its course. Not too soon and not too late.

The soft launch fouls up budgeting and corporate planning. It might even cause problems with manufacturing and distribution.

So be it. In marketing, as in life, timing is everything. The right product at the right time with the right PR support is an unstoppable combination.

Advertising is the opposite. An advertising program is usually tied in directly with the product's availability. The first ad runs on the first date the product is available for sale.

Most advertising campaigns for new brands are planned around a D-day, the day the product hits the beach supported by advertising airpower and promotional landing craft.

A military metaphor makes for a rousing speech at a sales meeting, but it lacks the flexibility to deal with the real world. No one can predict the course of a PR program. How long it will take, what new ideas and concepts will be unearthed.

Writing in the *New York Times*, Michael R. Gordon said, "The common assumption is that wars begin with a bang. In fact, they often start with limited airstrikes, stealthy border movements and psychological operations to weaken the enemy's resistance."

Marketing wars should start the same way.

Before divergence.

After divergence.

A COMPANY CAN GO FOR YEARS RIDING A SINGLE HORSE AND THEN THE
CATEGORY DIVERGES AND ALL HELL BREAKS LOOSE.

Chapter 17

Wrapping Things Up

THE CRITICAL EVENT IN A COMPANY'S HISTORY occurs when the limb it has been riding branches out.

Divergence creates opportunities and divergence also creates problems. Companies that try to ride both branches with the same brand name are in an exceptionally dangerous position.

They're like a circus performer who rides standing up into the ring straddling two horses. Nice display of horsemanship, but what would happen if each horse went in a different direction? Rider and mounts would part company in a big hurry.

In the ring, it doesn't happen because the rider keeps the horses under control. In the marketplace, it's a different matter. A company in the mushy middle gets pulled apart by evolution of the branches.

It happened to Western Union. It happened to Wang. It happened to Polaroid. It happened to Xerox. And it is happening to Kodak.

This is a phenomenon that traditional marketing is not trained to cope with.

The Five Functions of Marketing

A classic marketing book lists the five functions of marketing in the following order:

1. Defining the market.
2. Selecting the market segments.
3. Designing the appeal.
4. Generating support from other functions.
5. Monitoring performance.

Take the first function, defining the market. Let's see, a lot of markets are out there, which one do we select? Automobiles, batteries, beer, cola, cellphones, detergents, etc. Obviously, Anheuser-Busch is not going to go into the automobile business, and General Motors is not going to go into the beer business.

For an existing company at least, defining the market is really asking yourself, what business are we in? Anheuser-Busch is in the beer business. General Motors is in the automobile business.

Take the second function, selecting the market segments. Here again, successful companies have already defined their brands in terms of market segments. Busch is Anheuser-Busch's low-priced beer. Budweiser is its regular beer. Michelob is its high-priced beer. The same type of segmentation has already taken place at General Motors, from Saturn at the low end to Cadillac at the high end.

The other three functions (appeals, support, and monitoring) are in reality just ways of "fine-tuning" a marketing program.

Traditional Marketing Is Not Enough

While the five functions of marketing may be the way to maintain a brand, they are clearly not the way to build a brand.

Red Bull didn't become a big brand by going after the energy drink market. There was no energy drink market. Red Bull became a big brand by creating a new market and labeling this new market "energy drinks."

Duracell didn't become a big brand by going after the alkaline battery market. There was no alkaline battery market. Duracell became a big brand by creating a new market and labeling this new market "alkaline batteries."

And how were these new markets created? By divergence of existing markets. Energy bars/energy drinks. Zinc-carbon flashlight batteries/alkaline batteries.

Most brand-building success stories leave out the essential ingredient, the creating of a new category or new market. They focus on all the exciting things a company is doing to create interest in the brand.

Take Nike, for example. Why has Nike been successful? If you believe what you read in the papers, Nike was successful because they hired Michael Jordan to endorse the brand and spent millions of dollars on an advertising program called "Just do it."

Well, Raytheon hired Michael Jordan, too. They also spent a bundle of money advertising a line of rechargeable batteries. And where is Raytheon today? In dire need of recharging.

Whoever writes the books on marketing successes like Nike always leaves out chapter 1. How the brand was created in the first place. If you dig deeper into the situation that existed before the brand was launched, you will always find the same answer. The new brand owes its success to the company's ability to create a new category.

Before the rise of Nike, teenage America wore sneakers, preferably Keds. What Nike did was to create a new category, "athletic shoes," and then go on to dominate this emerging new category.

Matching Competition Is Not Enough

How did Uniroyal, the owner of the Keds brand, react to the Nike upstart? They introduced Super Keds.

How did Eveready, the leading zinc-carbon battery, react to the Duracell upstart? They introduced Eveready alkaline batteries.

How did Smirnoff, the leading vodka brand, react to the success of Absolut, a superpremium vodka brand? They introduced Smirnoff Black.

How did Tanqueray, the leading premium gin brand, react to the success of vodka brands like Absolut and Stolichnaya? They introduced Tanqueray vodka.

How did Gatorade, the leading sports drink brand, react to the success of energy-bar brands like PowerBar and Balance? They introduced Gatorade energy bars.

As you probably know, line-extension brands like Gatorade energy bars, Tanqueray vodka, Smirnoff Black, Eveready alkaline batteries, and Super Keds have gone nowhere. What leads companies to make these classic marketing mistakes?

It's a belief shared by many managers that marketing is a battle of brands. My brand versus your brand.

That's why the typical brand owner will invest considerable sums of money in advertising, displays, promotions, and merchandising to outdo the competition. May the better brand win.

Keeping Customers Happy Is Not Enough

Then there's the current emphasis on keeping customers happy. Billions of dollars have been spent on customer relationship management or CRM software. (CRM market leader Siebel Systems alone has recorded $5.5 billion in revenues in the past three years.)

Nor have marketing managers lacked professional advice on the subject. Amazon.com lists 2,634 books on customer satisfaction with such titles as *Delivering Knock Your Socks Off Service* by Ron Zemke and Kristin Anderson, and *Customer Satisfaction Is Worthless, Customer Loyalty Is Priceless: How to Make Customers Love You, Keep Them Coming Back and Tell Everyone They Know*, by Jeffrey Gitomer.

"Be obsessive about making your customers happy," advises Tom Peters, who says little about getting customers in the first place.

Furthermore, thousands of companies and brands are on life-support systems. What would you do if you owned the Kmart brand, the Polaroid brand, the Royal Crown brand, the Schlitz brand? Be obsessive about making your customers happy? We think not. There are basket cases in brands, too.

There's nothing wrong with improving customer satisfaction scores. But that's only half the story. Every brand should evolve via constant change and constant improvement.

Even Evolution Is Not Enough

Evolution, the first of Charles Darwin's revolutionary concepts, gets all the attention, and divergence, his second concept, gets overlooked. A brand can't evolve until it gets created in the first place.

Divergence first, evolution second is the order of things in nature. So, too, in branding. Companies need to pay more attention to how they create their brands in the first place. If you do the brand-creation job right, you can build a brand position that's insurmountable.

In the foreseeable future, will a competitive brand overtake Dell or Red Bull or Starbucks or the *Wall Street Journal*? Divergence created these brands. Evolution will keep them on top.

Brands live and brands die. Brands don't die because they didn't keep their customers happy. Brands die because their categories die. Wang (word processors) and Polaroid (instant photography) are two examples.

In the long run, every company will die unless it replaces its obsolete and dying brands with new brands built around new categories. In addition to investing in customer relationship management software, companies should also invest in a category replacement management system.

Divergence Is the Key

The biggest single source of new brand opportunities is divergence. But unlike nature, categories don't diverge in response to environmental conditions. (Think consumers.) Categories diverge in response to companies that introduce new brands that are divergent in concept.

Timing is critical. You might not want to introduce a new category (via a new brand) because that might make your existing category obsolete. But if you wait and let a competitor introduce the new category first, you will lose out in the long run. Survival of the firstest.

Even a sensational product like the Apple Macintosh remains a niche machine because it wasn't first.

Unlike nature, in marketing a company gets a second chance.

If you're not first, it's possible to build a strong No. 2 brand by being the opposite of the leader.

Dell was late in the personal computer game. The other brands were sold through distribution channels, primarily retail stores. So Dell did the opposite. They sold direct, first by phone and currently by the Internet. Survival of the secondest.

Consumers Buy Categories, Not Brands

With all the talk of brands and branding, the truth is that consumers buy categories, not brands. The brand name is shorthand for the attribute represented by the category.

People who want to buy a "prestige" automobile usually buy a Mercedes-Benz. It's easier, quicker, and psychologically more satisfying to say "I drive a Mercedes" than it is to say "I drive a prestigious automobile."

The day Mercedes-Benz loses its connotation of being a prestige car is the day the Mercedes-Benz brand loses much of its value.

The ultimate proof that consumers use brand names as surrogates for category names is the increasing tendency of brand names to become generic: Kleenex, Xerox, Scotch tape, Coke, Jell-O, Rollerblade, Palm computer.

Many marketing experts warn about the need to protect brand names with circle Cs (©) and other techniques to keep them from going generic. The dangers are vastly overstated.

How Many "Generic" Trademarks Have Been Lost?

Very, very few.

Aspirin, a trademark once owned by Bayer, is often cited as a brand that fell into the generic trap. Not so. After Germany lost

World War I, Bayer was forced to give up the Aspirin trademark as part of the Treaty of Versailles in 1919. (The Allies should have asked for Daimler-Benz.)

Having a brand name that is also used generically is an enormous marketing advantage. A generic brand like Kleenex is exceptionally strong and will almost certainly never lose its leadership as long as there's a market for pocket tissue.

What does *becoming generic* really mean in the mind of the consumer?

If you look in a dictionary, you will find that many words have secondary meanings. *Coke*, for example, means cocaine, Coca-Cola, or coal burned in the absence of air.

When a brand name becomes generic, the same thing happens. Consumers will actually assign two meanings to the same word in their minds.

In other words, a consumer will use *Kleenex* to mean the category as well as *Kleenex* to mean the brand. The same word means two different things in one mind.

That's why brands that become generic don't generally lose their branding power. Kleenex dominates the tissue category. Scotch tape dominates the cellophane tape category, and Jell-O dominates the gelatin dessert category.

A Strategy for Leading Brands

If you are blessed with a powerful leader brand (Visa, Budweiser, Coca-Cola, etc.) in a category that exhibits little or no evolution, then life is sweet.

The rich get richer, the poor get poorer. Not only are you unlikely to lose your leadership, chances are good that you will increase your lead over the No. 2 brand.

Most companies are not so blessed. Most companies are like short trees in the forest. Their bigger, stronger, taller competitors block the sunlight and make it difficult for them to grow.

A Strategy for Also-Rans

Instead of pursuing a branding strategy that has little hope of success, these companies should forget about brands and think categories.

"How do we invent a new category? And then give that category a new brand name?" This strategy will allow your company to move out of the shade of the leading brand and into an open area. This is perhaps the only chance for a smaller company to win big.

Electric toothbrushes have been on the market for decades, but most brands cost $50 or more. So John Osher and three other Cleveland-area entrepreneurs developed a battery-operated electric toothbrush that could be sold for $5. Called SpinBrush, the product was introduced in 1998.

Two years later, SpinBrush was sold to Procter & Gamble for $475 million, a big payout for an investment that totaled $1.5 million.

Every Category, Bar None, Will Ultimately Diverge

No one brand can cover all diverging branches. Especially not in the face of specialized competition.

Witness IBM's losing battle against Dell and Compaq in personal computers. Against Microsoft in personal-computer operating systems. Against Intel in personal-computer microprocessors. Against Toshiba in laptop computers.

In nature, branches seldom, if ever, converge. In the marketplace, branches (or categories) will sometimes converge, but only in areas where convenience is an important factor. Shampoo/conditioner. Convenience store/gasoline station. Camera/cellphone.

Convergence can sometimes mean convenience, but it always means compromise. That's why convergence will remain a minor player in the branding game.

One of the most difficult things to understand is the dynamics of a marketplace. Why some companies win and others lose. Why some consumers prefer one brand and other consumers prefer another brand. Why a brand that is hot today can get cold tomorrow.

Charles Darwin provides the theoretical concepts to understand the dynamics of the marketplace. The laws of nature apply equally as well to brands and categories.

Brands Evolve and Categories Diverge

If properly handled, brands can evolve over time to become stronger and more dominant. But there's always the danger of divergence.

A brand that tries to cover every aspect of a diverging category faces the almost certain possibility of losing its dominant position. A better strategy is to constantly prune the brand so that it continues to stand for a single idea in the consumer's mind.

In the long run, however, brand maintenance is a loser's game. Unless a company has the courage to introduce new brands to take advantage of new categories created by divergence, that company has no future.

Evolution is a powerful force, but evolution alone cannot account for the hundreds of thousands of brands that can be found in supermarkets, drugstores, clothing stores, shoe stores, discount stores, and convenience stores.

High-tech brands, low-tech brands. Expensive brands, cheap brands. Modern brands, traditional brands. Adult brands, kid brands.

Urban brands, country brands. Global brands, local brands. Female-oriented brands, male-oriented brands. Consumer brands, professional brands.

Divergence has created this incredible variety of brands. From a single tree, multiple limbs will form. From each limb, multiple branches will form in a process that has no ending. What we see today is just a small sampling of the many marvelous new products and new brands that are certain to arrive in the future.

There is grandeur in this view of brands, with its several powers, having been originally breathed into a few forms or into one; and that, whilst this planet has gone cycling on according to the fixed law of gravity, from so simple a beginning endless brands most beautiful and most wonderful have been, and are being evolved.

E unum pluribus.

INDEX